WHAT THE ORTHODOX CHURCH OWES TO THE WEST

D1524519

WHAT THE ORTHODOX CHURCH OWES TO THE WEST

Metropolitan Emilianos Timiades

HOLY CROSS ORTHODOX PRESS
Brookline, Massachusetts 02146

Published by Holy Cross Orthodox Press
50 Goddard Avenue
Brookline, Massachusetts 02146

Cover design by Mary C. Vaporis

Library of Congress Cataloging-in-Publication Data

Timiades, Emilianos.
What the Orthodox Church owes to the West/
Emilianos Timiades   p.   cm.
Includes bibliographical references.
ISBN 0-917651-96-0
1. Orthodox Eastern Church — Relations — Catholic Church.
2. Orthodox Eastern Church — Relations — Protestant churches.
3. Catholic Church — Relations — Orthodox Eastern Church.
4. Protestant churches — relations — Orthodox Eastern Church.
I. Title.
BX 324.3.T56   1991
281.9 — dc20   91-37-169
CIP

"Hail East and West, for whom both we fight and from both we are fought"

"Χαίροις, 'Ανατολή καί Δύσις,
ὑπέρ ὦν, καί ὑφ ὑμῶν πολεμούμεθα."

Gregory the Theologian: Oratio supremum vale 42, 27; PG 36.492

CONTENTS

1. What the Orthodox Church Owes to the West

God sent his only-begotten Son for the salvation of humanity and all creation. There is, therefore, one Savior for the entire universe. Indeed, for the entire cosmos there is one Gospel and one Church. Everyone, in the West or East, has been given one faith from the very earliest times. If we genuinely desire to overcome our divisions, we must rediscover this common faith which was entrusted by the Apostles to all generations. We must return to our common sources, to our common roots.

Such a return implies a transconfessional and transhistorical approach. The early Fathers of the undivided Church, before all separations and divisions, drew living water from the same fountain, even though they belonged to different cultural, linguistic, ethnic and geographic backgrounds. One of the ancient Church hymns expresses this oneness and togetherness in convincing poetry: "O Christ by extending your hands on the Cross, you brought all nations together. Thus you have shown the oneness of the Church, which praises you before those on earth and those in heaven by one voice . . . "
(Troparion: Sunday Matins, tone 4.)

In moments of theological crisis, reference is usually made to the priceless debt of the West to that contribution made by the Eastern tradition, with all its remarkable spiritual values. Sometimes we even see evidence of Western "nostalgia" for the mystery and awe of Eastern worship.

Yet there is equally a debt which the East owes to the West. Untouched by the distortions caused by scholastic and casuistic theology, and by the quarrels of the sixteenth century and onwards, the Eastern Church has been able to preserve intact and undefiled the faith of the undivided Church, including certain essential characteristics of asceticism and a healthy spirituality. The East is bound to share this heritage, however, with the West and to make it widely known, without any trace of paternalism or feeling of superiority, but in all humility. By so doing, the Christians of the East can render an immense service, a fraternal diakonia to their fellow Christians of the West.

That such a heritage should be shared is an imperative law of love and solidarity. The East can bridge many of the gaps which exist in the West, not to elevate its own confessional merit, but for

1

Christ's sake as such. In our ecumenical era which so emphasizes the "community" of human beings — the sharing, participating, just, and sustainable society — the East can take seriously its own duty to communicate the reality of so many common values which have been hidden, ignored or misunderstood by some Christian communions up until now.

What are some of the contributions the East can make to the West? At least the following could be included: the importance of the "inner man"; the primacy of "being" over "having"; knowing and possessing the mystery — the parousia (the ever presence of God's love in history) — *versus* an emptiness or deplorable vacuum in life; the coherence of doctrine, a continuity *versus* a discontinuity, overcoming the alarming confusion concerning what should remain and what should be changed; and an optimism emanating from the Risen Christ as opposed to an anemic Christology which is inadequate for spiritual warfare.

If throughout this study more emphasis is put on the crisis of the West, this does not at all imply that the East has not its own problems. Both parts of Christendom have entered a period of crisis with alarming symptoms of frustration, secularism, and confusion. Both must be reminded of the great need for a return to the saving sources of "the living water," in order to recover and be renewed. Gregory Palamas briefly has described the goal of all Christian families:

> Since the Son of God in his incomparable love for man, did not unite his divine hypostasis with our nature, by clothing himself in a living body and a soul gifted with intelligence . . . but also united himself . . . with the human hypostases themselves, in mingling himself with each of the faithful by communion with his holy body, and since he becomes one single body with us (Eph 3.6), and makes us a temple of the undivided Divinity, for in the very body of Christ dwells the fullness of the Godhead bodily (Col 2.9), how should he not illuminate those who commune worthily with the divine ray of his body which is within us, lightening their souls, as he illumined the very bodies of the disciples on Mount Tabor? For, on the day of the Transfiguration, that body, source of the light of grace, was not yet united with our bodies; it illuminated from outside those who worthily approached, and sent the illumination into the soul by the physical eyes; but now, since it is mingled with us and exists in us, it illuminates the soul from within.

Upheavals and frustrations are not signs of this century only. Throughout history the Church has confronted them in a conciliatory manner whenever they appeared. Thus, today we must know how to meet the challenges, standing upright and not becoming stagnant but, rather, contemporary. We can thereby prove that our faith remains ever-present and relevant as the old meets the new in the human wilderness.

In such a context, the following objection might be formulated: "You really are living in a completely different world, with a different temperament, and with an alien way of thinking. There is an abysmal gap; one wonders how it can be bridged. You are children of another confessional setting, bearing all its cultural and historical particularities."

These are indeed legitimate points. But there is one answer which meets the challenge: the march toward common sources and roots in no way violates the fact that each "East and West" — keeps its own particular physiognomy. We must avoid any identification of the essence of the one Faith with that morphological pluralism manifested in a variety of cultures, languages and historical events and their distinctive characteristics.

Such a variety — that "polychromy" and "polyphony" which was described by Irenaios of Lyons — is actually the composition of a genuine symphony, not a cacophony. The Church was never intended to absorb culture and destroy local traditions at the expense of a local community's physiognomy and identity. Instead, it is intended to infuse Christ's spirit into all cultures and traditions. Then they all take on a new meaning because a metamorphosis has taken place.

Needless to say, the impoverishment in question became inevitable when the Latin Church, after the great first Schism of 1054, began to march along alone. Deprived of its sister-church in the East, the Latin Church tried to confront all the emerging problems with its limited means, without a complete and wholistic theology.

2. Towards Our Common Sources

The presence of Orthodox theology is a welcome breath of fresh air in the ecumenical movement. It has moved out of its isolation into the mainstream of Western life and thought. Yet its faith remains a strange exotic import. While a variety of good books appear on icons, ascetic writings, and spirituality — an impressive array each year — the input from Orthodox life into the agitated West remains minimal. This is not to blame the theologians, for the culture in which we live also plays a negative role and there is a lack of adequate communication. In these days, religion is either so deadly serious that it is made to become a private affair very marginalized (the absurdities of the electronic church are but one example), or else it degenerates into a kind of infantile hobby, one of many aspects of our modern permissive societies. There is no difficulty in attacking all this confusion, but the problem is how to rise above it, and find our way within our daily life as we actually meet it.

Western culture protects itself against Orthodoxy by transforming the Orthodox faith into a quaint cult, attractive to seekers of the archaic — those interested in the antiquarianism of Byzantine icons. On the other hand, Orthodoxy itself is in danger of becoming a self-defensive community by intermarriage and the considerable exodus of its ill-prepared youth. Another factor is the mobility of students and workers from traditionally Orthodox countries; instead of creating a coherent national Church in the countries where they go to live, a collection of parishes arises, all imprisoned within their ethnicity, family pride, and individual peculiarities which are expressed in religious garb.

What is lacking is the sense of witness and outreach and a personal responsibility for bringing the witness of the undivided ancient Church to the "outside" community. How many parishes have any sense of obligation to reach out to the pluralistic, technologically-advanced Western world in which they live? In most cases, Orthodox people tend to think of religion as a private concern rather than as a living faith which can bring life to others.

Orthodoxy must emerge from its ethnic ghetto and culture and engage itself creatively within the contradictions and confusions of a pluralistic culture, just as the early Christians had to overcome the ancient pagan culture in which they lived. But the prospects do not look especially good. There is a great deal of work to be done. We cannot take refuge in the glories of the patristic age and the light of the past. The vision of a minority is always full of distortions. Like Lot's wife, it tends to look back nostalgically, and is always in danger of being turned into a pillar of salt.

We live in an age when the accumulated problems cannot be solved by one Church alone but by all the churches together. We need one another. A Western society in crisis badly needs to be complemented by the Orthodox ethos and theology. Present-day subjectivism and frustration could lead many into being lulled into a pleasant an esthesia and even render them victims waiting to be devoured by, God only knows, what sort of predator. Christians should know the true worth of unchanging changelessness. They could even find themselves experiencing a dimension closer to paradise than they ever imagined possible in this heavily-burdened modern society. Orthodox worship is ineffable. It has a quality which makes the passage of time full of meaning. It has a sense of reaching out to eternity, something which is the fruit of so many centuries of prayer and liturgy. Only when we have experienced this to its fullest do we turn to icons and their deep insights with genuine interest. Then we experience tangibly the bringing of the ephemeral life of humanity into contact with the timelessness of a primordial magnificence. The lasting impression is that of reaching out to the heavenly Jerusalem, where we are constantly conscious of holy things transcending the process of doctrinal or ecumenical disputation.

3. The Orthodox Church's Debt to the Ecumenical Family

While the Orthodox family emphasizes its eagerness to contribute effectively to the ecumenical family out of its resources, it senses at the same time its inadequacies and shortcomings. Proceeding to self-criticism with the humility that is called for, it confesses and deplores the shortage of qualified persons who can serve as spokesmen articulating the spirit and witness of Orthodoxy. Up until now, our policy has been one of small hesitant steps rather than of massive presence in all the sections of the WCC. It must be said that Orthodoxy does not regard itself as one confessional church among many others but as the Church which has remained faithful to its calling and to its distinctive heritage. It should not be identified with a certain geographical area — the East, the Orient, Byzantium or Russia — but rather with the oneness of the ancient Church, the embodiment of the *didaskalia* and the worship of the undivided body of Christ.

From this standpoint, it has shared in the work of the WCC from the very beginning, as a founder member, and worked for the development of the existing fellowship, offering its best to many consultations in both bilateral and multilateral dialogues. As well as offering, it also receives, from the experience and generosity of the member churches, striving to advance the process whereby broken Christendom is being reconciled. In what follows, we want to offer a few suggestions as to how Orthodoxy can make a further positive and constructive contribution from its common resources. We highlight a few selected areas wherein the Orthodox Church can effectively and dynamically contribute and participate.

We have used the word "debt" in the title of this study, keeping in mind the words of St. Paul in his letter to the Romans: "I am debtor both ... " (Rom 1.4) and again: "We are debtors, not to the flesh ... " (Rom 8.12), and endorsing some parallel comments of St. John Chrysostom: "This debt does not refer to material needs, namely, to how our bodies should be fed, treated and well looked after. While not disregarding such needs, it is a fact that we should not make the body the master of our lives. A body must follow, not lead. The rules of the Holy Spirit must be accepted as our guide. Without the Spirit, even someone supposedly alive is in reality already dead ... " (*Homily 14.1-3 on Romans*; PG 60.524-25).

6

4. Toward a Better Understanding of Orthodoxy

To a Western theologian, Orthodoxy is still a relatively unexplored territory. We are able to sense that it is firstly and most naturally an outgrowth and expression of, precisely, "The East." That is, many of the characteristics of Eastern cultures provide a base for our understanding of this form of Christianity. Eastern societies, including Byzantium, for example, are more at peace in the presence of mystery and the irrational than are, say, the Latins. And "patriarchy" happily exists alongside a strong sense of "the feminine" in many Eastern countries. Complex rituals involve all the senses — and the dead as well as the living. The past, for an Orthodox, is somehow a key to the present and to the future in a manner which many Westerners recognize but cannot enter into themselves. And certainly in nearly all non-Western countries the *family* is still of more importance than "the individual." All these traits are fair, if over-generalized statements with regard to Eastern countries, whether one is speaking about them in the framework of their religious or other practices. And they are also statements one can make after only a fairly superficial introduction to the Orthodox Church. But it is, I believe, precisely this Eastern aspect of the Orthodox which causes many of the difficulties, as well as the fascinations, in our ecumenical discussions.

The kind of *shift* in mental and imaginative gear which is required to even approach an understanding of that Tradition takes *time* and attention which few of us can really spare. It is, therefore, much easier to fall into the temptation of dealing superficially with issues or pretending that the differences are not as deeply rooted as, in fact, they are.

The Orthodox, on their part, have tried to adapt to the discursive, rational approach *which is always used by Protestants*. The real problem is that Orthodoxy by its very nature *cannot* really be talked *about. It must be experienced.* There is only one way in which we can begin to understand Orthodox doctrine, and that is by actually entering into Orthodox devotion. Without entering into its rhythms, its spirituality, its colors, and its communities, we cannot really pretend to have understood its views on this or that theological issue. This is why, for example, when a person expresses a desire to "become an Orthodox" by conversion or development of Christian life or

7

whatever — it is required that he spend a considerable length of time in the Orthodox community before the actual steps are taken towards membership. This is because it is considered to be more than a mere mental decision. It is a style and orientation of life which touches all the levels of human experience — many of these non-verbal. We cannot even begin to talk about Orthodoxy without a firm grasp of the place of the non-verbal, particularly iconography.

Orthodoxy then has to do with "looking," at the ineffable reality with a different perception, far more than it has to do with speaking or even hearing. It is the eyes of the heart which are the important image-making faculty. And it is at this level that ecumenical exchange must take place. Through looking beyond the screen, by mental contemplation on the mystery behind the iconostasis — the Tradition is learned, tested, developed. In order for Orthodoxy to be sufficiently understood, this Tradition must be the central focus of our piety.

It is primarily from this living, unbroken Tradition that all teaching and questioning emanate. Any modern insight must cohere with and be tested in the light of this living and organic Tradition. What is more, the Orthodox Tradition is not *just* Christian, or even predominately Christian. It is *Jewish-Christian.* I find it difficult to emphasize this enough. Many speak easily of our "Judeo-Christian heritage." But when they do so, they do not infer the same thing as the Orthodox do. These people tend to think, despite their conscious attempt not to do so, that the New Testament superceded the Old Testament. They sweep their hand over the Old Testament and mutter something about "old things pass away and behold all things become new." They look upon the Old Testament much as the Muslims, after the revelation of the Koran, look upon the New Testament. That is, they take sort of a poetic interest in the Psalms and a few of the stories; and they lump it together vaguely under the category of "holy writings." However, *they primarily do their theological homework from the passages of the New Testament.* The Orthodox do not do this. The Orthodox Tradition is evolved from *laminated* material. That is to say, it is layered. And the layers all define one another and illuminate one another; so that the Old Testament and church history are always *necessary* and interconnected to any New Testament event or saying, and vice versa. Eve, Mary, Hagia Sophia must be seen together, for example; as must Easter and Passover or the Church and the Temple (with its Ark and Holy of Holies) or the Old Testament Trinity and the Holy Trinity, etc.

This is why the icon of the Transfiguration is so central a parabolic picture to the Orthodox. Jesus stands with the Old Testament on either side, represented by Moses and Elijah. There is the Law and the Prophets, the verbal and the visual, the maintainer of the past and the dynamic of the future, the outer and the inner. Gazing at this trinity in all icons of the Transfiguration is the new trinity, represented by Peter, James, and John. They thread the old in with the new and carry it forward. In so doing, *in the joining*, is the glory. All of the law and the prophets are transfigured by the New Church. But they are, at the same time, the very material out of which Jesus always comes and from which the Church eternally and always is born.

For the Orthodox, holy Tradition can be divided into Tradition concerning the Faith and consequently of equal authority to the Holy Scriptures, and traditions of a more ecclesiastical character . . . with only relative authority and which do not affect the faith and dogmas of the Orthodox Church.

This icon, like that of the Old Testament Trinity or those of the Virgin Mary and Jesus, (the Virgin Mary is never pictured alone, while Jesus is only pictured alone in relatively modern and relatively Western icons) or those of the Crucifixion with the Apostle John on one side and the Virgin Mary on the other, indicates the concept of fellowship, the communion of Saints. This *communio sanctorum* is central to Orthodoxy, that is "spiritual reciprocity, a union in love, a oneness in thought . . . an organic rather than an organized principle." *Basic* to this organism is the Old Testament. Somehow the writers of Leviticus *have* to be able to be included in the dance along with, say, St. Luke. To do one's theology about women and men in the Church is to make as much use of the Old Testament and the cultural history of the Church as to use the New Testament and modern insights. This is, perhaps, why it is always a more painful and difficult process for Orthodox theology and Reformation theology to find a common *use* of language with which to discuss the issues of common importance to both.

And again, as the Old Testament is a necessary "connecting link" to the New Testament, so, too, is the historical Church in time and space. It is only in the Church that the seed sown by the Word does not remain barren, but brings forth fruit. And this fruitfulness of truth, as well as its capacity for being fruitful, is called Tradition. This, for instance, is important with regard to the person and place of the Mother of God, the Theotokos, in Orthodoxy. She is pre-eminently "the figure of the Church," her beginning and her continuity. The the veneration-cultus of the Mother of God, which when viewed externally, might seem to be in contradiction with the biblical data, is spread far and wide in the tradition of the Church and is the most precious fruit of tradition. All the sacred history and tradition of the Jews are the tale of the slow and laborious journey of fallen humanity towards the "fullness of time," when the angel was to be sent to announce to the chosen Virgin the coming Incarnation of God and to hear from her lips the *human act of consent* to that which the divine plan accomplishes through her. Thus, according to a saying of Saint John of Damascus, "The name of the Mother of God contains all the history of the divine economy in this world" (*The Orthodox Faith* 3,12; PG 94.1029). Orthodox theology continues to indicate the highly organic and masculine/feminine process as it is understood by Orthodox ecclesiology, namely, that all children of God constitute this community of the redeemed, living or dead, on earth and in heaven.

> This divine economy preparing the human conditions for the Incarnation of the Son of God is not a unilateral one; it is not a matter of the will of God making a *tabula rasa* of human history. In this saving economy, Divine Wisdom is adapted to the divine challenge. It is thus that Wisdom hath built herself a house through the generation of the Old Testament righteous . . . resolves the tragic problem of fallen humanity. All that God required of human liberty, since the Fall, is accomplished.

Now this is just one example of the way in which Orthodoxy is able to take biblical events and intertwine them in order to elucidate doctrine. In this instance, it is apparent that the Virgin Mary, i.e., a woman, is the pivot upon which salvation is accomplished. In other words, Jesus by his incarnation through the Virgin becomes what he was, is, and always will be, our Redeemer and Savior.

That the Virgin Mary's importance is beyond any Marian piety in the narrow sense, and bears deeper connections with the whole Christology, is seen from the condemnation of Nestorianism by early Ecuomenical Synods. Nestorios claimed that the name "Theotokos" suggested that Mary gave a beginning to the divinity. This was an absurd charge, which the Fathers had little difficulty in rebutting. The Virgin gives birth in the flesh to a divine person who has existed from eternity before her. Cyril of Alexandria writes to Nestorios:

> He who had an existence before all ages and was born of the Father is said to have been of a woman according to the flesh, not as though his divine nature received the beginning of its existence in the holy Virgin, but since, for us and our salvation, he hypostatically united humanity (*to anthropinon*) to himself and

came forth of a woman, he is thus said to be born in the flesh (*Second Letter* 4; PG 77.54).

His passion could not have any salvific value. Gregory the Theologian exclaims: "We needed an incarnate God, a God put to death, so that we might live" (*Oratio* 45.28; PG 36.661). If it is someone else, not the person of the Christ, suffering humanly on the cross, then the crucifixion is no more than the shameful murder of an innocent person; a tragic defeat and not a victory. As Sophronios, Patriarch of Jerusalem, states: "In his *philanthropy* he became consubstantial with us men, in the passible and mortal flesh he took from Mary" (*Oration on the Annunciation* 31; PG 87.3256).

Thus, the rejection of the Theotokos is the rejection of the voluntary "kenosis," self-emptying, of the Logos. The Fathers view the entire saving economy of God from the womb of Mary to the descent into hell, as a continuous process, as the descent of a loving Savior, as a condescension-synkatabasis of the third person of the Trinity. Quite the opposite is Nestorianism; by its repudiation of Mary as Theotokos, we have the rejection of the humility of God incarnate, of the kenosis, self-emptying of Bethlehem and its climax on Calvary, and thus of the foolishness of the generosity of his love for the whole cosmos.

Christ chose to live out his life on earth under the conditions of the Fall. He did not contract the defects of suffering and death, as we humans do; he accepted the whole human condition from conception to the last breath. He condescended to be conceived and carried in the womb, to take on flesh from and to be born of a woman. He became a woman's tiny baby. This baby in Mary's womb, in the manger, is God, God incarnate. Orthodox hymnography sings with lyricism:

> O marvel. God is come among men; he who cannot be contained is contained in a womb; the Timeless enters time; strange wonder. His conception is without seed; his emptying is past telling, so great is the mystery. For God empties himself, takes flesh, is fashioned as a creature when the angel tells the pure Virgin of her conception . . . (Matins, Feast of the Annunciation).

It is his human nature, not his divine nature, which receives the beginning of its existence in and through the Virgin. Gnostic Docetism influenced Muslim theology to such a great degree that it denied the real humanity of Christ, by rejecting that Christ took on himself anything from Mary, his mother. For the Valentinian Gnostics, he merely "passed through Mary like water through a channel."

The Church Fathers emphasize the fact that we are related to Christ precisely because he took on flesh from his mother. It is through taking flesh from this daughter of Zion that he becomes a Jew, a son of David, a son of Abraham, a son of Adam. Jesus is truly human, a man like us all in all things but sin, precisely because he is from Mary. So, the name "Theotokos" sums up the whole mystery of the incarnation. In championing its use and explaining its meaning, the Fathers were witnessing to the truth that is Christ and, thus, fighting for an authentic soteriology.

This is so because, if the Virgin Mary is not Christ's real mother, then he cannot really be man, could not have really suffered on the Cross, and as a result, we are not saved. On the other hand, if the Theotokos is the mother of a mere man and not the mother of God, the second person of the Holy Trinity, the Son in his human nature, then again we are not saved, because only if Christ is truly God can he save us.

If Mary's Son is not the incarnate God, then it will not be God made man, like one of us, who suffers on the Cross but someone else. For Nestorios God comes near and is joined, in an emotional union, to a suffering and mortal man, but he remains sublimely uninvolved. On the contrary, the Church states, that this suffering and mortal man is the God-man, the *Theanthropos.*

If there is still a primary value attached to Father-Creator and Son-Redeemer-Spirit in Protestantism, in Orthodoxy there is an interaction, a continuous communion of saints with the Holy Trinity. The entire Church, the assembly of the faithful enter into communion with the Theotokos. The Second Eve is as significant as the Second Adam. And, wisdom is as central as the Logos in illuminating the divine to humanity. As for the Spirit, in Orthodoxy, there is a dependence and fully central place given to it, which gender-less places it above and beyond the mind of humanity to categorize, but which, nevertheless, acts like a silence over the name of God. This apophatic attitude to the nature of God was present in the Old Testament times.

Spiritual mystery signified by the Spirit, the epiklesis, stands between man and expression of God; therein lies its power and its efficacy. It both guards and preserves, the icons of God and the Tradition which they window, and yet it keeps them from becoming idols. The invocation of the Holy Spirit, the angel of the Annunciation, and the glory at the Transfiguration are all means of both revelation and veiling.

5. Collegiality and Co-Responsibility

We are all chosen for God's service. If the Orthodox Church, as we say, has preserved an unbroken continuity of the apostolic faith, this fact imposes a great responsibility on her. It is a binding duty to make this faith and spirituality known, not only to her own members, but also to the others, with all humility and charity. This idea of being used for the transmission of this treasure seems odd, because it may imply a crypto-arrogance and favoritism. Let us consider an analogy. A headmaster calls a boy to his study and says: "We have a new boy from your village, a place well known to you. I want you to help him settle in." This brings out two points. The boy was not chosen because of any merit he possessed but because, within the mind of the headmaster, he was the appropriate person to do a particular task. "It was not because you were more numerous than any other nation that the Lord chose you, for you were the smallest of nations; it was because the Lord loved you (Dt 7.6)."

This means that God seeks human cooperation. To those who have been given certain blessings, he asks at the same time that they be shared by others as well. The undivided faith of the Church is destined to become the personal possession of everyone. Christ said: "I call you friends, because I have made known to you everything I have learned from the Father." We have been taken into a *koinonia* with God and his teachings through the Apostles and the countless martyrs and confessors of the faith. This is why we are commissioned to share this fellowship with others.

In the earlier eras of the history of the Church, Christians were more conscious of the ecumenical dimensions of their community and the consequent binding intra-faith aid and solidarity. Parochialism was rejected as contradicting the very essence of the body of Christ. This ecclesiological principle incited a general concern and responsibility, so that no one could be exclusively preoccupied with the affairs of one's own given local church and thus ignore the developments next door. Catholicity — an essential mark — was not taken lightly as a vague article of faith, but as a serious commitment and the guiding principle of mutual concern, the sharing of tribulations or upheavals as if it were one's own. All scattered local communities, separated by national geographic frontiers, essentially constituted one church, one ecclesial assembly, one body, one congregation, and employed one and the same governing ministerial system. St. John Chrysostom underlines the fact that because of there being one body, no factor whatsoever could bring about any separation, neither time nor space (*On the verse: "Do Know This"* 6; PG 56.277). If, in a geographical sense churches were at a distance one from another, yet the one and same Lord united them, He who was common to all (*Hom.* 1.1 *On 1 Cor*; PG 61.13).

Gregory the Theologian similarly states that because of this unity, no local, particular church is allowed to digress from the common faith, under the pretext that it belongs to the West or to the East, or due to different interpretations concerning the episcopal primacy or doctrinal issues. Regardless of such distances and in spite of the fact that each one keeps its own physiognomy, our faith remains one and unchanged. He asks, in a dramatic way: "How long will they pretend to be separatist factions, claiming that one particular view is more valid than another, insisting that their own belief is more genuine because it is older, more tested and more spiritual than the other, which is younger and less representatively spiritual or worthy?" (*Oratio* 42.21; PG 36.484). General warnings were, therefore, addressed to the faithful in all parts of the *oikoumene*, to keep away from heretics and schismatics, because by disobeying the catholic faith, they are self-excommunicating themselves from the Mother Church. They are indeed blind and full of arrogance, seeking to guide others, who are also blind. So, St. Basil of Caesarea states (*Moralia, horos* 40; PG 31.760 and *Letter to Amphilochios* 188; PG 32.665).

Such being their conviction, the Fathers fought this error wherever it was found, because if an evil was not confronted in one place, it might contaminate and pollute another part of the Church.

In current theological and cultural essays, the term "debt" is often used to indicate the gratitude of the West to the East, with the assumption that Eastern theology greatly influenced the West. This fact cannot be denied, because the cradle of civilization and religion is in the Middle East and in the surrounding areas of the Mediterranean. Thus, frequent reference is made to Jerusalem, Antioch, Alexandria, and also to Athens. Here sprang forth early Christianity, and

Greek philosophy was already widely diffused throughout the Roman Empire so as to greatly influence it. This area, therefore, naturally attracted those people interested in making long journeys in order to profit and receive light from the centers of high theological and intellectual wisdom.

In addition, westerners visited the sources and very centers of monasticism and liturgical life in order to learn and to build up the newly converted Germanic regions and other areas. We know of the Spanish abbess Etheria's or Egheria's "Peregrinatio" to Egypt, the Holy Land, Edessa, and Constantinople at the end of the fourth century. In 374 St. Jerome, living in the home of Evagrios, where Greek was spoken, set out for Antioch. In Palestine he settled as a hermit in the desert for five years; then he went to Constantinople. On his return to Rome, he established numerous monastic centers and finally settled in a monastery in Bethlehem in order to improve his Greek.

Similarly, St. Melania (342-410), an aristocratic Roman lady, left for Egypt and Palestine, and founded a double monastery with Rufinus of Aquileia on the Mount of Olives, but later she returned to Italy. Another such pupil in the school of the East was St. Melania the so-called Younger (383-438). With her husband they founded two monasteries at Tagaste in North Africa and on the Mount of Olives. A mother of five children, St. Paula, a Roman matron (347-404) followed Jerome to Palestine where she studied the ascetic discipline in the Egyptian deserts.

Every time a spiritual crisis attacks the Church on earth, instead of seeking its causes or who is responsible for all the well-known historical quarrels of the past, it is better to put forth honestly a common question, a challenging perennial problem: Why doesn't the Christian faith transform the life of our faithful? Why don't Christians of the West and East radiate their faith and diffuse the redeeming message of the Gospel in the surrounding darkness? Why are they not a race apart, thankful to be different from everyone else, consistently living according to binding promises of the Gospel in every act of everyday life? We certainly are not all saints, but we could be better, more consistent with the demands of our faith.

Christ can transform our everyday life in new ways. It is the same faith that has transformed the world of the senses and the world of reason to a new single world of the spirit and the inner life. It is precisely on this point that Orthodox spirituality has preserved the sense of awe and mystery. It is absurd to be ashamed of this. On the contrary, here lies the strength of our faith. Because in this way it speaks more directly to the unconscious mind. It is the product of our inextinguishable sense of the supernatural, of the unseen forces, since our life is followed by guardian angels. It is very wrong to regard such views as primitive in a derogatory sense. They are perennial. The mystery, found in apophatic theology and in the sacramental life, speaks powerfully to that part of our minds which is our purest inheritance. In every liturgical act we are participating in that which is timeless and universal — of cosmic dimension.

The time has passed when one could proceed alone to a monotherapy or self-therapy. Challenged by so many threats, we need to undertake a collective diagnosis of our unhealthy symptoms and to find common means for restoration and renewal.

The holy Apostle Paul uses the words ''I owe a duty'' in the widest sense (Rom 1.14). In principle this applies not only to St. Paul, but to every member of the Church where its apostolic commission and witness is as wide as this. What one receives from one's Church makes him a debtor. We should think of this when we covet great things: all that we have received puts us in debt. We are but stewards of the faith inherited by the Apostles and safeguarded by the early Fathers and Ecumenical Synods. Such a rich heritage has made Orthodoxy a debtor. The Orthodox Church has improved her talents, elaborated her theological and ascetical writings through various doctors, confessors, and martyrs, and has done as much good as any other Christian Church. Yet, the Orthodox still remain debtors to the people of the Church and to others.

St. Paul says, ''Debtor to the Greeks, and to the barbarians, to the wise and the unwise.'' In fact, the Greeks fancied themselves as having the monopoly of wisdom and looked upon the rest of the world as barbarians. The holy Paul was a debtor to both and looked upon himself as obliged to do all the good he could both to the one and to the other. Every man owes more than he can ever repay to the people with whom he is linked by baptism and the same Savior. The unaltered Christian faith is God's gift to us. And we can only repay him by passing on that gift to others. Freely we have received it from him; freely let us give it to those who do not have it.

Orthodoxy owes much to the protection of the Holy Trinity, St. John Chrysostom says, ''The Holy Trinity administers the whole Church by providing the economy needed'' (*Hom.* 87.4 *in John* PG 59.472). Christ gives power and joy, restoration to the preadamic state, liberation from the ancient world's idols and pagan philosophies. The mystical head of this body sustains, defends, and protects it from visible and invisible enemies. When the Gnostics and heretics tried to lead Christians to the old errors, with God's help, the Councils and brave Fathers fought to save the apostolic faith. Such saving truths of unspeakable blessing could not be kept hidden. They had to be shared. Orthodoxy's debt to the Triune God's protection and guidance became a duty to others. In proportion as we realize the value of the saving truths for ourselves, only shall we be driven to pass them on to others who do not possess them. What is precious for us, must also be relevant and good for others, too.

In the most critical moments, facing schismatic bodies, Arianism scandalously being protected by emperors and state officials and even perverted patriarchs, such as Nestorios, and Eutychios (not a patriarch), the faithful Orthodox, although a small minority, took refuge in prayer, invoking the succour of the blessed Trinity. Thus, pneumatology and trinitarian theology became intermingled in the daily life of its historical upheavals and to all manner of attacks.

St. Hilary of Poitiers (ca. 315-367) in the fourth century defended the integrity of Christian dogma with such learning and efficacy that he was called the Athanasios of the West.

We are sometimes disturbed and disorientated by the experiments of those who anticipate a future in which they themselves already fix the character. In the fourth century the Church's situation was far more difficult, and that which was at stake in the struggle was far more critical and decisive.

Committed Christians, having emerged from the catacombs into which they had been driven by the persecutions, which were the fiercest, but still limited to a clandestine type of existence, were suddenly recognized as the equals of their persecutors. Christianity became a legal religion; moreover, for the masses, it became a victorious religion. The emperors, in the person of St. Constantine, had recognized that they had made a mistake in trying to destroy Christianity. Instead of attributing the evils of the times to the impiety of the Christians as had so often been done with fervor, would it not have been more correct to seek their real causes in Rome's long rejection of the new law?

It was possible to learn by experience that nothing acquired is acquired for all eternity. That is the state of man and the deepest condition of the Christian. St. Hilary was under the illusion that the return of Arians to the Catholic faith was around the corner. He was clearly heartened, amid many disappointments, by participating in many conciliar gatherings with brothers of the Middle East.

The Church, with every honor given to the members of her hierarchy, endowed with sumptuous buildings for worship — those Constantinian basilicas that glittered with mosaics — was about to meet the insidious danger of her history, for it was not a question of attack against her members or her possessions, but one against the sacred deposit of her doctrine, the essence of its message — Arianism.

Arius rejected the very divinity of Christ, as if he were not God in essence, but had become God in some way, like an ancient hero, through his heroism, holiness, and merit.

Never in two thousand years was there to be so fundamental a heresy. If Christ is not God, the whole of Christianity collapses and the faith loses all substance. No longer is there an incarnation, no more is there a redemption.

To confront this danger a Synod gathered at Nicaea in 325, in the presence of two representatives of the holy Pope Sylvester who was himself absent because of his advanced old age. Arius was condemned and the Creed that is still recited, with a few additions, during the Divine Liturgy, was drawn up, proclaiming the Son to be *homoousios* — consubstantial with the Father.

But Arianism did not simply disappear as a result of this, for after energetic evangelism among the barbarian peoples, the latter adopted Christianity in its Arian form. Their opposition to the Empire was henceforth to be not only political, but, and this was far more serious, also religious.

Only with the baptism of Clovis, thanks to St. Clotilde the Princess of Geneva, did the barbarians, after returning to Orthodoxy, and after many vicissitudes, make possible the flowering of the Christian Middle Ages. These historical facts demonstrate the immense debt of gratitude which Christians owe to St. Clotilde. She made possible not only the Christianization of Gaul, but also and above all, the religious unity of the West and the survival of the true doctrine among us.

The role of St. Hilary was fulfilled at the beginning of this crucial period, which started with the Council of Nicaea and ended with the baptism of the king of France at the end of the fifth century. He was born into a rich family in 315 at Poitiers. He received a complete and cultured education. The reading of the Gospel of St. John made a very deep impression on him, especially the sentence from the prologue: "The Word was made flesh and dwelt among us."

Married, and the father of a little girl, St. Hilary asked for and received baptism, and was then appointed bishop by the voice of the people, so greatly were his knowledge and virtue valued by his fellow citizens. At that time the marital status of the clergy had not yet been settled, and marriage was not an obstacle to episcopal rank.

Then began a long and harassing contest against Arian doctrine which, although condemned at Nicaea, had vigorous partisans in Gaul. Constans, an emperor of the Arian persuasion, was offended at this resistance. He, therefore, made use of a method that was then in practice to uproot the opposition; he sent the holy Hilary into exile in remote Phrygia.

It is said that there is no ill wind but bloweth some good. These few years made it possible for the illustrious exile to study Eastern theology by meeting monks and theologians in the Middle East. His fame became widespread in the East to such an extent that the Emperor preferred to send the outlaw back home where, so he thought, his influence was limited. In 359 he had already defended the cause of Orthodoxy at the council of Seleucia, thus becoming the leading and most respected Latin theologian of his age. St. Hilary was indefatigable in the writing of dogmatic treatises and commentaries on the Scriptures and in settting forth to his contemporaries the beauties of the monastic ideal that his disciple St. Martin was to help spread in Gaul.

That is why, at a time when there is a tendency to greater liberty of expression, one may regret that the translations from Latin into French weaken and sweeten the admirable definitions of a past age by substituting in the Credo "of the same nature as the Father" for "of the same substance as the Father," and by diminishing the dogmatic force of the preface on the Holy Trinity by the same substitution. What would the Fathers of the Church have said to this weakening of the proclamation of dogma?

At every turning point in the life of the Church, providence brings forth exceptional men whose mission is to prepare the future without denying anything of the unchangeable deposit of the faith. The faithful, disoriented sometimes by unofficial peripheral manifestations, find, through their fidelity to the successors of the Apostles, new reason for belief and hope.

The early fathers never presumed that the life of the Church and its survival, in spite of all the assaults by the heretics, was due to their own merits. The victory of Christianity against pagan philosophy must not be attributed, St. John Chrysostom states, to "those simple fishermen, neither the teachings nor those miracles; all those extraordinary events were due to the power of Christ operating through them" (Sermon on Babylas the martyr 3; PG 50,538). This trust in God's power is also proclaimed in the hymnology of the Church: "That creative, uniting all things, the wisdom and power of God, power immovable and everlasting is that which sustains the Church" (Ode 3, 15 of 15th of August during Matins service). On another occasion a troparion states: "Your Church, that is all the people, sings and rejoices, shouting: You are, O Lord, my strength, my refuge, and protection" (Ode 3, of the first Sunday of the Triodion). And again: "The holy Church in a divine way sings, shouting: Christ my strength, God and Lord" (Ode 4, Sunday of Publican and Pharisee).

Consequently, this theanthropic community of the redeemed people of God remains beyond human scrutiny and comprehension. St. John Chrysostom says in this regard: "By how many was she fought, and yet never was conquered? How many tyrants, generals, kings, rulers, men of high powerful intellect attacked her, but they did not succeed to uproot her? The paradox is that while her enemies are forgotten and passed over in silence, the attacked church is going up to heaven" (*On the verse I saw my Lord . . . Homily* 4,2; PG 56.121).

As Christians redeemed from the bondage of evil, we can never discharge our obligation to those Church Fathers, martyrs, and ascetics of the desert who have enriched our lives in every eucharistic service and who challenge us, being in constant communion with them, to repay them in the present as well as the future. What the past ages have communicated in their writings and doctrinal pronouncements as Tradition's most precious treasure, compels us to transmit this tradition enriched by our own contribution, to the ages to come. Thus, metaphorically, let us pay our debt to our parents in faith and to our children, to our brothers and sisters in the Lord. If one examines the life and activities of any saint or ecclesiastical leader, he will find this constant eagerness and sense of interdependence burning in his heart, this inner calling for sharing, anxious always not to keep the faith to himself only but to share it. It was a trust, something to be enjoyed, but also to be shared, and to be shared most with those who needed it most.

This sacred heritage, *parakatatheki*, which includes worship, spirituality, creeds, doctrines, sacred hymnography, iconography, etc., is not to be hidden away in a chest or locked in a safe, but to be dispensed in blessing. Neither is bread to be wrapped up in a cloth and stored away, but the very bread of life is to be broken and distributed to others. Nor is water to be kept in tanks and reservoirs, but the very living water is to quench the spiritual thirst of all. Here lies our debt, reflecting the community of our baptismal binding duties and the solidarity as children of the same family of God. It is this indebtedness which led many missionaries from the East in the past to go to the West: such as St. Irenaios from Asia Minor, Theodore from Tarsus, later archbishop of Canterbury, and so on, also leading them forth into other lands. There is a secret in the nature of our common faith, as St. John Chrysostom says, "that we possess it only as we share it."

If we are dealing with material things, the more we give them away the less we have. But if we are dealing with the truth and the Gospel, the more we pass them on, the more we own them. Our certainty of grasp is increased by the process of expansion, diffusion and sharing. The more we make them known to others, the more we possess them for ourselves. There is something creative about the very act of giving. Sharing is possessing. The coin which comes from this mint has no significance except that it is in circulation. Orthodoxy found its vitality in the act of proclaiming and sharing the common Tradition with the others, her sister churches. In this deep fraternal sense, we, as Christians, are all under the compulsion of the same sort of debt. In this sense, the Holy Cyril of Alexandria pointed out that St. Paul had called all the churches scattered throughout the world as being the one Church. This is because they have only one Lord, one and the same faith, so that in spite of being many in number, in reality they are only one" (*Comment. on Psalm 44,10;* PG 69,1041).

The Christian community is sharing and participation. What belongs to one particular church, also belongs to the others. Inactivity and introverted enjoyment of spiritual or material goods contradicts the very term "Body of Christ." Inactivity, furthermore, is a symptom of an unhealthy or even a dead organism. This dispensing and sharing is the continuation of Christ's diaconal commission, which is so well illustrated by Tertullian: "*Ecclesia ab apostolis, apostoli a Christo, Christus a Deo.*" Reception of the faith and promulgation are closely interrelated. Human capacities vary greatly. They can in part be measured, tabulated, assessed and their probable development anticipated. Yet, the element of the incalcuable and unpredictable remains. No man's life is precedented. Applied to the ecclesiastical body, we see this same variety to which the holy Apostle Paul refers when he wrote, "there are diversities of gifts." Eastern Christianity is not culturally and phenomenologically in some way like the Western, and vice versa. Here we are before a ground of variation, many gifts of mysterious nature, in that they are gifts from

God. None may justifiably be proud of these gifts. Every church of Christ is given enormous charismata clearly manifested in its particular history. Certain achievements should cause gratitude rather than triumphalistic arrogance, to be charged instead with a great responsibility for the right exercise of that which has been given, and never for its own self-interest.

Whether they be great or small, God's gifts are intended for use. They even increase with use; in being given afresh to others, they return as a more valuable and more permanent possession than ever before. A Christian, like the local Church, knows that he has nothing which he did not first receive. There sometimes may be too many ethnic and/or cultural elements, and the differences in another's temperament may help to point this out. But these diversities, above all, point to the Holy Spirit, whose ways are not those of man, not his thoughts as man's thoughts. They prompt a fresh humility and a sense of pluralism, inevitable in a communion of human beings, each one having his own peculiarities.

6. Towards Unity

Contrary to what has sometimes been asserted, the Orthodox Church has been involved in seeking Christian unity long before the founding of the Amsterdam Assembly and was ecumenical before the ecumenical movement. The western churches may have become aware of the scandal of division in recent decades, but the Orthodox Church has been aware of the tragedy of division from the earliest times. Despite his advanced age, the holy Polycarp of Smyrna made a long journey to Rome to discuss with Pope Aniketos the date and common celebration of Easter (Irenaios: *Adv. haer.* 3, 3, 4; PG. 7.853). In many instances, when errors emerged in either the East or the West, pastoral letters were written and local synods or peace-making conferences took place with the goal of resolving disputes or of taking the appropriate steps to re-establish church discipline and order. The following are some examples: the Byzantine delegation at the Council of Lyons (1274), and at the Council of Florence (1438), not to mention generous bilateral meetings with the Armenians and other Monophysite bodies and even with Muslims. Eagerness and passion for the restoration of the broken unity can be found in the written records of these meetings. If the pace and rhythm of the movement for reconciliation later slowed down due to unfavorable historic conditions, it would be wrong to attribute this decline of unity efforts to a lack of concern or to isolation in a confessional ghetto.

The Orthodox can be both helpful to and make a dynamic impact on the ecumenical movement because of their historical depth. They have offered not only delegates and qualified theological scholars, but also produced the largest number of martyrs and confessors in the effort to safeguard the unity and purity of the Faith. Councils were convoked and frequent appeals sent to local communities and churches where the unity was endangered by schismatics or actually broken by obstinate champions of heterodoxy. The fact that the terms "guardian," "custodian," "watchful," "vigilant," "stewardship," and similar terms are often incorporated into conciliar decrees, shows how sensitive the Orthodox were on questions of faith and the importance they placed on loyalty and fidelity to the heritage — to the deposit of faith (1 Tim 6.20 and 2 Tim 1.14 - mistranslated by Tertullian as "magisterium"). Rather than bargain away or betray the oneness of faith, they were prepared to die. How unity was preserved despite so many attacks and doctrinal upheavals is explained not in terms of human triumphalism on the part of Eastern Christians but rather by Christ's constant presence, thus assuring us that he will never abandon his Church.

For the Orthodox, the term "concepts of unity" (Document of Faith and Order) as a formula for the rediscovery of the true nature of the One Church requires correction and in its place the singular term "concept" must instead be used. There has always been only one concept and model of unity proclaimed and accepted by the universal Church. Once sectarians or deviationists introduced different concepts, they were vigorously disowned and cut off from Christ's Church by the decisions of the Ecumenical Councils. Gregory the Theologian writes the following: "Let us not permit the Church to be divided and cut into pieces. Whoever divides the beautiful Body of the Church will incur damnation and will have to give an account to God on the day of judgment" on the tenth chapter of Galatians: (*Letter 101 to Kledonios*; PG 37.193). The severity of this warning recalls the words of Irenaios: "Those who cleave asunder and separate the unity of the Church shall receive from God the same punishment as did Jeroboam" (1 Kings 14.10) (*Adv. haer.* 4, 26, 2,33). The early Fathers were conscious of the oneness of the Church and the indivisibility of the Christian faith.

In line then with all these patristic testimonies, we regard any doctrinal pluralism and different forms of unity departing from that proclaimed in the Apostlic Church as contradicting the continuity and fidelity of the Church and therefore its very essence and meaning. They threaten its homogeneity and consequently threaten its durability. To attain a true unity, it is not enough to propose a change of methodology or to compromise its truth for the sake of fellowship. This painful tension must be faced. The root of the crisis of our divisions lies at a deeper level. We have to return to effective and acceptable solutions and listen more attentively to the voice of the ancient Church.

How far can it be said that there is a complete absence, a disappearance, and an eclipse of unity? Let us remember just this one point: the churches (those which have remained solid historically) have constantly strived for the purity and survival of the Christian faith unspoiled from the time of Christ and the apostles until this day. To point to schismatic upheavals in history as proof of an absence of unity is to ignore the importance of the witness of these historically ancient churches. It is also to display an ignorance of the fundamental biblical principles established by Christ and stemming from his incarnation. He assured his disciples that the Church, being the depository of truth, will remain forever the guardian and the witness of his faith and life. From this standpoint, we think that a disproportionate emphasis is given to unity in comparison with truth. Simply being "united" horizontally does not mean that we possess the truth. Unity depends on the precise contents and the criteria by which it is established.

Unity is usually contained in an agreed, unanimous homogenous corpus. This unanimity and consensus cannot be the result of whatever is elaborated upon in the course of any bilateral dialogues by agreement in human terms at the expense of truths inherited from the apostolic teaching. There can be no compromising of the faith's integrity and/or respect for the truth, for the sake of fellowship, friendly relationships, and "unity." Ambiguities also arise when the very nature of unity is discussed, as is the case in the ecumenical text of WCC: "It is never achieved once and for all, and it has constantly to be renewed and re-created" (Faith and Order document). In such a case, we would be confronted with a fragile, superficial, short-term, opportunistic unity, the child of a minimalistic theology, without solidity and therefore easily broken again at the slightest divergence, conflict, and peril. False witness to the truth is possible at any time and by any member of the Church, but the Church itself, as the Body of Christ, because of its mystical ties with its head, remains faithful to him. Infallibility belongs to the entire Church. Nor will the Spirit permit the Church (*in toto*) in time and space, to proclaim falsehoods and/or to mix truth with error. It is not only ontologically impossible but also soteriologically inconceivable that the Church should be "unfaithful" to Christ.

In other words, we may be united on a certain human basis and may have attained a degree of mutual consent and understanding and still not have attained the true unity. Such human unity depends on the quality and apostolicity of fellowship formed between the partners involved. Throughout history there have been many unions and alliances negotiated which have lacked authority and durability precisely because the constituting partners had not fully adhered to the fullness of truth of the Church. Repeating what had already been stated by Aristotle, St. John Chrysostom distinguished between false peace and true peace — "In the days of the apostles, Paul rebuked and attacked all those unanimously opposed to him . . . Unanimity cannot be praised in every case, since even robbers can agree among themselves. It was his intention not to disturb them, but the dispute arose owing to their persistent divergences . . ." (*Homily 35,1 on St. Matthew*, PG 57.405).

Unity of faith will result and be manifested in ecclesiastical and sacramental unity, organic unity, a natural consequence of the achieved consensus, i.e., the symphony, harmony, agreement, and unanimity of all baptized believers. Unity will become the eloquent sign of that which already exists among the homogeneous members of the community. Unity, in other words, is operational. It has a functional distinctiveness derived from what it contains and expresses in reality. It is difficult to speak of unity if its ecclesiological implications have not been solved. Basically, the solution of the urgent problem of unity depends on what we think about the Church. This inviolable essence of the divine nature of the Church is clearly defined in the brief description given by St. Cyprian:

> The spouse of Christ cannot be adulterous. She is pure and uncorrupted. She knows one home. She guards with chaste modesty the sanctity of one couch. She keeps us for God. She appoints the sons whom she had borne for the kingdom of heaven (*De Unitate* 6).

Cyprian's language is biblical. The word "adulterous" means unfaithful and refers to the conjugal relationship that existed between God and the Jews and which now exists between Christ and his people, the Church. In this context, "infallibility" means "fidelity." The Church is always faithful to Christ, her bridegroom, to whom she is ever united. And, since his divine nature is hypostatically united with humanity, the Church is also theanthropic, human and divine, though essentially the latter, inasmuch as Christ is one divine person of the Holy Trinity in two natures, as proclaimed by the Council of Chalcedon (451 AD).

This unity consists of a single-minded understanding of doctrine and of the actualization of life in Christ. What one believes, all believe. Personal awareness and experience does not imply an individualism, a private "gnostic," relative, or peculiar apprehension of the truth. Maximos the Confessor used to say: "I have no private doctrine, only the teaching of the catholic Church."

The apprehension, the experience, even the verbalization, of the truth emanates, issues from the life of the Church, nourishing all with the same blood and truth. They are "catholic" and mystical. In other words, life in the Church brings assurance, the confidence that God loves humankind, that he has spoken to us in his Son, that the Church is deifying, and that its teachings were given to this end.

We remain rather skeptical of statements which declare that unity can never be achieved once and for all, that it has constantly to be renewed and recreated. This view seems to imply that unity has disappeared from the Church and we are asked, therefore, to start *ex nihilo* to discover a new unity. Even worse, it has been suggested that the various "concepts of unity" can be melted down and a new and more inclusive concept forged. If in such a fellowship we mean that one is more "catholic" and another less "catholic," the perplexing question remains. How is this inconsistency to be bridged?

We realize that there are some who are allergic to the term "return" to the ancient faith and *didaskalia* of the ancient and undivided Church. Is the proposed solution logical, however, that consists in venturing upon future experiments and acrobatics on unity? Whatever convergence may emerge from our discussions, the same doctrinal issues will resurface, once more challenging us all and calling for the same answers and solutions. We cannot introduce a selective consensus into our dialogues. Truth, like unity, is indivisible and integral. For all future models of agreed statements, the permanent prerequisite of oneness in faith remains catholicity and continuity. It must also be insisted that unity is not an ethereal concept hanging in the air. Unity cannot live outside the Church.

Authentic church unity is something which cannot be externalized in rational formulae. It is a moral intuition of an inward nature, its interiority being especially clear from its mysteries. The true Church, which is intrinsically indivisible, is wherever the Eucharist is presided over by the bishop. Many criticisms were formulated against the ecumenical councils to the effect that they had adapted the apostolic faith to the needs of the ancient Greek, Latin, etc., speaking society by producing definitions which were binding on, and, therefore, readily intelligible, to all members of the empire. These critics go on to argue that the externalization of the Christian intuition in formal dogma, reinformed by a philosophical confidence in the ability of reason to discern spiritual truth, meant that the diverging traditions of the Latins and the Greeks were felt to be mutually exclusive, with each side treating its own position as absolute. The dispute over the filioque thus reflects a profound difference: the West magnifies the position of the Pope as monarch and, for certain Orthodox theologians, reduces the significance of the bishop, as the head of the local Church.

The unity of the Church remains the most central concern of the ecumenical movement and the Orthodox can only welcome the fact that "concepts of unity" and "models of union" have again come to the fore in Faith and Order. Discussion of the subject of unity inescapably raises the basic question of how the divinely given indivisible unity of the Body of Christ was realized and preserved in history. Two positions are held: on the one hand, there is the belief that this unity exists continuously and uninterruptedly in the Orthodox Church, in its doctrine, sacraments and order. On the other hand, there is a tendency to think that true church unity exists wherever human beings meet in faith and obedience and that it cannot be the monopoly of any of the existing confessions. Clearly the whole ecumenical problem takes on a different focus depending on which of these two positions one holds.

If we are to stay together in one ecumenical movement, we need a working methodology which pays full attention to both of these positions and suggests to each side the right questions to be asked of the other side, so that the answers may lead to an ecumenical advancement leading to union. Reformers, for example, should be encouraged to ask the Orthodox to define their view of life outside the one Orthodox Church, with all its implications, in particular, for conciliarity. The Orthodox, on the other hand, should challenge Protestants to explain how the ontological unity and identity of the Church are to be expressed if there is no permanent and visible criterion of unity in the midst of so many upheavals, endless variations, and even contradictions in creed and church structure due to historical change.

These studies should be accompanied by a parallel study of "factors of division" which would allow us to make an appropriate distinction between legitimate pluralism and sinful divisions. Being quite diverse in character (some being doctrinal, others sociological or ethical), these latter are the "works of the enemy," and a common struggle against them should be part of the search for unity in Christ.

Fellowship has been overly dominated by the pursuit of middle-range objectives. The result has been a monolithic concept of research, planning, and sociological analysis which fails to recognize the extent to which true objectives and values have been deviated in concealed assumptions. Such a concept is totally insensitive to such major structural problems as the likely development of its envisioned ecclesiastical body.

Unfortunately, even the alternative to this kind of unity — that based on an overly sentimental and esoteric love in Christ — turns out in the last analysis also to be a mechanical approach which can be adapted almost arbitrarily to any kind of middle-range brotherhood. Thus, theologians realize sooner or later that they must return to the classical view, not simply out of respect for the authenticity of present-day ecumenists holding this classical view, but because they find that among the patristic writers themselves there were men of great intellectual stature who were confronting the problems of bringing about unity.

7. Seeing the Present and Not Thinking Only of the Past

Theologians are often inclined to judge the profiles of particular churches, laying stress exclusively on what has been taught and practiced in the past. In this we are in a certain way slaves of past evaluations. It is the past which often determines and influences our views in many things during bilateral theological dialogues. This rule is also applied in the relationship between Rome, Canterbury, Lutheranism, Utrecht, etc. This imprisonment to the past hinders and distorts the real identity of a particular Church. In fact, many things have disappeared in the course of time. Others have been modified under pressure of quite objective theological observations by honest and impartial theologians. Self-criticism, fortunately, is not a rare phenomenon among our theologians in this ecumenical era. Therefore, we need not adhere to the archaic and the outdated in judging one another's views and conceptions, that is to something which is no longer valid in the life of one of the two churches concerned. In fact, we are moving from division to reconciliation.

In reality, many of those quarrels which in the past shook the peace, and brotherly relations between the East and the West, have ceased and are now considered irrelevant. It would not be wise to repeat the polemical issues of the past, without considering the immense improvement and the real change in positions which have occurred. But even if we do so, we must not consider these existing divergences as isolated from certain external, accidental elements, which have influenced this or that established formulation or practice. History, political tension, antagonism, linguistic misunderstanding, and a defensive attitude towards heretics, all these have caused many theologians to exaggerate minor issues and to overdramatize their significance. The past, since it is constituted both of history and life, is a complex affair and consists of a variety of issues and causations, both theological and non-theological.

Our theologians, therefore, should examine before anything else, the present reality. The Church is not a monolithic organism. She is changing. Many things have been changing for some time. We must see the Catholics and the Reformed as they are today, and not as they were yesterday. Between the Schism of 1054, the first Vatican Council, the second Vatican Council, and the official bilateral

29

dialogues, there have been many changes. In comparing the West-East theological self-understanding and ecclesiological outlook, westerners are more keen in regarding "theology" and doctrine as an adaptable and changing thing, answering new rapid changes within a given ecclesiastical life. So many changes have occurred in Roman Catholic theology that certain observers do not hesitate to describe this trend, not only as an "evolution," but also as a "revolution." Hopeful signs are the commonly agreed to statements, and the numerous convergences during frequent consultations.

Another important fact is that many honest efforts have been made for a better knowledge of Orthodoxy. A considerable number of fruitful and astonishingly creative consultations and study groups have taken place, and their finds cannot be ignored or minimized. We mention only a few of them: the Colloquia of Pro-Oriente at Vienna; meetings at Regensburg, Germany; consultations in the United States of America between Orthodox, Lutherans, Episcopalians, Roman Catholics, and others; and the extremely relevant publications by patristic scholars and other eminent theologians, which bring to light all the best that the undivided patristic period and its liturgical wealth can offer to us.

Of course, in this quest each partner must clarify and restate its position on controversial issues, in light of the new and useful results of honest and impartial research. In this respect, it is necessary to strictly keep to the basic issues of our faith and of our salvation without mixing the purely theological with the non-theological problems. Here we must give another warning, namely, to distinguish between (1) *adiaphora* — indifferent issues, not relevant to the question of salvation, (2) *theologoumena* — that is, problems for which there has been no official statement, and, (3) *mythologoumena* — that is, only customs, piety, or religious practices which are the product of the particular devotional style of a local church or country.

In terms of methodology, let us say that there are two ways of approaching our dialogues: the minimalistic, where the least possible number of agreed points is to be asked for, or the maximalist, where we hold out for the maximum of our demands to be met, rejecting any kind of review, re-statement, or compromise, and not allowing any serious consideration of the essentials of our faith, which cannot be altered. In this respect, our common ancient experience during the time of the debates of the Ecumenical Councils can teach us many precious lessons: to what extent should we use *akriveia*

or the exacting (accurate) approach? Or, where is *oikonomia*, a more
lenient, charitable, and comprehensive attitude needed? For certain
conservatives among our people, perhaps it would be useful to clarify
the status and the identity of the two partners in a dialogue. What
makes one a "heretic" and not merely a "schismatic"? In other words,
have our divisions and extended separation so deeply undermined
the structures and our basic doctrines that one of us could be qualified
as a "heretic"?

8. The Ecclesiological Intra-Structure

It has recently been noted in the West that there exists a certain bi-polarization in the collegiality between the bishops and the priests as well as the clergy and the laity. Is this a resurgence of clericalism or just an "impasse"? One can always say that in theory at least, in western ecclesiology, and especially in the Second Vatican Council, a co-responsibility exists among the bishops in the Church. Important decisions should be taken by the body of bishops, surrounded by the clergy and the laity. But one becomes aware during the work of the episcopal synods, that neither the bishops, nor the priests, nor the laity do in fact participate sufficiently, for certain decisions are revoked by an inexplicable "centralism." We also note that there is a tendency to build up the picture of an idealized Church in the best of all worlds, that a species of computer-bishop is being perfected that will provide each new question with a precise answer. Such confusion depends upon a false vision of the Church — which is too often identified with a hierarchical system — and such distortion is also based on a certain scorn concerning what the majority of church members are actually experiencing today. The people of God, who constitute the foundation and the guarantee of the Church, express their opinion with too feeble a voice and more often than not present the impression of remaining dumb and amorphous.

Collegiality must be a permanent reality. The people of God should never be considered dismissed, unemployed, or even on holiday. In communion with their clergy, they must play their part in the labors of the whole body of Christ. One will be committing a sin against collegiality if the guidance of the laity becomes anonymous and the clergy become mere executive agents of the upper hierarchy of the Synod. The ancient Tradition speaks about the active contribution of the people of God (λαὸς τοῦ Θεοῦ). The bishop is not separate from his community, nor the community from its bishop. And yet scant attention is often paid to this community.

Another misunderstanding or ambiguity seems to be due to the very nature of the Synod, which identifies itself, albeit unconsciously, as a parliament where the majority is not in the habit of yielding ground to the minority. And yet, a synodal decision should reflect the consensus of the whole body of Christ, and not this or that divergent tendency. The bishop is the representative of the catholicity of the Church, the world-wide episcopacy; he does not express the voice only of his own particular church, but is responsible for the Church universal. Hence, a bishop must not be considered as a sort of robot, but as the defender of the aspirations of his people and those subordinate to him in the universal Church. The actions of collegiality often come up against juridical dispositions and other such things. But the task of the Church lies in the hands of bishops, priests, and laity, all of whom must share the responsibility for this mystical body which constitutes the greater family of the redeemed.

The dark side of the causes of separation is that through the course of time questions of secondary importance assumed a position of primary importance. After so many centuries of separation, we now see how ridiculous certain distinctive elements are which in and of themselves do not bear any significance, but nevertheless became the boundaries which separate one church from another, though they are often so close to one another. One of the bishops in the Middle East reflecting on this tragic situation made the following comment with regard to the variety of denominations in the holy City of Jerusalem: "By their hats you shall know they are clergymen and to which church they belong, since each church adorns its priests' and bishops' heads with a variety of headgear. All too often to Moslems, Jews, and other outsiders we are only known as Christians by our hats, not alas by our fruits."

It is true that animosity has since disappeared in most parts of Christendom, but mental or spiritual eye-gouging is still alive and well in many quarters. Religious bigotry is no respecter of persons, and the Orthodox who looks no further than his own parish and then beyond the borders of his country may be as a Christian segment as unattractive as the "sectarianly" exclusive non-conformists.

Nowadays we are all living in a more or less Christian era; consequently, it is rather difficult to appreciate the difficult battle of our fathers in the faith to preserve the purity of the inherited apostolic doctrine. Let us take, as an example, St. Hilary, bishop of Poitiers (315-367). In his days the part of the empire which was then known as France was threatened by Arianism and rationalism. The danger was immense. For Arius, only God the Father counts. Jesus is only man. Surely, an exceptional man, even a divine one, but not in his very nature, but only by adoption by the Father. Undoubtedly, Jesus is a man of great value, to whom God has given certain divine attributes. Arianism was thus denying not only the mystery of the Trinity, but even refusing the revealed truth in Christ, not seeing in Him the true Logos of God. In fact, the entire unity of revelation was at stake. Thus, Arianism attempted to replace religion with a man-centered rationalism which limits faith to its proper measures. Religion — *religare* in Latin — unites us to God. Rationalism limits us to man. The Arian emperor Constans convened a Council in Arles in order to counterattack the authority of the Nicaean Council (325), which stood against Arius, and then sent St. Hilary into exile in Asia Minor. There in exile, the holy Hilary wrote the famous *De Trinitate*, a systematic exposition of the true faith and a refutation of the Arian errors. Even from his exile he gained wide fame for his orthodoxy, sustaining the weak clergy in the West, and encouraging the pastors to keep the faith intact, thus copying the adamant example of St. Athanasios of Alexandria. After his return, he restored confidence among the Gallo-Roman clergy, and with astonishing courage wrote to the emperor Constanse in the following fearless terms: "I will speak in strong terms, Constanse, as I should have spoken similarly to Nero, to Decius and to Maximilian. You must not have any illusions, because in reality, by your philo-Arian attitude, you are making war against God and against His Church."

At the same time, he writes exhortations to those weak Arian bishops who had taken bribes, drawing their attention to their grave responsibilities, in a new treatise known as *Contra Auxentium*. Like any other true fighter, the holy Hilary's ministry was a continuous march in continuity with all those confessors of the faith. *Ex fide in fidem*: From faith to faith. The Church workers' task will always lie between faith and the incredibility or error held by corrupt people. In all ages, there will always be supporters of falsification rather than respect for the faith entrusted by Christ to his Church. Such battles do not only occur in the intensive dangers of the well known classical heresies, but also in the fight for the propagated ideas of secularism, and doubts, undermining the ecclesiastical order and putting into question all transcendence, especially in the field of evangelical ethics.

Many martyrs and godly workers of the Church of Christ have spent their entire lives in the quest for the reconciliation of their entrusted flock with God and with their fellow-men. Priority was given in this respect to unity among Christians who, although belonging to the same Christian family, were not in full union. Thus, it is generally recognized that this full reunion is a long and painful process. It requires many steps, often resulting in tears, prayers, disappointments, and stagnant situations as well as setbacks and certain impasses. Their unfulfilled desires, therefore, remain a precious legacy for us, but also incite us to a more active commitment. Restoration of unity is not an easy task. In addition to adequate preparation and the creation of favorable conditions, we need to find the most efficient means of dialogue, to find a common language, to make every effort to overcome psychological and deeply rooted prejudices and misunderstandings, so that when we use a theological term and a certain theological language, we can immediately grasp the same reality without such language becoming a source of division.

It is true at the same time, that history and past events have created a wound which awaits to be healed and that still weighs down our steps and slows our progress on the way to the unity which we seek. Consequently, we have to proceed with perseverance, but also with wisdom, so that the building may be solid and not endowed with a merely outward appearance. The risk here might be that an idealized picture of the ancient Church's unity before the schism between East and West (1053) might lead to an idealized model for the restoration of unity. We have to keep in mind the necessary distinction between differences compatible with unity — what we call *adiaphora* or *theologoumena* — and the differences which make it necessary to find a common solution and agreement. A study of such problems regarding ecclesiology and soteriology would normally lead to an examination of additional aspects of faith without departing from the character of existential experience which is fundamental for theology.

This leads us to accept a solid historical criterion which will test the common experiences of the living reality in the Church. On the one hand, this means that it is not necessary to seek a totally new model of unity. (See the unusual method of the Faith and Order document: seeking new models of unity.) The history of patristic theology offers to us a model that has somehow already been experienced. On the other hand, this reference to past experience should not be considered to be preclusive. The communion we seek to re-establish is in line with the existential experience which follows and develops this experience. Our research must guide us so that together we do not seek for a model literally found in the past. Rather, we are called to remember the historical developments, the "modifications of terms and language" which due to rupture and the isolation, have taken on a different meaning throughout history. We are equally advised to be careful when comparing the ways of thinking, formulating, and accepting terms and interpretation of the revealed Truth between the East and West. What for one Church may be a sensitive priority, for another is not. We meet this difference in many encounters. If this point is not solved, then there will simply be the joining together of an old piece of creased and ill-fitting patchwork with a bright and expensive new piece of clothing. The unity we seek must transcend sociopolitical and cultural factors which impede any progress. Because of the philanthropy of Christ, manifested in his incarnation for the unity of alienated people, the sin of division is healed, so that all forms of separation contradict God's design. In the ecumenical movement it is often stressed that this future unity is not isolated from another unity, that of the whole of humanity. Thus the Church's unity becomes the prototype.

Identification must not be seen as an exclusion of distinctive elements which certainly do not touch upon the oneness of our faith. But neither is it wise to isolate issues from their totality and fullness since all particular items are interrelated. If not, such a selective approach might result in our returning to the same themes with differently labeled words, e.g., the next meeting, like the last, would be concerned with the sacraments, the Church, etc. No item must be put in the margin or underestimated because of any disagreements that might be expressed. At the same time, without being imprisoned in absolete vocabulary, we must avoid existential language that is incomprehensible because it is far from traditional definitions and may leave the way open for unilateral, subjective interpretations. Thus, while this healing of the painful rift is an awesome duty, it is also a humbling one. It is difficult to amalgamate, humanly speaking, to find an acceptable terminology after centuries of separation and estrangement. We must foresee in this respect the blessed repercussions of such a consensus between the two major historical churches, namely, that they will influence and facilitate other dialogues belonging to the same confessional family.

We need also to be aware that often, in official statements resulting from Christian dialogue, an objective reader finds a kind of schizophrenia. One kind of declaration is plunged in friendly and ecumenical feelings, while quite different statements are made after a few days, on the same topic, for internal consumption, as if two criteria and two different approaches are being used.

9. We Are Christ's Body

In view of so many distorted interpretations concerning the nature of the Church, Orthodoxy cannot but remind us all of this faith and its living reality. Strengthening the concept of the body of Christ in both segments of Christianity becomes one of the urgent tasks which must be addressed in the pursuit of full unity. This fundamental belief that the Church is the body (*soma*) of Christ constitutes an essential element of our ecclesiology over and against any other wrong approach.

In recent years, for many reasons, the community attracts many followers and yet has embraced strange, divisive, and secular ways. What is therefore needed is to clarify the very nature of our assemblies that they are not simple, friendly, of one-minded fellowships but that we are gathered because Christ invites us, consolidates us, remains the chief, the head, and we, either alive or dead, constitute the members of his body. It is even proper to add the quality of that body, namely, that it is mystical and organic. Such a view, then, explains why we pray both for our beloved ones on earth as well as beyond the grave. Thus, in our liturgical texts, we pray: "And be mindful also of all those who sleep in the hope of the resurrection unto everlasting life. Give them rest, O God, where the light of thy countenance shines."

Now, praying for or on behalf of the departed saints is an affirmation of the existing unity of the body of Christ in which all believers are living and none is really dead. Death is a removal from bodily existence to incorruptibility. Our God is not the God of the dead, but he is God of the living. All believers are joined to one another in the bond of love. And that love is manifested by praying together and praying for one another. Death does not break that living, prayerful relationship of mutual concern. Such exchange of supplications shows that we are and we remain one family. Individualistic prayers ignoring the communal dimension are rejected by God. Whatever is selfish is condemned. In the Old Testament distorted offerings, partial and defective, are displeasing to God. Thus, Amos the prophet says: "I hate, I despise your feast days, and I will not smell in your solemn assemblies . . . Take you away from me the noise of thy songs" (5.21). And Isaiah: "Your new moons and your appointed feasts my soul hateth. They are a trouble unto me. I am

37

weary to bear them ...When you make many prayers, I will not hear" (1.14).

The fact that Christ remains forever the head of this ecclesiastical body implies that he is continuously transmitting his gifts, his "energies" as the Church Fathers tell us, thus transforming the whole body and its members "in his likeness." Consequently, each one experiences the same attributes of Christ; he becomes christified. All such members are linked among them with a spiritual communion, equally with those on earth and those in heaven. So, heaven and earth constitute one single united entity, the one impossible to exist without the other. Eucharistic sacrifice offered and renewed by the militant members on behalf of the living and the departed members keeps this inner unity unbroken. It reflects as an echo a continuity of heavenly praise to God, offered by the angels to the most blessed Holy Trinity.

Thus, the Church is united, inseparably embodying earth and heaven, eternity and present. What happens with all members leaving this earthly life is that they are registered or inscribed upon arrival in "the book of life of the Lamb" (Rev 21.27). Here on earth we are sojourners, foreigners, while our permanent home is the upper Jerusalem. We all are marching towards that direction. Gregory the Theologian says: "This upper Jerusalem, invisible to our earthly eyes, is our final city to which we march. Its main citizen is Christ, and we are the Church, namely the co-citizens, of the first born, registered in heaven. In this feast around the great Citizen, all are celebrating with that vision of the glory and dancing the endless dance" (*Oration* 8,6; PG 35.796).

Isaak of Sarouk, a Syrian theologian and poet, (c. 6th century) has written many profound pages about this Christological link with the mystery of the Church. The following is an example. It is clear, that he was greatly inspired by the typology of the Old Testament, precisely that of the Song of Songs: "Women are not as closely united to their husbands as is the Church to the Son of God. Who among the bridegrooms except our Lord ever died for his bride, and which bride has ever chosen as her husband a crucified person? Who ever gave his blood before his spouse, if this is not he who died on the Cross, and who with his wounds sealed his nuptial union? Who has ever seen, laying down dead at the wedding feast with his spouse present nearby embracing him for consolation? In which other feast is distributed to the guests the body of the bridegroom in the form of bread?

Death separates brides from their husbands, but here, it is exactly death that unites the spouse to her very beloved one. He died on the cross. He delivered his body to his glorious spouse and beholds that every day she takes him and consumes him at his table.

From the most precious blood that came out of his pierced side, he offered to her a cup which she ought to drink in order to forget her innumerable gods. With him she was covered with oil. In the water she attracted Him to her. She consumed Him in the form of bread, and in the form of wine she drank so that the world might recognize that: the two have become one. After the death of her Bridegroom on the Cross, she did not exchange Him for another one, but she loved His death because she knew that by His death she received Life (*Homily on the Veil of Moses*; Ex 34.35).

Such being the nature of the Church, as the body of Christ, the oneness is manifested, among other ways, in the same faith. Diversity or pluralism on non-theological factors, often misinterpreted, cannot effect its doctrine. All members have to confess one faith, one Lord, one Baptism (1 Cor 12.13). Consequently, there is none other but only one way to salvation. All local ecclesial communities, inspite of cultural diversity or geographical distance have the same teaching and doctrinal structure. Even that one which is isolated, John Chrysostom states, "is part of the same Church spread out throughout the oikumene, and that body constitutes the wholeness of the Churches. Because if locality of space separates one from the other, the Lord unites them, being the same and common for all" (*Comment. on 1 Cor. Homily* 1,1; PG 61.13).

This explains why heretics were always seen as the worse enemies of Christ, cut off from communion. The Church during the Ecumenical Councils was fighting not so much the heretic as a person, since he has merit out of charity, but rather heresy, the error, both so that it might not pollute the whole body and also that the evil be healed, John Chrysostom remarks (*Sermon on St. Phokas*, 2; PG 50.700-01).

First, we have to refute any misconception about the purpose of our prayers for the dead. They are not meritorious as such, neither do they have the effect attributed by some, that such prayers can automatically change the place of an unpenitent to the place of the righteous and just. Prayers help us to recollect the saints of past generations who not only have set an example of faithfulness to Christ for us but have made it easier for us to live our own commitment of faith because of their enriching the heritage of the church both spiritually and doctrinally. Such links with present generations must not be taken as the laurels of the past, or that the Church is involved in spiritual ancestor worship, but rather it is because it delights in affirming over and over again its identity with the previous generations of saints, martyrs, and confessors in terms of the unchanging Gospel and a common experience of redemption. In this context, the absence of such links in many reformed worship experiences leads to a vacuum and consequently to a searching for spiritual roots. Perhaps the alarming symptoms of loneliness stem from the absence of such an ontological koinonia and association. And the centrality of Jesus in all these, is not diminished or even lost. As a matter of fact, it is enchanced by remembering that we are "encompassed about with so great a cloud of witnesses" (Heb 12.1). We are not alone or isolated. They exist ontologically but not bodily. Honoring the departed saints is simply a continuation of the honor which they enjoyed while they were still with us. They share this peace and joy in terms of their spiritual state.

When St. Paul in his epistle to the Hebrews defines the meaning of faith, it follows with a long list of men and women of the Old Testament who left behind great feats of faith. Early post-apostolic texts make reference to godly people who left behind them striking examples of faith and consecration to Christ. Thus, Clement of Rome (circa AD 96) states: "Let us fix our gaze on those who have rendered perfect service to his excellent glory . . . mentioning Enoch, Noah, Abraham . . ." It is true that since the time of the Reformation, many Western theologians have been known to repudiate the practice of commemorating the saints, and especially their intercessions on our behalf. Undoubtedly, this was a reaction against the abuses that had prevailed in the Latin Church, thus distorting the whole issue of intercessory prayers for the dead. But is it right to throw the baby out with the bath water?

We must again repeat that only Christ is our unique intercessor and high priest who perpetually intercedes for sinners at the throne of the Father, pleading the blood shed of Calvary's cross (1 Tim 2.5). This practice is seen in the worship of the early Church which combines Christ's intercessions with those of believers who are still living their earthly pilgrimage. Thus, Basil of Caesarea in his eulogy for the martyrs states: "How much have you labored in order to find even one person beseeching the Lord? And here there are forty in one voice offering up supplications . . .O Choir of saints, O holy order, O steadfast alliance, O sentinel of the generation of men, gracious partakers in our cares, most powerful, intercessors" (Homily on the Forty Martyrs).

It is precisely in this frame of reference that we must understand the special honor attributed to the Mother of God. A distinction should be made between Mariolatry and Mariology. We venerate Mary, as we do venerate all the saints dear to God. And if this is so for the ordinary faithful who are departed, much more gratitude does Mary deserve for her contribution and our praise for what she has done and offered in God's design for humanity's redemption. Mary is not a substitute mediator to the Father, but rather on our behalf, an intercessor to her Son. We petition for her intercessory prayers, as we would petition a fellow believer for intercessions for a specific need in time of adversity. All the ancient liturgical texts plunged in religious poetic style with delightful superlatives and rhetorical expressions, behind such rich vocabulary try to convey the importance of inner communion between all the living Christians on earth with those in heaven, and above all, the Theotokos.

Saints can more easily intercede for us since they are nearer to God's throne. It is dangerous when Christians lose their sense of accessibility to Christ. It is an affront to his loving concern and care for man. It is a violation of the Incarnation — that the Father's Son emptied himself and took on human nature simply out of his concern and mercy for man in his need for salvation. Jesus is not some transcendent power in heaven who looks down or a judge who is waiting to meet us only on judgment day. He is very close to us and he lives within us, seeking our meeting and final communion.

The paradox of the Church is that, while it has suffered a great deal throughout the ages from divisions on all sides, outside and inside, it has remained one and faithful to what it received from its founder. Indeed, the divisions were grave and could have destroyed its existence if it were a mere human body. Monophysitism, the famous *Henotikon* by the Emperor Zeno, the Exposition of Faith by the Emperor Heraklios and the conflict of Iconoclasm have disturbed the peace in the Church and have caused a great number of internal dissensions. The Church must not be seen as a monolithic body. Although it has suffered and still is suffering, it preserves its identity, purity, integrity and authenticity, held by its invisible head, that is, Christ.

It is the *hierarchia veritatum*, the existence of a real hierarchical order which determines those things necessary for salvation and those which are not.

The frequent interventions by secular power within church affairs were a constant threat to the integrity of the faith. Thus, in addition to the scandalous support of Arianism by several Byzantine emperors, later during the Christological conflicts, the Emperor Zeno (476), while showing interest in Orthodoxy at the beginning later joined the camp of the Monophysites by his ambiguous and compromising attitude. His *Henotikon* rendered no real service. While Nestorios and Eutychios were condemned and the formula of the Council of Chalcedon was defended, yet the catholic faith on the whole was left at the mercy of passionate debates. The *Henotikon* tried to introduce a middle way of reconciling the opposing views, but in fact left everyone free to give his own interpretation.

Concerning the dispute on the two wills, dyothelitism, the Emperor Heraklios (638) issues, in his turn, the decree of the "Exposition of Faith," by which he imposes Monothelitism. This document was unfortunately signed even by several patriarchs of the East, Kyros of Alexandria, Makedonios of Antioch, and Sergios of Jerusalem.

10. Living the Mystery of the Church

The inaugurating link with Christ, the initiation sacrament of Baptism, incorporates us at the same time into him and his brethren. Together, head and body, constitute from now on a complete wholeness, human and divine in its character, earthly and heavenly. How can we live this reality? Of course, such a life is and will remain a mystery. Nevertheless, we have to touch on certain distinctive elements, which differentiate the Orthodox ecclesiology of belonging from other conceptions. Such a theme acquires substance in view of our bilateral dialogues.

Living this reality of membership in Christ's Church is vital for the Church. This corporate aspect has an important repercussion on a Christian's character, his way of feeling and seeing persons and things around him and within himself. In spite of human weakness and imperfection, it was to such a community of redeemed people that Christ was referring when he guaranteed the unconquerable nature of the Church, i.e., that no powers of Hades will prevail upon her (Mt 16.18). Repeatedly Christ promised that he would sustain his Body by bestowing graces, or charismata. The dialectic between the human and divine factors, as often distinguished by the Reformers, seems artificial. The one does not preclude the other. Throughout the history of salvation, God has used man's power, ability, and cooperation for his divine plan — his economy.

In formulating the order of the Christian faith, the Fathers of the First Ecumenical Council of Nicaea saw no objection, to putting side by side faith in God, faith in Christ, and faith in the Church. The records of the Acts are centered on the Church's reality — historical, redemptive, evangelizing, and growing through the Apostles. Nobody was relying on an individual, closed and self-centered, or on an inner witness of the Holy Spirit. Christians were living this reality not by themselves, but with their pastors, with the community. The absolute criterion for verifying the Gospel's message was not a person's own view, but that of the whole hierarchy of the *Ekklesia*. The Bible was read before the Christian assembly, and understood by the Church as a whole. "Securus judicat orbis terrarum," St. Augustine wrote, and this security has supported Christians down through the centuries.

There is a certain reality surpassing human understanding that is faith in the mystical body of Christ, the Church. The ninth article

43

of the Nicaean Creed expresses this common faith by describing the Church as "one, holy, catholic, and apostolic." Of course, faith in the Church is not a substitute for faith in God. To believe in the Church is to believe that she is the mystical fountain of grace on earth, where man receives sanctification, the abode of the grace of God throughout all ages (Mt 16.8, Eph 3.21). To have faith in the Church means to venerate the communion of Christ and his people. It is through the Church that man can rightly know the oneness of God in the Trinity. The Church is the image of this Trinitarian unity. Through spiritual striving, as a member of the Church, one can apprehend something of the ineffable divine essence and the redeeming action of the Holy Trinity within the Church.

Being the body of Christ, the living symbol of Christ's incarnation, the Church is fully in possession of all that is required for man's sanctification. We must commune within the shrine in which the Holy Spirit permanently abides, and which we call the Church. In other words, faith in Christ leads us to the Church. Life in Christ is life in the Church. Thus, he who does not believe in the Church is unable to understand the fullness of Christ's incarnation. The words of St. Paul apply only to those who believe and abide in the Church: "Now you are no more strangers and foreigners, but fellow-citizens with the saints, and of the household of God; and are built upon the foundation of the apostles and prophets, Jesus Christ himself being the chief cornerstone . . . In whom you also are built together for an habitation of God through the Spirit" (Eph 2.19-22).

A Christian's life is incoherent and inconsistent without his membership in the Church, without abiding in this sacramental communion. For the Church is the climate in which we achieve our union with God in this present, earthly life. This union will be completed in the life hereafter, following the resurrection of the dead. It is impossible to understand Christ's soteriology without the Church. Our life consists of a gradual merging with the life of the Church. It is this Church which generates and renews all those who enter her. She vitalizes and elevates man, making him fit for a new and holy life in Christ. Whatever we might need for our salvation, we will only find in the Church.

There is nothing accidental or arbitrary in the Church. Everything in the Church takes place through God's appointed means and his assigned people. Faith in Christ has ecclesiological dimensions. It cannot be limited to an individualistic principle, by neglecting or underestimating the inner relationship between members of the same body and the head of this body. Consequently, faith in the Church is not an abstract belief or an isolated element, but implies and produces the Christian life in its fullness, proceeding from the foundations of moral or ethical being, and is behaving accordingly. Christ articulates his saving grace by incorporating each human being into his Body. Thus, a Christian feels the power of divine grace acting upon him through the Sacraments, the liturgical setting, and the whole spiritual order of an ecclesial life. As one lives this life, one attains an unshakeable conviction of the truth of one's faith in the Church of Christ.

11. Living a Corporate Reality

Many people live by a "natural" or individualistic piety, without a "church-centered" life. They look like a traveller in motion, neither knowing where he is going, nor how he is to arrive at his final destination. The scope of a man outside the liturgical life is a duality of thought and action. He thinks that he alone hears the angels' concert, while in reality, he hears the voice of his own ego.

The first fruits of membership in the ecclesiastical community is the broadening of the human personality striving for a common action or purpose. Outside, it is restricted to a narrow ego. My ego in the Divine Liturgy finds many other egos. There, I am more conscious of myself; for I find my place in the community, the Church. This is not the achievement of an instant. It requires a slow process, waverings, hesitations, exaltations, indifferences, and the sacrifice of personal interests for the common good.

It is true that the natural man often wants to go beyond himself. He breaks out of this imprisonment. But he only finds similar types who suffer from the same agony and perplexities. He cannot raise his head towards heaven. Within the liturgical life, however, he finds all the vital elements for his growth and progress in the light of God's grace. This light is sought after in vain by non-sacramental efforts. Man, in this case, may display some qualities, but they are so atrophic, so anaemic.

The stimuli provided by our own capacities is not sufficient to overcome the dominion of our carnal being. Just as our soul becomes sclerosed when nourished only by its own substance, so, too, it becomes alive, creative, and dynamic when it is plunged into the Liturgy.

By including the natural world in the sharing of the glory of the Resurrection, Orthodox eucharistic theology shows the breadth of Christ's redemptive work. It wants to show that everything in creation is part of the universe, and that everything may be sanctified, and not rejected as unworthy. Especially the body, which is the temple of the Spirit, requires our respect. It is the instrument of the unseen world within us. It is the image of God, an *alter Christus*.

It is for this reason that the Divine Liturgy, although a great mystery, is very human and comprehensible. It speaks not only of our spiritual needs, but a great many of the petitions deal with our

46

earthly needs. There are prayers for the sick, for rescue from insom-
nia, for wells, for animals, for protection against tree diseases, for
good weather, for fishermen that they may have a good catch, etc.
Our welfare, in the real sense of the word, consists of many detailed
factors. The Church takes good care of every aspect, and neglects
nothing. We can easily understand, after all, why all those bodily and
material elements find such a considerable place in our worship, which
must be grounded in spirit and in truth. Because the whole of our
human existence needs to glorify God, both body and spirit, must
equally be sanctified.

In other words, the faithful live within the Church, relying upon
the Church's offered spiritual resources. One relies upon the prayer
and help of his fellowman. The Epistle to the Hebrews warns against
a separatist conception of worship when it says: "Do not forsake the
assembling of ourselves together as the manner of some is; but ex-
horting one another" (10.25). We find a similar statement in Psalm
78.52: "He made his own people to go forth like sheep and guided
them in the wilderness like a flock."

Here the equivalent of the Hebrew word for "flock" to the Greek,
translated by the Septuagint as "synagogue," has been the subject
of a sacramental and liturgical interpretation by the great doctor of
the Alexandrian School, Origen. He finds here the real physiognomy
of Christian worship. Being together means praying together, obtain-
ing strength together from the same chalice and the same bread. Any
departure from or abandoning of this fellowship leads one astray,
towards all the dangers and enemies of our soul, lying in wait to catch
their victims:

> By observing these assemblies, we keep the mystery of the flock.
> But if we neglect them, we follow the example of those sheep
> who run away from their companions. Then as a consequence,
> the wolves, their enemies, attack them and catch them, as we see
> in practice. But when a sheep stays together with its flock, even
> if it be attacked, it will resist assaults more easily. You see how
> many dangers beset the isolated sheep.

> If we do not want to fall prey to the power of our adversities,
> let us not abandon the assembly, but be eager to meet and honour
> the day of the resurrection of Christ, in order that the bones of
> Christ may join the other bones, the nerves, the skin, the hair,
> the bowels. Forget not that you are the body of Christ, and it

near the beginning as Western thought does, but it takes it seriously. At any rate, Orthodoxy puts great emphasis on man's participation in God's nature — *methexis*. The Divine is not inaccessible. Since
Christ's incarnation and God's *philanthropia*, man can become a partaker in, and a coheir of God's blessings.

Consider the related problem posed by the notorious *Filioque*
clause added by the West to the Nicene Creed's description of the
origin of the Holy Spirit. Since the West was preoccupied with the
problem of applying Christ's merits on one's salvation, it thought
it appropriate to define the Spirit in relation to the Son. But Orthodoxy
thought it dangerous to suggest that the Spirit had some secondary
relationship to the Son in contrast to that which he enjoyed directly
to the Father. A moot point indeed, especially today when theologians
show such diffidence in probing into the inner divine life. The
Paraclete then becomes the main leader of the Church, sanctifying,
guiding, inspiring, and sustaining the faithful. Pneumatology is closely
related, in fact, to the active participation of the laity in the mission
of the Church, since each person becomes *pneumatophoros* (a bearer
of the Spirit).

In order to understand this controversy, one must bear in mind
the inner conflict of every human being. As God, Christ willed and
acted differently than he did as man, although remaining one and
unchanged. He acted according to his will, whether human or divine,
interchanging both roles whenever necessary. In other words, as soon
as his human will grew weak and shaken, then at once his divine will
intervened, guided, and prevailed. He was acting in a "perichoretic"
way, in full communion. Of course, in all his deeds and thoughts,
his divinity was the leading power and his humanity, because of its
perfection, followed suit. John Damascene states: "Human nature
is conquered and coming after the superior. It enacts those things
which the divine will desires" (*The Orthodox Faith* 3.6).

His human will submitted to the divine. Thus, Christ left us a
precious example of how to perform what is good and virtuous and
how to resist the attraction of evil in all its forms: "Since Christ himself
was very God with all his humanity, and perfect man with his own
divinity, he as human in himself and through himself did submit his
humanity to his Father and God, thus offering to us the best model
— *typos* — and example, becoming obedient to the Father" (ibid.
3.18).

Man is not excused, in view of the amount of evil and adversities
to overcome, if he overestimates his personal resources. He is

empowered with divine strength, having accepted the victorious promise of the Savior who conquered death and evil by his death.

12. This Is the Time (*Kairos*) of the Church

God revealed the mystery of the Holy Trinity progressively and in different stages in the history of mankind. Gregory the Theologian perspicaciously explains this process in his sermon "The Holy Spirit." He says that the Old Testament revealed the Father plainly, but spoke of the Son only in an obscure manner, through typologies and prophetic prefigurations. The New Testament manifested the Son most clearly and openly for all to understand. The Logos, hidden since before the aeons of time, now becomes man with man, assuming human nature. But the New Testament did no more than hint at the divinity of the Holy Spirit. Finally, there is the third and last stage, the period in which we are now living, the *kairos* of the Church, extending from Pentecost to Christ's second coming. This is precisely the period during which the person of the Holy Spirit reveals its energies and saving action by indwelling the Church. He particularly emphasizes the pneumatological structure of the new Israel, where the indwelling of the Spirit promotes spirituality and liturgical life: "Today the Spirit dwells among us and makes himself ever more and more clearly known. By gradual additions, God's people progress from glory to glory" (*Oratio* 31, 26-27; PG 36.161).

In similar terms Gregory of Nyssa underlines the important role that the Spirit plays in the Trinitarian economy's manifestation, especially in the sanctifying field of worship:

> It is not the blessed water — were it even the sublimest of elements in all creation — which bestows this benefit upon us, but the commandment of God and the descent of the Holy Spirit which mystically leads up to our freedom. And the water serves as a sign of purification. It is because we are accustomed to calling the body clean when we have washed it of dirt and mud with water, that we also use water for the mystical Sacrament, making the incorporeal splendor manifest through an object of the senses. If you agree, we shall discuss baptism by water in further detail, taking as our starting point the biblical commandment, as if it were a source and spring. "Except a man be born," Christ says, "of water and the Spirit, he cannot enter into the kingdom of God." Why are both of these, and not the Spirit only, considered necessary for the performance of baptism? Man, as we know well,

52

is a complex and not a simple being; that is why for the healing of what is double and joined together, similar and related medicines are chosen; on the one hand, for the visible body, physical water; on the other, for the invisible soul, the unseen Spirit, invoked by faith and ineffably descending. For he who is at work is great, and the things He accomplishes are prodigious in proportion. For just as this holy altar before which we stand is, with regard to its nature, only a common stone, in no way different from other slabs, such as those used to build our walls and to beautify pavings; yet, because it has been consecrated to the service of God and has had a blessing bestowed upon it, it is a holy table, an immaculate sanctuary, which is not touched by all men but only by the priests, and by them only with respect. Likewise, the bread which has hitherto only been common bread, after it has been sanctified by the sacrament, becomes and is called the body of Christ. It is the same with the holy oil, the same with the wine; being of little value before, being blessed, each operates wholly differently after sanctification by the Spirit. It is the same power of the world which renders the priest holy and worthy of honour, setting him apart from the community of the people. For, although he had been until yesterday just one among the people and the public, suddenly he is seen as the head, the president, the teacher of piety, the initiator into the hidden mysteries. And he accomplishes all this without undergoing any change insofar as his body or person is concerned, but always remaining the same as to his appearance, albeit, transfigured, by a certain power and an invisible grace, for the better, as to his invisible soul (*In Baptismo Christi*; PG 46.581).

We need to bear in mind that early Christianity appeared everywhere as a liturgical fellowship, eucharistic community. Sacramentalism was not confined to this or that locality. The primitive Church did not produce a sacramental system in one district and a non-sacramental type in another. Liturgy was co-extensive with the preaching of the Gospel. The Church, after Pentecost, was everywhere a baptized and eucharistic community. This universal identity is deeply significant. The eucharistic structure, everywhere prevalent in the age of the fathers, was the natural product of the eucharistic life of the apostles. There are early evidences of the uncompromising foundation of Baptism and Eucharist, as indispensable requirements in the life of the Church to the last degree, sometimes in argument, sometimes in exhortation, wherein the reception of both baptism and/or Eucharist is represented as simply indispensable to the salvation of any human being since the time of Christ. No human power invented sacraments. No other form of worship, however beautiful and scriptural, can take the place in Christian esteem of the rite of which Christ himself said: "Do this . . ." Whatever else they might do in addition, they must assuredly do this. Such was unmistakably the conviction of the primitive Christian centuries. In addition the fathers explain that this principle agrees profoundly with the twofold nature of man. St. John Chrysostom taught his contemporaries: "If you were bodiless, bodiless gifts would be appropriate. But since you are a soul inserted in a body, it is through things of the senses that intelligible things are perceived" (*Homily 82 on Matthew 4*; PG 58.743).

The divine economy is operating ecclesiologically on the level of the Church. The community of the baptized is the most visible sign that the unseen God meets his people and is working out their progressive salvation. In this perspective, Gregory the Theologian's brother, Kaisarios, sees the expansion of the Church as an extension of Christ's incarnation: *Ekklesia estin Christos kata sark*a. Here is an extract of this important comment: "Those who, as St. Paul says, were baptised, have put on Christ himself, that is, they constitute an ecclesiastical body bearing Christ. All newcomers are received as attached members, as if Christ receives them. The Church is Christ in the flesh . . ." (*Dialogue 3, Interrogatio 127*; PG 38. 1024).

The Church has perfected the mission of the synagogue. Liturgical rites were never meant to cease. The Jewish signs needed to be replaced. They were anticipations. Eucharist is retrospective. The first looked forward on that which was to be; the latter looked backward on that which had been fulfilled, as St. Augustine says: "The very intention of the Jewish observance was to pre-figure Christ. Now that Christ has come, instead of its being strange or absurd that what was done to pre-figure his advent should not be done any more, it is perfectly right and reasonable" (*Reply To Faustus*, xix, 11).

More importantly, the liturgical life was the natural sequel to the principle of Christ's incarnation, which is the supreme example of communion with the human being through material channels. The fact that "the Logos became flesh and dwelt among us," could not consider the outward as an inconsistent means for the manifestation of the esoteric, or as an unnecessary element for the communication of the spiritual. Faith and praxis came first and elaboration followed. Faith in the Trinity preceded and only later bcame a matter of theological formulation. The same thing happened in the whole Church-Eucharist question. The Church in celebrating the Eucharist adhered to certain observances before any explicit principles were defined.

Basil of Caesarea, with his exegetical sensitivity, full of wonder for the dimension of Christ's incarnation, sees its saving effects throughout the whole cosmos, above our inhabited universe as well as below. The Son of God's kenotic descent to earth, where time and space constitute existential criteria, remains a deep mystery. He recalls the admonition of Isaiah: "Ask thee a sign of the Lord thy God; ask it either in the depth or in the height above" (Is 7.11). Here Basil finds the answer to inevitable questions, asked even in his days by the baptised, as to whether the incarnation should be understood in a limited sense, concerning mainly the locality of Bethlehem where Christ was born, and only a particular time of history, namely the fifteenth year of the reign of Tiberius Caesar, under Pontius Pilate (Lk 3.1). And he makes the following comment in which Christ's birth transcends all space, time, and history, becoming a permanent feature, connected with all, with everlasting results, touching all:

> Since the Logos was made flesh, this prophesy by the word "depth," implies all the earth, and the flesh which offers itself to Christ. By the word "height" is meant the supracelestial Logos, who is above all power and dominion, who from the very beginning was with the Father, thus being the Logos truly God (John 1.1). Or again, it might mean by "depth" the lowest region of Hades, and by "height" the firmament above heaven, as in this context the apostle says: "Say not in thine heart, who shall ascend into heaven? that is, to bring Christ down from above; or who shall descend into the deep? that is, to bring up Christ again from the dead" (Rom 10.6-7). Since "He that descended is the same also that ascended up far above all heavens, that He might fill all things" (Eph 4.10), "both the depth and the height signify the descent of the Lord" (*Comment. on Isaiah*).

The present ministerial and liturgical structure of the *Ekklesia* depends on the very nature of the Church, indwelt and guided by the Holy Spirit. Both cannot be simply accounted for and/or explained by influences which are merely either human or historically accidental. For the Church is God's new creation, the extension of the Incarnation, expressly designed to perpetuate and complete the purpose of redemption. To suggest any other interpretation is to misconceive its nature, and to incapacitate ourselves from a right judgment on the principles it has maintained. There is no reason to doubt that the Church was profoundly conscious of itself as being God's creation. It was deeply understood that its formulated faith, its Eucharist, and its ministry were the products of the guiding and directing influence of the Spirit. The Church was serenely certain, with a certainty that nothing could disturb, that these distinctions, characteristic of its life, were not the result of any human prudence or sagacity or even to a sense of what seemed expedient or appeared to be for the best at the moment. They were due to the power of the ascended risen Christ, who after he ascended to the Father, sent the Holy Spirit and pledged himself to be with his Church even unto the end of the world. If the Incarnation means God's *epiphania* within the human, then the promise, that "the Spirit will guide you into all the truth" is exactly what the present situation involves. If the faith that has been entrusted to the keeping of the Church, God's guidance enabling it to bear that responsibility and to fulfill the awesome and solemn trust becomes simply indispensable. Nothing was more characteristic of early Christianity down through all the centuries than the claim of its identity and consistency, with the living Church. And the classical expression of the means of securing the truth is that which Vincent of Lerins in his *Commonitorium* has recorded for all time.

Since the Church embodies the double theandric nature of its head, Christ, its main task consists in transforming its members into that which the Church is in reality, that is: one, holy, catholic, and apostolic, the last signifying its bond with God in Christ. The Church seeks to unite all who exist on earth. Unity means reconciliation with God and with each member as a person in one body, also reconciling all creation into a cosmic dimension. In order that this universal peace, this symphony, be established, a continuous catharsis is needed, since in daily reality the members of this mystical body are not always what they ought to be. Any moral idealization of the component members risks a Montanist view overstating the ideal state at the expense of daily reality. On earth, failure and shortcomings are not excluded. For this reason, precisely, there are always sacramental remedies available, the Eucharist above all, as the means of restoration, purification and gradual sanctification. Membership in the Church should thus be viewed in a dynamic way, involving the development of the whole individual, as well as his social outreach. If the early fathers saw the Church as an ark or a "vessel," that is because it illustrated typologically the Ark of Noah, in which all those in danger from a rough sea could enter. The future of mankind thus germinates within the Church.

Since earliest times this faith in communicability with Christ became the very content of liturgical hymnology, so that worshippers were singing what they believed. Synesios, bishop of Cyrene (c.409) has left us some masterpieces in praise of the Savior, colored by Greek and Semitic phraseology: "Jesus, Savior of the human race, shepherd, husbandman, helm, bridle, heavenly wing of the all - holy flock . . . ."

It is the frequent use of antitheses, characteristic of Semitic poetry. which denotes the double identity of God, being the Giver of all and, at the same time, through his condescension (*synkatabasis*) assuming the human condition. God did not, once and for all, accomplish his duties and withdraw himself. He is a continuous Savior. Thus Synesios introduces in his hymns the language of the prophets:

Thou art the Generator, Thou the Generated; Thou the Light that shineth, Thou the Illumined; Thou what is revealed, Thou what is hidden . . . (*Synesius Cyrenensis: Hymni et opuscula*, vol. 1; Hymni 1st Ode, verses 191-96. Ed. N. Terzaghi (Rome, 939).

Another hymn-writer, Makarios the Egyptian (300-90), underscores the dimensions of Christian worship. It is not limited to utilitarian motives, just demanding and then thanking. It is more than that. In prayer we become spirit with the Spirit, entirely light, joy, rest, charity, peace, mercy, sympathy, and goodness. Just as the stone in the abyss of the sea is surrounded with water, similarly such people are interwoven with the Holy Spirit, and become Christ-like, bearing upon them the virtues of the actively operating Spirit (*Homily* 18.10). In such pure souls the Trinity dwells, not as such, since the Spirit cannot be limited, but inasmuch as humans can receive. They become the throne of glory for the Lord. The celestial icon, Christ, mystically lights the soul and reigns in the souls of the saints (*Homily* 2.5).

From the above texts we can see that although God is immutable, he is not foreign to his own people. He transcends the bounds of history and accommodates himself in appropriate ways in order to be perceived. But the deity remains without any form (*aschematistos*), always retaining his own hypostasis. In this continuous dual operation,

stability on the one hand and continuous flexibility and change on
the other, is found the attitude of God to his people. Nothing can
hinder this communion. With godly people, he has manifested himself
differently to each, taking on different forms in different circumstances: differently to Abraham, Isaak, Noah, Daniel . . . God in
his theophanic contacts adjusts himself to those who are worthy (*Homily* 4.13).

Spiritual renewal through God's energies does not consist purely
in human action within an ethical framework. God does not promise
happiness in human terms, with our understanding dictated by earthly desires and meeting expectations of this world in time and space.
It is based on a continuous ascesis, a spiritual war, a resistance of
the spirit over fleshly appetites. It goes, therefore, beyond the human,
the temporal, the perishable. As such, it remains a real mystery,
because it follows the ascending narrow path of Christ's teaching.
Before such a life one becomes a seeker not of mere happiness, but
rather a seeker of salvation, of inner "death and resurrection of the
old man" whom we all carry within us.

Man has to renounce any reduction of Christian standards in order
to be united with Christ. As Clement of Alexandria says: "In him
and by him alone we become at the same time saved and saving agents,
real saviours for others" (*Stromateis* 7.2). Again, elsewhere, he
describes the impact upon the Christian of this outpouring of divine
energies. Each transmitted gift progressively produces a new state:
"By being baptized, we become illuminated; being illuminated, we
become by adoption sons; having been offered sonship, we are perfect;
being perfect, we become immortal" (*Paidagogos* 1.6.26.1).

Christ's conversation with Nikodemos, etc., leaves no doubt that
in the community of the baptized, the Church, the action of the Trinity
finds fulfillment. The basic New Testament events serve as a concrete expression of this fact. At Jesus' baptism, the Father wills, the
Son is baptized, and the Spirit descends. At the Transfiguration, the
Father commands (Lk 9.35), the Son is revealed in divine light, and
the Spirit permeates and illumines (Mt 17.5; Lk 9.32). In the Crucifixion and the Resurrection indivisible from it — the final act of the
economy of salvation, where, seemingly, the God-Man Jesus acts alone
in the face of evil and death — all the persons of the life-giving Trinity
participate. The Father gives away the Son, receives the Son's spirit
into his hands. He resurrects him with his spirit. The Son suffers and
accomplishes salvation. The risen Christ gives the Spirit to the disciples
and the Spirit descends into the world as a consequence of Christ's

death upon the Cross (Jn 16.7).

Needless to say, such action becomes effective only when human beings fully participate. The Fathers had much to say about this *synergia,* a proportional sharing of the two partners for salvation, God and man. The famous expression of St. Augustine leaps to mind: "God who has made you without your consent, will not save you without your consent" (*Sermo* 169,11; PL 38.923).

We must keep in mind in this context, the different approach of Augustine in other cases on the same topic. What is the place of free will on God's offer? Precisely because of such ambiguities, a sort of determinism and the doctrine of absolute predestination are attributed, thus making Augustinian theology defective and unorthodox.

God, the Creator and Lord, the ruler (*Pantokrator*) of all creatures visible and invisible, is a "spirit" who is not bound by space, time or anything else. He is everywhere at all times, and he is aware of everything. The Godhead is, in some mysterious form, a Trinity. There is an incomprehensible union of the three Persons of the Trinity in one Godhead. We humans can and do communicate with our God through prayer. This is not some sort of symbolic type of communication. Rather it is a genuine communion, *koinonia* with the Spirit.

In prayer we go beyond the realm of the analytical and can in reality communicate with our God in a realm we call the spiritual. Even death cannot restrain us. Through Christ, who defied death, we can be raised after death and united with God eternally. For we were created in the image of God to share in his divinity; but through sin we have stained this marvelous image and thus perhaps have suppressed certain parts of our total consciousness. By choosing to sin, man has chosen to refrain from exercising such a global, existential consciousness. Thus, death has a hold on us and we become limited beings, noticing our nakedness, our limited resources and our inadequacies.

Precisely for this reason, Christ has stated that anyone who does not welcome the kingdom of God like a little child will never enter it. A little child is a typical example of innocence, acknowledging his various needs and his dependence on others, without having to resort to formal logic. The child is genuine and expresses what he feels without suppressing his feelings. Thus through faith we may become innocent, like a child, in opening our total selves to God. A Christian is one who realizes that there are other ways of seeing things other than in the way that we may now know.

The early Church Fathers set the soteriological direction that was to become the pivot for subsequent theological thought among contemplative and ascetic writers. Man was created so that he might be indwelt by the Creator. The world as it was created was a paradise in which God walked. Man was in constant communion with God. What the soul is for the body, God is for the soul. The soul lives as long as God, by his love, dwells in it.

This communion with God, destroyed by the fall and disobedience of Adam and Eve, was restored by Christ, who remade the image of God, since he was the one human being capable of reflecting the perfection of the archetypal divine image, and once again establishing the kingdom of God on earth. In Christ the faithful, too, may come to lead a heavenly life even on earth, because for the soul washed by the sacrifice of Christ and for the liberated Christian consciousness, everything on earth is restored to purity and becomes a means to salvation. The earth is a mirror reflecting the heavenly, a "book" that can be read by anyone who has the "mind of Christ."

Such is the outlook and approach of a true member of the Church. Crossing himself in the name of the Trinity, the "newly born," restored human being enrolls himself in the service of Christ and commits himself to him, and to the Father and the Spirit, promising to work faithfully. Thus, a Christian life consists not only of God's salutary intervention in the life of a given human soul, but is also an act, a concrete commitment on our own behalf. A vital element in our "deification" — theosis — is our personal contribution. Here, in this world, we sow; there, in heaven, we shall harvest. The new heaven and new earth are created by convincing Christian deeds. These constitute the best guarantee, proof, and witness, *martyria* of the authenticity of our membership in the Church. Not only the spirit but also the flesh is sanctified and deified; so, too, are all manifestations of our existence in the world. The flesh is that common factor which unites man with the cosmos and the whole creation. Saved himself by Christ's grace and sustained by the liturgical life, the faithful servant of Christ saves all creation.

Faith is imbued with the need for complete inner birth, the subordination of one's entire life to the task of salvation and deification not only as an individual, but also as one who is dedicated far beyond to the salvation of the entire human race. The divine economy embraces the whole creation from its very beginning down to the accomplishment of its "restoration" (*apokatastasis*). For those who have taken up a position of spiritual isolationism, the incarnation of Christ (Jn 3.5,16) is at the same time a stumbling block and their primary accusation against him. There is no question that the revelation of the Trinity originated in the Old Testament. Such an approach makes God's manifestations to the prophets thoroughly unintelligible. This created world is also God's revelation (Rom 1.20). The biblical narrative of the creation shows that it was preceded by the "council" of the three persons. This implied already an incompletely expressed Trinitarian economy, one to be completely revealed in the New Testament.

13. Diversity in Unity

This theme is profoundly important for the restoration of our communion with one another. We should, therefore, clearly explain our thinking about diversity and certain pluralism. In approaching any particular theme, it is essential that we examine all of its aspects but especially its various connections, the elements associated with one another and their organic dependence. Nothing in nature or in human life is absolutely self-existent, or autonomous, existing by its own power and exclusively for its own sake. Everything is interrelated. If we look, for example, at the component parts of the human body, we can legitimately concentrate our attention on the eyes, the legs, the ears, etc. But instinctively we want to go further and study the inner connection and relationship of each part of the whole. Only a synthetic, global, and wholistic approach can provide a complete and full identification of the object. This truth especially applies to the basic elements of our Christian faith. We cannot absolutize one member and ignore the rest, together with which it constitutes a coherent whole.

Nor can we isolate a human being from his context. You meet someone and immediately you want to know more about him. Who is he? Where does he live? What does he do? What is his background, his affiliation, his cultural, ethnic, social, and religious history, even his hobbies. Only with this information can you have a full picture of the person concerned. But, however revealing for us a situational or contextual overview might be, there is a danger of overlooking other further elements.

We consider poverty, for example, to be a crying injustice, a social anomaly, and a scandal. But it is the result of various contributing factors. There can be no adequate solution to poverty if certain underlying causes are disregarded. This is the mistake of economic planning which relies solely upon an assessment of certain human symptoms, while ignoring the broader human situation. These plans may inevitably engender conditions in which human beings, in fact, exploit one another.

14. Turning Points in History —
in Retrospect

Many streams united to influence the emergence and shape of divided Christendom. All of us, but especially the Orthodox, have to keep in mind a variety of factors, visible and invisible, which produced this explosion. Slowly and silently, but increasingly, it became a flood which threatened the whole Church with grave consequences for unity. Since the schism of 1054, the Roman Church walked alone and was to some extent cut off from the sources of ascetic, patristic spirituality, as it developed a legalistic and scholastic theology all its own. The entire ethos of the Church was affected and the gap between east and west was widened.

The reformers, on the other hand, ignoring or knowing very little about the Orthodox Church, tended to discredit everything that was not "reformed." A campaign against the Church of the primitive Byzantine period was launched, especially against the "Constantinian Church." This, it was said, was dominated by the civil authority of the state and threatened with the introduction of anti-evangelical elements affecting the life of the faithful. A number of historians systematically cultivated this attitude. On the other hand, the primitive apostolic Church was overestimated — as the only pure, immaculate and authentic Church. There was a tendency now to idealize everything connected with early Christianity as the only period which could be relied upon and provide the point of reference. Reformers considered the Byzantine era to be too pietistic and sacramental, overloaded ritually and less evangelical: they saw it as relying on the outcroppings of Caesaropapism and very feeble in evangelical missionary activity. Such pessimistic views were also widespread in the days of Symeon the New Theologian (949 AD) who vigorously had to refute such charges: "There is no worse heresy in these times than of those who proclaim that the Church has fallen into error and gone astray and consequently lost the fullness of grace which she had in the days of the apostles" (*Catechesis* 29).

However, the last thing we want to do is to deny the sad and inadmissible events which have occurred in Church history. There have certainly been periods of deplorable decline, darkness, stagnation and triumphalism. The last claim we would want to make is that of any angelic perfection. A human-divine body living on earth cannot remain wholly unscathed and unspoiled. It is precisely for this reason that

63

the Church exists — to heal and to restore those struck down and wounded by all sorts of evil, by means of its therapeutic pastoral care and spiritual worship. In any event, it is dangerous to over-idealize the family of the baptized. It is also extremely difficult to trace the boundaries where church history and secular history meet. Even in the days of the great church fathers such as Athanasios, Basil of Caesarea, Gregory the Theologian, John Chrysostom, Maximos the Confessor and others, there were scandals, liturgical ignorance, cases of simony and lamentable quarrels about ecclesiastical policy among high-ranking bishops. But the church fathers often engaged in frank self-criticism and deplored the attitudes of self-arrogance. Some people exalt the number seven as applied to the ecumenical councils, as if the Church were unable to convoke further councils in the future. Others argue that only four sacraments are indispensable, analogous to the four gospels and the four rivers of paradise. The saddest feature of such an approach is the incoherent nature of such a conclusion — the divorce between orthodoxy and orthopraxy. While the goal of sacraments is renewal, as rivers of divine grace, they are sometimes diverted from their purpose and become static forms of outward observance without renewing the heart and all the interior world of the believer. But we should not blame the sacraments as such, but only the obscurantism, the unprepared and superficial attitude that exists towards them, as well as the subsequent abuses.

While considering unity as the most precious of gifts, the teachers of the universal Church, nevertheless, used different forms. They had no problem interpreting the ineffable mystery in allegorical, analogic, and even in symbolic, apophatic or cataphatic if necessary, terms. For example, Athanasios of Alexandria and Serapion, Bishop of Thmues, preferred as an epicletic prayer for the consecration of the offered gifts not the descent of the Holy Spirit, but that of the divine Logos. Either *akribeia* or *oikonomia* were applied. Basilica style or the octogen were used for the architecture of the house of worship (see an admirable analysis of such pluralism by Photios of Constantinople: Letter 3rd to the bishops of the East; PG 102.742); the last was strongly defended by Gregory of Nyssa (*Letter to Amphilochios*; PG 46.1093-100).

What might trouble them, however, was the danger of using forms which implied a departure from the *paradosis* and which neglected the catholicity of the faith. The Church is an historical "communion" in time and space, of persons gathered from different backgrounds. It is the "new humanity" gathered around the risen Lord-nourished, perfected, and growing according to particular gifts. Such a variety in unity is described by Maximos the Confessor:

> It will be shown that God's holy Church, an image conforming to its archetype, does God's work in us. The men, women and children coming into the Church, reborn and recreated by her in the spirit, are just about infinite in number; they are very different from each other in race and appearance, they are of all languages, lifestyles, and ages; there are great differences in their mentalities, customs and interests, in their social situations, their skills, and their professions; their fortunes, their characters, and their abilities are all very different, but the Church confers one and the same divine character and title equally upon all: that they be, and be called, Christians. The holy Church is an image of God! It works the same unity in the faithful as God has in himself, even though the people unified in her through faith vary in their particularities and come from different places and different ways of life; it is God's nature to provide this kind of unity which he has in himself, in the substance of things, without any kind of "fusing." In fact, He softens the diversity in them and unifies them (as has already been shown) through their relationship and union with Him, their cause, beginning, and end (*Mystagogia* 1, PG 91.666-67 — translation: Dom Jul. Stead p.66-67).

Our inherited faith is not monolithic. As it had been applied to life, it was necessarily subject to a certain adjustment to temperaments and particular needs of given local communities. It operated in terms of human nature and understanding, in accordance with the memorable, last words of Moses: "My doctrine shall drop as the rain, my speech shall distill as the dew, as the small rain upon the tender herb, and as the showers upon the grass" (Deut 32.1-2). Each of us has to live the truth of the One Church within his or her own culture, taking into account, in its application, the human condition as well as human desires and needs. The Church has shown its creativity by generating its teachings which can be matched to the challenges of history and the needs of all human beings. For the faith to become the possession of the people, it had to be clothed in the forms which satisfy their longings and needs. Only in this way was a balance possible between a permanent unity, on the one hand, and a pluralism of expression, on the other.

St. Cyril of Jerusalem (*Catechesis* 16; PG 33.932) shows in a poetic way how God's spirit operates, using the wonderful analogy of the rain. One and the same rain produces different effects in the vegetal world, in the plants and flowers. The color of the lilies differs, as also that of the roses, tulips, rhododendrons, chrysanthemums, and so on. And not only is there a profusion of colors, but also a variety of aromatic scents and a multitude of different shapes.

The one Church has accommodated itself like this, and thus has produced a wealth of cultures, rites, traditions, religious customs, and missionary and catechetical patterns. Philosophers and others have always been preoccupied with the problem of the one and the many. The apparent difficulties with this, as regards the Church can be solved only upon the assumption that when human beings accept the revealed truth, they act as individual persons or communities of persons. God's action within the framework of unity is expressed by physical coercion, taking into account all the particularities which free persons can possess, but at the same time without violating the very unity itself. This diversity in oneness is reflected in the saying: "As faces are not similar to other faces, neither are the thoughts of men" (Prov 27.19,LXX).

This means that in the process whereby the invisible is articulated in visible forms, various stages have to be passed through, harvesting all that human intelligence and personal feeling can contribute.

It would be disastrous if, in equating unity with uniformity, we were to concentrate upon marginal matters whereas, in fact, flexibility and pluralism are the most desirable. Our attention should focus, rather, on the most essential and elemental components of our faith. Perhaps it would be relevant to our present dialogues to remember the words of Peter III, Patriarch of Antioch, expressed during the conflict between the Patriarch of Constantinople, Michael Kerularios and Cardinal Humbert on the eve of the Schism of 1054:

> If the Latins were ready to withdraw the addition of the Filioque clause in the Nicene Symbol of our common faith, then I would require nothing more than that. All the other issues I would consider as secondary, marginal, belonging to the adiaphora ... must leave the beards to the barbers, the forms of clerical vestments ... We must also leave aside the controversial question of celibacy, liturgical practices, different church traditions concerning discipline, etc. .... (PG 120.812-13).

A closed mind may engender dangerous misinterpretations. This is the case concerning apophatism and liturgical theology. Christians, who mistrust anything strange and unusual, may absolutize and exaggerate this to themselves and even consider the unusual elements to be suspect or heterodox. There has always been and there still exists a real danger of absolutizing the *adiaphora* — things not essential to our salvation. Every *difference* then becomes a cause for conflict, whereas our division may be over accidental symptons, connected to such facts as culture, language, or historical experience.

From childhood we are reared with the idea that theology is, could be, or should be divisive, and little mention is made of our common faith. In this connection, it may be helpful if we bear in mind that from the eleventh century, the West underwent a real intellectual revolution. In order to become more efficient within the developing national societies of Europe, religious thinking came to be organized more on a rational basis. Theology sought the support of logic, rationalism. The first scholastic writings are a mixture of dogma and largely based on rational arguments and logic. We thus pass from the symbol to the dialectic. In face of the revival of Aristotelianism, western theology became apologetic and tried to become an autonomous science, using natural reason to serve revelation and the Church. If Thomism, in the end, preserved a balance between faith and reasoning, it was, nevertheless, unable to escape from a certain compromising of the mystery with philosophy. We observe a departure from the liturgical communion, *koinonia,* because of the invasion of subjective and individualistic forms of devotion and expression.

During the same period, the East experienced its own kind of transformation. The Eunomian crisis of the fourth century and the occasional nostalgic movements of return to the sources of Hellenic culture, compelled theologians to place less emphasis on the speculative or rational approach. There was an amazing growth in an ontology of the "mystery." Knowledge of God can be obtained, on one hand, within the totality of man's inner nature, and on the other, within the eucharistic communion of him with his brothers. Man is reconciled with his very self by the union of his heart at that very place where the light of Tabor is shining. All the theology of personal communion and of energies of God which influenced the fifth, sixth, and seventh ecumenical councils, placed the emphasis on the individual liberty of the human being created in the divine image.

Dorotheos further applies this principle of causality to the analogy concerning suffering and physical illness. The lack of attention in matters has recently borne unexpected fruit in the contemporary West. St. Gregory Palamas, widely read today, underlined the unity of man's experiences in the sacraments and the possibility of man's theosis through the uncreated energies of God.

Later authors would begin more and more to emphasize the way to achieve a spirituality based on the "imago Dei." We find a departure from the "gnostic" view so copiously developed from Origen by Clement of Alexandria. The question which arises is rather that of *koinonia* and the transformation of human nature. The theology of grace was felt to be inadequate and a more ontological approach came to be established. Grace is the fruit of personal communion. The trinitarian God is a tri-hypostatic, tri-personal "fellowship" in himself which comes to each and every one of us. Because of the Incarnation, we become partakers, sharing in the *methexis* of God, as Gregory the Theologian states: "The Son of God became man so that you might become a God for him" (*Oration* 40.45; PG 36.424).

After the Schism of 1054, Western theology went off by itself. It showed persistence but was often frustrated, becoming polemical, impassioned, or arbitrary and thus deprived of the help of Orthodox theology. Today it remains somehow isolated. The sister Church of Rome, the Church of the East, every now and again has raised her voice to warn Westerners of the theological abuses and deviations always possible to a church having a tendency to follow a false road. She has tried to make the Western Church conscious of this evil, and to make it realize the seriousness of its occasional arbitrary acts. But the Western Church just keeps on going its way alone. This solitude can be dangerous or even disastrous. The Western Church has developed a juridical, authoritarian, scholastic, and casuistical theology, which colors its worship and church administration, as well as the piety and moral guidance of its flock. For, in fact, the faithful are the product of their church and reflect all its characteristics. Such, alas, was the position of the Western Church in the Middle Ages. Orthodox theologians foresaw the gathering storm clouds foretelling new tempests and turmoils. They took the few opportunities that were offered to try and put their Western brothers on guard against a number of dangerous innovations. At the Council of Florence (1438-39), for example, Mark Eugenikos, the metropolitan of Ephesos, protested against certain decisions concerning the practice of the faithful which were, in fact, "supererogatory," against the punitive spirit, existing in the sacrament of penance, against purgatory; he was a reformer before the Reformation, a "Protestant" — in the best sense of the word — long before our modern period of protest.

Such anaemic and atrophied theology affected Western ecclesiology. Today the East, in a fraternal spirit, comes to remind us of the true face of the Church.

15. The Struggle against Evil

An unbalanced approach to vital questions of sin and death is due to an insufficient development of Christology. A great deal has been said and preached about Christ's life with emphasis on and implications for Church life, but soteriology as well as the quality of piety were weak. Attending church services is not enough if it is not accompanied by a growing spirituality nurtured in eucharistic worship. Religion in modern times has been prone to be a religion more of the head than of the heart. Faith does not demand any difficult assent. Rather, it demands only that we be moved to an "orthopraxia."

Secularism is concerned with philosophical skepticism when faced with the claims of religious dogma. But dogma in and of itself is not secular at all; each one in his own post-baptismal way experiences this life as the *kairos* in which the rules of the world are suspended, homage is paid to other values, and inarticulate hope is refreshed. Those who cannot enter into its spirit are to be pitied indeed, for they are confessing their total captivity to wordliness, and denying the existence of another kind of life which is inherent to all. Christian life and membership in the Church is not a periodical bringing to mind thoughts about God and his mercy, when man takes leave of his senses, but rather is how things ought to be in a permanent coherent attitude; it is an empirical taste of an otherworldly reality.

The saint's vision of "living Christ day by day" is not absurd; it should be the goal of all human effort. The one sin is to give up that effort, to abandon the world to its normal nastiness, as a hopeless mess. We have to remind ourselves of the difference between option and fulfillment. Life is not only a promise; there is also the test of it, death, no less awesome, no less central to its meaning. In order that there be a sense of God's presence — *epiphania* — every day, there has to be a struggle against death, a victory like that at Easter. The ultimate rejection of Christianity is to refuse to contemplate that price.

The early Church demanded more than just enthusiastic promises for its support. As Paul explained to the Galatians and Philippians, the gradual unveiling of truth, which in God's *oikonomia* constitutes our education and gradual maturity, could not stop short of a full and loving demonstration in the universal language of a human life.

70

The Fathers were well aware of the difficulties involved in making an infinite God responsible for creation in time and for interventions in history. They regarded as providential the fact that the Word- Logos or Wisdom-Sophia, proceeds from the Father and acts as his personal agent in the process of putting into the world and also illuminating the heart of man. Anaxagoras, a Greek philosopher (6th century BC) maintained that the wisdom of God (in terms of the *Sophia* found in the Book of Proverbs), the active agent of Godhead, pulsing through the world and cooperating in such perfect harmony with the transcendent Deity, was "daily his delight." Clement of Alexandria assumes that God is love and as such underlines the course of history. The Logos, he explains, has always been in the world as the Instructor-*Paidagogos*, speaking with the voice of the human conscience. God pitied mankind from times of old, but more recently he has appeared and saved him. Thus salvation, *soteria*, is to be understood as union with God.

Origen argues in precisely the same way as does Clement, that divine love is revealed in a gradual process. The disclosure of the Incarnation is so radical and decisive in nature that after it, things can never be the same again. The event, he explains, reveals how man in his ascending course is compared with the steps leading up to the holy of holies in the temple; the ascent is a gradual one until finally God is known in himself. Origen sees the Incarnation as a cosmic radiance lighting up the entire cosmos, universal and personal worlds throughout history.

He says:

> Let us imagine a statue of such size as to fill the entire world and so vast that no one could contemplate it. Then let us imagine that another statue was made, identical with the first as regards the shape of the limbs, features, and the whole outward appearance but much smaller in size. The purpose of this miniature would be that those who could not properly grasp the nature of the enormous statue would look at the tiny copy and assert that since this copy is an exact likeness of the former they had gathered from it the essential character of the original.

Origen is here crystallizing the third century argument that, after due preparation in the works of nature and in the heart of man, God is obliged to proceed to a certain abnegation, or *kenosis*. This self-emptying forced on God by his own will, this condescendence, *synkatabasis*, is in order to cut himself down to a recognizable size. "He became one of us in order that we might become like him," Athanasios of Alexandria would later say. Thus God could speak to his people in a language which the simplest of them could hardly fail to grasp, or that the keenest mind of any philosopher could think inadequate as a theme for lifelong contemplation.

Origen at the same time considers Christians not as passive or withdrawn, but as active beings engaged in spiritual warfare, since passions and enemies surround their souls. In his usual allegorical way, he concieves of the beasts of Jeremiah as the mind's demons (*Contra Celsum* 4,93). They are those fantasies which, in certain ways, reflect activities of a spiritual world, for animals are not rational (*De Principiis* 1,8,4).

Just as an ordinary animal can never become a thinking, willing, choosing, and speaking being, so bestial images are the soul's fantasies. These demons carry the deep pathos of the soul struggling with aggressive movements from within, and that pathos is the place where the outer man is pierced and wounded by glimpses of the inner man. The beasts are the sensuous embodiments of the unexplored spaces of the self, and grappling with them brings an awareness of the soul's deeper frontiers. Therefore, self-awareness and awareness of the demonic form a pair. Origen, elsewhere, treats the confrontation between the Israelities and the inhabitants of Ai (Joshua 8) as a drama of the soul. Ai is chaos. When a soul dwells in this place, it is ripe to a bursting point with demonic hosts, inhabitants of chaos and masters of the abyss. Like the Israelites killing their enemies of Ai, each of us has to kill the demons. We have serpents in the soul; yet those beasts are the turning points for the transformation of the outer man into the inner man (*Homily on Lk* 8.3).

One of Origen's images for this metamorphic process, which consists in the ontological turning from homo-animal to homo-homo, is the metaphor of the mask. A mask, defiguration of the face, implies a distortion of the "imago Dei," the fatal mistake of Adam. His descendants we replicate to "clothe" the heavenly image with the terrestrial, the image of clay. Thus we make the inner, luminous self into an opaque, clay-like exterior. Mistaking the earthly for the heavenly, we turn the angel into a beast. In place of Christic images, we wear the mask of the lion, the dragon, the fox, and the pig. The animals are masks. They are the personifications of the earthly selves and, as scriptural images, they make visible the unconscious depths of the soul. If we are willing to understand that in us here there is the power to be transformed from being serpents . . . let us learn from the apostle that the transformation depends on us. For he says this: "We all, when with unveiled face we reflect the glory of the Lord, are transformed into the same image." We must not only wear the animal mask, but see through it as well, thereby unveiling the inner reflective self. It is the word which touches the soul and empowers the metamorphosis. Christ's word, indeed, breaks through the iron bars of all our liberalisms and releases a healing power. That healing power is the discovery of Christic perspectives in the soul, and this discovery is intimately tied to interpretation of scriptural image-masks. In Origen's words, the one who possesses the dynamic-effective (*ton aistheton logon*), is governed by the divine word (*Hom. in Jer.* 2,1; *Dialogue with Heraklides* 13-14; *Comment. on John* 1,28).

Our souls are dominated by bad and good thoughts, but all carry optimistic possibilities. By the word and order of God, Origen says, we are to bring all these forward for the inspection and judgment of God so that, illuminated by him, we might be able to distinguish the bad from the good. Christians have to have adversaries so that their faithfulness is tested and more opportunities be given for their progress in Christ. "It is because of the saints that the beasts which oppose them are good, because the saints are able to conquer them and that victory brings them greater glory before God. After all, when the devil demanded that he be given power against Job, the attacks of the enemy were for Job the occasion for a glory twice as great following the victory . . .Thus the Apostle said that "no one is crowned unless he contends according to the rules" (2 Tim 2.5; *Homily on Genesis* 1,10). Like Jacob, then, our struggle is with spirits. We do not summon them; they come to us. They are the vessels of the soul's movement toward reflection. Animate beings are moved or impelled from within themselves when there arises within them an image which calls forth an impulse. When such fantasies arise, the imaginary nature sets the impulse in ordered motion. Origen's example for this process is a spider weaving its web: a weaving image arises and prompts an impulse to weave; the web results from the incitements of the spider's imaginative nature. When Origen speaks about "order" in this context, he does not mean to imply that imagining is an irenic process. The real situation is, if anything, the opposite, for the impulses which fantasies summon are frenzied (*De principiis* 3,2,2). Now, in this struggle against evil, the hopeful assurance of victory continues to be communion with God.

Already in the Old Testament there is evidence of God's promise that he wants to be so near to his children as to *make habitation* in them (*katoikeso*). Religion was never understood as a supplemented, additional piety, but as a coherent life of faithfulness to

God, as close communion, co-habitation. Christ developed this further, referring to the analogies of the vine, the body, the divine household, etc. The climax of eucharistic oneness reflects to what degree God and man became united and answers the soul's deepest needs. The soul is longing to be visited, inhabited, loved, forgiven, uplifted and united. It is not satisfied with its present state, but looks forward to its becoming different, through self-emptiness on the one side and reception of Christ on the other. Emptiness is not for despair; indeed, a new birth occurs. This vacuum is to be filled by another kind of host, so that *the self does not return again to its own familiar self.* In patristics this idea, how a soul provides space for the heavenly guest, is called *hospitium*, a guest-chamber. The term may mean both host and guest. The soul is a guest-chamber.

The book of the Shepherd of Hermas, repeating the same idea, states: "Two angels attend each human being. And whenever good thoughts arise in our heart they are suggested by the good angel. And whenever thoughts of the opposite kind arise, they are the inspiration of the bad angel." It is up to the soul, the hospitable guest which feasts on all this commotion, to decide how to work with and understand the agitations of the invaders. Many fathers of the desert, experiencing the presence of Christ, were distinguished by their extraordinary holiness, radiance in glory, and wisdom of sayings as visible bearers of this blessed visitor. St. Paul affirms the same truth when he writes that the old man no longer exists in him, but Christ who lives entirely in him. The Mother of God is called by the Byzantines "dwelling-house" (*katoiketerion*) of the Logos: *Chaire he tou achoretou chora.*

The life of a Christian is a continuous effort for further growth and expansion. It is not a complacent, static life, looking on what is achieved. Rather, he looks forward to Christ as the everlasting *typos* or model, in order to shape his own life. Such is the meaning of the term *teleiosis.* In the old martyrologia the term is used to denote the fulfillment of martyrdom in death (see *Martyrium Carpi* 47). St. Paul (Phil 3.12) refers to perfection as moral and spiritual. The apostle wants to reach the fulfillment of his life and his ministry by sharing in the passion and death of Christ. In the famous Lyonese letter, in spite of the horrible torments which they had so faithfully endured, the prisoners strongly refused the title of "martyr," which in their view was reserved only for those whose witness (*martyria*) Christ had sealed by their death. Therefore, they urged the continuous prayer of their brethren in order to be perfect (Eusebios *HE* 5 2,3). In the case of Agathonike, such behavior was not a rash suicidal act, highly condemnable because of the Church's rejection of self-sought martyrdom, but in fact Agathonike's death meant the fulfillment of her life: therefore, she ought to be regarded as a martyr in the fullest sense of that title; she belongs to the circle of "official" martyrs. In accordance with this, Origen in his *Exhortation to Martyrdom* warns his addressees against the devil's attempts to lead them astray, and thus to deprive them of the glory of martyrdom and perfection (*teleiosis*) (Eusebios *HE* 7 22,4).

16. The Dynamics of Incarnation

Liturgical texts abound with references to the theme of the Incarnation and birth of Jesus. For Pseudo-Dionysios it is "a mysterious truth which we have received" (*On the Sacred Names* 11.9). Great joy fills the congregation contemplating this mystery in which the transcendent God became man and visible in the flesh. This truth "which cannot be expressed by any languages or known by any mind," according to Romanos Melodos (*Kontakion* 11.19) constitutes in fact a sacred drama. In it and through it we withdraw from the passing moment of historical, profane time and enter into the eternal present of sacred time. We become contemporaries with the sacred event of Bethlehem. It is today (*semeron*) that Christ is born, and for the believer that "today" is any day. We watch and hear the Child, Mary, and the Magi as, with the intensity and solemnity of an ancient Greek drama, they act out the Incarnation drama, the universal and eternal Christian drama. This Incarnation is the genesis of a tremendous cosmic encounter of the divinity with humanity. Christ, the God-Man, the Theanthropos, unites in his person the disparate worlds of heaven and earth, the invisible and visible, the eternal and temporal, the infinite and finite.

The encounter thus begun by Christ, the new Adam, continues until the end of time, since God's descent implies man's ascent, since man's theosis completes God's incarnation. The star, metaphorically, becomes the "way" (*odos*), common to all religions. It drains the Greek vocabulary for verbs of coming, going, travelling, wandering, leading; and nouns for journey, road, way, path. The "journey" motif extends even beyond the limits of the present into the future. This inner journey of the soul is cosmic, uniting earth to heaven, matter to spirit. It is eternal in the human experience. It implicates all creatures and all of creation in its movement and action because it symbolizes process, change, becoming and evolution. It is the optimistic symbol of the final perfection. Hymnography expresses the confident hope that through Christ man will forever find the way from error to wisdom, from evil to good, from darkness to light. This is theosis, man's return to God, to the joys of Eden.

Fulfillment can be achieved only through and with God, because man is not self-created and therefore self-sufficient. He depends, he needs his Creator's continuous help and assistance. Modern humanism, asserting that "self-fulfillment can be one's motive," is unrealistic; it is rather like making one's own happiness one's motive. If one sets out each day with a conscious intention of achieving one's own happiness, one would fail. One might succeed in providing oneself with a number of pleasures, but they are not the same thing. Pleasure results from the satisfaction of an appetite, whereas joy, inner peace, or happiness result from the satisfaction of one's whole life and self.

If a person does whatever he has to do as well as he can; if he uses his gifts in the way in which they were meant to be used; if he sets about his relationships with those who cross his path that day — then he may well find that he has been happy. Happiness does not come to those who seek it; it comes to those who live as they are meant to live. Happiness and fulfillment seem to us to overlap considerably, if not totally. God created each one of us for a purpose. It is as if he had laid down a path through life for us to follow. When I am walking on that path I am living as God intended me to live when he created me.

Of course, like all mortals, I err and stray from his ways. But there are times when my path coincides with his, and it is as if it were a live line: I light up. I feel! "This is what I was made for. This is the true *me*."

It may be as a husband or as a father; it may be as a pastor; it may be as a teacher or as a friend; or it may be in the exercise of a particular gift. The feeling, "This is what I was made for," is both fulfillment and happiness. We are aware that there are people who would put a different, and even an immoral, meaning to the world "fulfillment," but they would be using the word in a different sense, perhaps as something more like self-indulgence. According to the thinking of the ascetic fathers this might produce pleasure, but could never produce happiness or fulfillment.

It is no small struggle that is needed if one is to lead a life joined as closely as possible to God amid so much wordly clamor, falsification of purpose, and so much agitation that easily distracts the mind from the one unique end, "the one thing needful" (Lk 10.42). Here the comments of St. Augustine are apt:

> The sound of the external voices is heard for a time, then is silent, but the sound of the internal voices must be continuous. When you come to church to pray a hymn, your voice sounds forth the praises of God; you have said as much as you could, you have departed; but let your soul sound forth the praises of God (*Comment. on Ps.* 102.2; PL 37.1317).

It is obvious that this spiritual nourishment rightly orientates one's thoughts to achieve the right and not the wrong.

The ancient world could not believe in such a transcending action of God to man. The ancient Greek attitude toward God, life and death was that God remained inaccessible, far too distant and that communication was limited. In the highest period of religiosity, it was accepted that a man, not during his life but after death, would be caught up by the gods and wafted to the Elysian Fields, there to consort with Tiresias and similar heroes; but knowing that he was not of semi-divine origin, he believed that he was not going to share in any more than that. And Pindar, the epic poet of Greece, reflects a meagre conception of man's relationship with God: "We must seek from the Gods such things as befit our mortal minds, knowing what lies before us and to what portion we were born. Seek not, my soul, immortal life (*bion athanaton*) but explore such resources as are practicable" (*Pythia* 3.line 59).

Moralists of the past have distanced the present and the blessings of eternity, excessively setting forth rather what separates us than what unites us. Everything concerning God's promises, his peace, his kingdom, his reward, were considered to be inaccessible during man's earthly life, the most frequent argument being his sinfulness. Only a few drops of grace could be obtained. And yet, his incarnation, Pentecost, the outpouring of his Spirit, the whole mission and sanctifying activities of the Church, makes the other world accessible, makes Whitsun ever-present. For even here there is another life that may be lived, a life wholly other than that which commonly bears the name, and yet one which may be lived out in this very place where one now is, be it the desert, in an anchorite's cell or the marketplace in this technological age.

This relationship with God makes life quite different. When Christ controls my will, then I am most free. When I obey his will, then am I most autonomous. And when I love my fellow men for God's sake, then and only then do I obey the requirements of love. I begin to love them for the sake of the deepest thing in themselves: that heteronomy in which God is the *eteros*, the highest of all autonomies. True love can be found only where the asbsolute, the divine, is somehow co-involved; in other words, true love, in a horizontal sense, is at the same time love of God, respect for the vertical commitment.

There are, of course, a few exceptions. Even a few of the ancient Greeks maintained a certain unity with the Deity. They foresaw that the gulf might be bridged, that God (*Theos*) might enter into man until he became *entheos*: he in God and God in him. The soul then "stood apart," the meaning of the word "ecstasy" became "enthusiastic" — a term derived from *entheos*. The hope naturally sprang into being that, when at death, the souls of the worshipers were completely and finally liberated from their bodies, they would be wholly united with God for evermore, so sharing in his own immortal nature. It was in the very act of communion with the divinity that the sense of its own divinity and therefore of its eternity was revealed to the soul.

There were in the Middle Ages people who even condemned innocent laughing, entertainment and joyful acts with the notorious pretext: "Jesus had never laughed." Selecting from among extravagant practices, they were trying to impose on devout Christians the most unusual eccentricities, as distinctively required characteristic virtues, assuring them that they must not behave like worldly people. Such models were badly falsifying the true spirit of the evangelical life.

Thanatology, in the course of time, degenerated into "thanatophobia." Consequently, fear of death became the most frequent theme for preachers, but not so much as teaching in the light and reassuring message of the Risen Lord, but rather in a melancholic way. Christians must be reminded of their last days. The arguments used mostly in certain historical periods were completely distorted, and were not in conformity with Christ's teaching. The error of Hell and of purgatory, no longer now, but for a long time in the past, had been two distinctive issues that were put forth in Sunday sermons, the latter being compared with Hell by the fixed length of the imposed punishment for miserable offenders. The prayers of the living relatives could reduce their sufferings while they were still in this intermediate state. But on the whole, purgatory played a significant role in religious instruction. Violent preachers unmercifully attacked sinners by referring to that devouring fire; fire in the eyes, fire in the bowels, fire in the whole body, sinners burning like a torch. Fire also around the body. A wholly unhealthy series of sermons appeared in the Middle Age, which in order to describe the desperate supplications of those suffering in hell, used images taken from daily atrocities, horrible sicknesses and cruel executions.

In Western European and Nordic countries around the same time, the encounter with fear was used in different degrees, according to given places and times. In principle, a preacher was at the same time threatening and consoling. This eschatological preaching included the trespasses of sinners, the unconditional despising of earthly pleasures, cultivating a horror for one's self by insulting its fragility and misery. Such self-accusations were considered indispensable preambles for salvation. To all these was added yet another element, namely, the uncertainty of one's divine election to be saved, in the context of a kind of predestination.

The irritating question chiefly preoccupying a Protestant was: How does one know that he is saved? How does one claim that one possesses the "right faith," which alone is deserving of the grace of God?

Fear and de-Christianization, in this context, are interrelated. A fear which undermines the spiritual life, consumes all energy, all appetite for constructive upward work, for joyful fellowship, diverting the attention to the peripheral rather than to the essential issues — such perverted fear can never be salutary but only destructive. Surely, it is an arm which is manipulated with considerable risks and dangers. How far were all these views from the optimistic teaching of the early Fathers, who underscoring the victory of the Resurrection were guaranteeing hope and the assurance that already the body can participate in God's glory. The world and history became different since Christ became one of us, sharing in our misery. Gregory Palamas was explicit on this question: "If in the age to come the body will share with the soul in unspeakable blessings, it is certain that it must share in them, so far as possible, even now" (*Tome of Mountain Athos*; PG 150.1233C). Many godly people, in fact, have experienced during this earthly life the springtime of bodily glorification. When Arsenios the Great of Egypt was praying, his disciples saw him aglow "like a fire" (*Apophthegmata*, Arsenios 27; PG 65).

When all is said and done, one may ask: "Why then such a deplorable distortion of the authentic spirit of the Gospel? What is the reason for this propensity to obscure the crystal-clear and joyful economy of Christ during his earthly ministry, who was incarnate precisely in order to bring light, to free the captives, to heal the sufferers, to conquer sorrow, deception, unbelief and anguish? Why have theologians and preachers for centuries, in the exercise of their ministry, done their utmost to cool enthusiasm with culpabilizing theories? The answer can be found in the "fear of the practising" themselves. The more church-goers became pious, the more incited by their preachers to be ashamed and afraid of themselves, the more they were dominated by a metaphysical fear, which in turn they disseminated around them. Religious life, therefore, being thus contaminated, lacked the creative ability, the strength for renewal, and the dynamism of the real disciples of Christ. This virus of a pathologically weak faith was unavoidable and created fragile types of Christians. Herein lies one of the main causes of the slowly developing de-Christianization of the West.

In countries that received the Gospel, the very essence of true religion, it was forgotten that above everything else is the daily experience of the love of God. Religion is not an occasional devotion limited to pious works or ritual signs, nor a sophisticated altruism but a most sure possibility that the ideal and the real can become to some extent identified one with the other. This is guaranteed by Christ's incarnation, by which we are enabled to overcome evil and the corruptibility of death. There the eternal discloses himself to us as one who loves us with a love greater than that which our minds can comprehend. Christ loves us better than we love ourselves.

The Incarnation conveys and at the same time encompasses the cosmic dimension of divine redemption. Christ became man in order to save us, not in a narrow limited sense, but including everything which is directly connected with us and our life in general, i.e., happiness, joy, peace, culture, all social structures, etc. Christ, having saved all creation, continuously seeks to liberate human nature from all forms of slavery, from depressive conditions which alienate us all from the very essence of life. Sin, then, in this context is a denial of God's love by man and consequently carries with it a degradation of the self of the individual. This vital perspective was developed from the very early days of the Church, which was living and developing its mission within a pagan or Jewish society, in relation to totally different or even hostile philosophies of life. Its growth was made within the midst of strange ideological settings and hostile, established rules. Early partristic thought was, therefore, wrestling with the question as to how to find points of common ground and how to overcome negative influences, so that the truth would not be ill-taught or hindered. Thus, Justin, a philosopher and martyr of the second century, although respectful of the then prevailing philosophy, was urging the newly converted, to engage in scrupulous research about the real meaning of the faith, arguing that the Logos is innate within human nature and asking the neophyte to understand the consequences of this realty (*Dialogue with Tryphon* 2; PG 6.476).

Christ, indeed, liberated not only the soul, but also liberated everything human which is connected with our existence upon earth. All human values were redeemed by him, thus giving, since this time, a new dimension and direction to the human reality in history. Because we risk falling into error, continuously tempted by evil, we need to be critically minded, watchful, testing, judging, and discerning of what surrounds us and what reaches us. Such an attitude makes us privileged, creative, watchful beings who stand beyond human cultures pressing social forces, as well as in whichever way they impinge upon us. St. Augustine rightly affirmed the dynamic and challenging strength of Christians: "If the faith is not engaged in thinking or questioning then it does not exist at all. Such lack of engagement is impossible. After all, to believe is nothing other than to think (cogitare), the human intelligence giving consent, stimulated by will" (*De praedistinatione Sanctorum*, 2,5; PL 44,964) And elsewhere he states: "It would have been impossible to believe, in fact, if we had not possessed a reasonable spirit (*rationales animas*)" (*Letter* 120, PL 33.453).

All of which is to say that God's transcendance allows man not to remain a mere passive spectator, inactive before challenging historical events and social realities, but to go further — to go beyond and through, controlling them, examining them as to whether they really serve a good purpose or not, and by his critical intervention, to improve them, thus becoming God's collaborator and co-worker. Contemporary societies make every effort to promote the individual as a production unit, as a consuming element, or as a recipient of superficial communications alienated from his personhood while in reality they do all which is possible to marginalize or eclipse the *person*, that which precisely is the most sacred in him, and what is of an irreducible value, namely, his proper identity. On television all casted heroes are really actors of quite cheap quality and banality, and millions are invited to follow the excesses of their "originality." In the same field, too, the extraordinary development of information does not hold much hopeful news. We are moving towards a new civilization in which there will be enormous difficulties of recognizing ourselves and others. Perhaps the only signs of our proper individual existence will be reduced to our life or accident insurance policy number, credit card number, or medical dossier — and all these will be hidden in the depths of a sophisticated electronic memory. Such an inhuman and depersonalized evolution is promised to us in the near future. We are threatened with becoming unqualified, anonymous beings, just members, which certainly will engender up to now unforseen psychic difficulties in the most profound areas of our divinely-created being. The time has now come to check such trends and to correct them.

The message of Christ's incarnation, a pregnant and inclusive term, is far too little and very rarely contemplated; all these are its fruits: liberty, peace, redemption, salvation but also joy. Pessimism and despair in view of evil's pervasiveness in humanity discourage many, and instead of keeping a joyful attitude, they manifest an inexplicable sorrow and sadness. We have seen this dark image of the religious and literary production of the West in the Middle Ages. We see it even today. Pleasure is widely sought, even angrily demanded, as man's right from nature and his fellow-men. The secular person, for whom the ultimate truth of things is meaninglessness, may have many pleasures. But he cannot have real joy. Pleasure deceives, as we see in today's dissatisfied society of which it became an idol worshiped by many.

Joy derives from intimate communion with God at the heart of all things. And even those whose creed not only admits but requires joy have largely lost it; they are far too often strangers to it. Some even appear to think that the Christian should not be joyful, that he should cherish a dour attitude of censorious condemnation. And although this attitude is increasingly rare, joy cannot be said to be the note of the Christian life. Such attitudes of the mind seem preoccupied with the sorrowful passion, as if Christ were still on the cross or in his tomb. A Christianity centered upon human sin, fear of a wrathful and legalistically rigorous judge, all this militates against the joy which should belong to those who believe God is risen from the dead, who has conquered death, thus showing us that life is restored and evil no more prevails on earth. Consequently, the love of the Risen Lord has been triumphantly revealed in Christ's defeating sin and transfiguring pain. Thus, not only is joy the logical fruit of faith but it is a gift of the renewing effect of the life in the Holy Spirit which is bestowed upon everyone. St. Paul considers it to be one of the many fruits of the Spirit, because the Spirit is joy. Nor is this joy simply a pleasant feeling or pleasure that has been refined. (It may coexist only where exists an absence of any sensual pleasure in the sensual experiences of this superficial world.) It exists right within the purity and innocence of the heart of reality, a real heaven, at once transcendent and immanent where the Spirit of God dwells and it gives perfect joy, which is he himself. Thus, Symeon the New Theologian refers to Christ, given in the Eucharist, not only as joy-giving, but self-joy (*autochara*), the spring of real joy. And because this joy is deeper and more real than pain and sin, its communication is a present triumph over those things in the center of the soul, and the pledge of their final defeat.

There is a great paradox in Christian joy, since its very nature does not depend on earthly and sensual pleasure. This cannot be easily understood by secular people, as can be seen from the episode of Pentecost when the crowd mistook the exuberance of the apostles for "intoxication" and drunkenness. A little of this exuberance in the widest sense of ecstatic joy, would do more to convince men of the living power of the Gospel than any amount of apologetic, denunciation or joyless social service. It would be now, as it was then, infectious. Nothing but a willful refusal to face facts can evade their testimony as to the spiritual joy communicated to men by the Gospel. It is not the joy of the illusory sought for upon earth, which people persist in seeking despite all their disillusionments. Nor is it the joy of heaven after death where too many expect it as their only reward. It is a present joy which, in fact, perhaps more than any other argument, makes the future joy of heaven credible. How different a landscape looks when the clouds have passed over and the sun once again shines out, as though the same land is not really the same. It is illuminated, transfigured, and glorified. So it is with the landscape of human life and experience when the soul receives the joy of God, the joy which is God himself.

Christ's Lordship and the firm conviction that he remains ever present in our history is strengthened by his promise that angels will be sent to be our permanent companions and helpers in crucial moments of our life. This question of the value of angels is quite important since our generation thinks less of them than did any previous generation. In fact, we may lose our concept of God himself by not thinking more of the angels, for it is certain that in the past, thinking about his angels made God a very vivid person in our eyes. The fact that God is surrounded by such an immense court of angelic hosts lifted him far above earthly monarchs in popular esteem. We, in our sophisticated way today think more naturally of the difference between God and every creature by imagining his absoluteness, his separateness, and his remoteness. But here we run the danger of assigning to him a loneliness which is quite contrary to Christian teaching. Our fathers in the faith populated the universe with his messengers. Even Satan, as readers of Job will remember, was at one time an obedient messenger of God.

A corollary to continual recollection of the immensity of the heavenly host is that it was thereby much easier to comprehend the individual care of God for each and every one of his people. We rely greatly on the thought that not a sparrow falls to the ground without

God's knowledge and that the very hairs of our head are all numbered. Jesus taught his hearers that in heaven the "angel" of each child (his spiritual representative, almost his other self) was continuously before the eye of God. This biblical concept was extended to suggest that not only has a child his angelic representative, but each nation as well. It is true that in the Bible there is no specifically elaborated doctrine of guardian angels, nor has there ever been one so defined officially in the history of the Church, where one would more properly have looked for it. But the Church is living this experience in its liturgical life, attaching importance to it in feasts and the consecrated dedication of churches. Thus, certain hymnography anticipating the second parousia of God, shows him surrounded by an angelic order:

> Into the splendor of thy saints how can I, who am unworthy, enter? For should I once dare to come into the bridal chamber, my vesture would betray me (for it is not a wedding garment), and as a prisoner I would be cast out by the angels. O Lord, cleanse the impurity of my soul, and by thy mercy save me (Tuesday in Holy Week, Chant First Tone).

Later, during the same feast day, Christ is seen coming to judge the whole creation, surrounded by angels:

> When thou, O Jesus, shall come in glory with the Heavenly Hosts, and shall sit upon the throne of thy judgment, O Good Shepherd, drive me not away. For thou knowest the ways of righteousness, and those on the left have turned aside: therefore suffer me not to perish with the goats, though I be savage with sin, but number me with the flocks on thy right hand, and of thy mercy save me (Ibid., Second Plag. Tone).

On Holy Saturday, after the burial of Christ, the hymnographer is surprised by the marvel of Christ's condescendence for the sake of fallen humanity: "The company of angels was amazed, beholding thee O Savior, numbered among the dead, who has destroyed the power of death and raised up Adam with thyself, setting all men free from hell" (Matins, Fifth Tone).

Another seasonal hymn: "The angelic choirs are filled with wonder, beholding him who rests in the bosom of the Father laid in the tomb as one dead, though he is immortal. The ranks of angels surround him, and with the dead in hades they glorify him as Creator and Lord" (First Tone).

What is clear from all this "angelology" is that it gives sharp support to the essential Christian doctrine of God's care of the individual, and that sharpness we must never allow to be blunted. In addition, it must be said here that the belief in angels included concepts of the continual use of natural forces. We today, of course, are lovers of natural beauty. The writers of the Bible, however, did not have quite the same attitude. They were not so impressed by the beauty of nature as by its superior quality. In particular they thought of it as an instrument of God's personal power.

There is a passage in the psalms which, properly translated, is an excellent illustration of this thought. "Who maketh his angels spirits: and his ministers a flaming fire." Correctly, the phrases should be turned around: "Who makes the winds his angels and the flaming fire his ministers." Another interesting example is to be seen in the announcement to David that the sound of the wind in the mulberry trees would betray the presence of the troops of Yahweh marching to war. Perhaps the climax of this type of thought is to be seen in the Book of Revelation, with its close association between the angels and the most tremendous cataclysms of nature. To believers in the Incarnation, God should be closer than thought in every detail of daily life. Recollection of the angels should quicken our sense of his constant care. "Turn but a stone and start a wing." We cannot miss the tokens of God's presence, if only our eyes are open.

Christ is mightier than our poor will. On almost every page of his letters, St. Paul pours out his heart as he pleads, "that I may know him in the power of his resurrection and in the fellowship of his sufferings." And then changes into a major key as he shouts: "They that are Christ's have crucified the flesh with the affections and lusts," and again, "I can do all things through Christ who strengthens me" (Gal 2.20). Nor is this so much verbiage. The Pharisaical bigot, who went up to Damascus to torture and harass the Christians, writes: "Love suffers long . . . the greatest of all is love," and so lives what he preaches that at the end he is glad to die for his faith.

There are many Christian heroes who have left a similar testimony. After Augustine's conversion, he suddenly came face to face with a woman whose very presence reminded him of the dissolute life he had forsaken. She sought to tempt him and faced him with an enticing smile as she said: "Augustine, it is I." But he was unmoved by the old enchantment and replied: "But it is not I." Or there is the story of the devil's coming to the door of Martin Luther's heart where, knocking repeatedly, he cried: "Martin Luther! Martin Luther!" To which came the response: "Martin Luther is dead; Jesus Christ lives here."

If such incidents mean little to us, it may be that we have far too static a view of redemption. We feel we have been redeemed like inanimate articles bought out of pawn, but in the Bible there is no such lifeless view. Because we have been redeemed, we are "in Christ," we are new creatures of a new creation, and because we are in him the *dynamis*, power, of the cross is ours. For in him all that he underwent we undergo. We died when Christ died. Sin has been killed in us as it was killed in Christ — and as he rose from the dead so we arise, dead to sin but alive unto God.

Prayer to the Guardian Angel of Human Life, consequently, occupies an important place in Orthodox worship:

> O Holy Angel, interceding for my wretched soul and my passionate life, forsake me not, a sinner, nor shrink from me for my intemperance. Give no place for the subtle demon to master me through the violence of my mortal body. Strengthen my poor and feeble hand, and guide me in the way of salvation. O Holy Angel of God, guardian and protector of my wretched body and soul, forgive me for all the insults I have given you every day of my life, and for whatever sins I may have committed during the past night. Protect me from every temptation of the enemy, that I may not anger God by any sin. Pray to the Lord for me, that he may strengthen me in his fear, and make me, his slave, worthy of his goodness.

Prayer of Intercession to the Holy Guardian Angel:

> O Angel of Christ, my holy Guardian and Protector of my soul and body, forgive me all my sins of today. Deliver me from all the wiles of the enemy, that I may not anger my God by any sin. Pray for me, sinful and unworthy servant, that thou may present me worthy of the kindness and mercy of the All-holy Trinity and the Mother of my Lord Jesus Christ, and of all the Saints.

Prayer to the Holy Guardian Angel:

> Holy Angel of Christ, I fall down and pray to thee, my holy Guardian, given me from holy baptism for the protection of my sinful

body and soul. By my laziness and bad habits, I have angered thy most pure light, and have driven thee away from me by all my shameful deeds, lies, slanders, envy, condemnation, scorn, disobedience, brotherly-hatred, grudges, love of money, adultery, anger, meanness, greed, excess, talkativeness, negative and evil thoughts, proud ways, dissolute madness, having self-will in all the desires of the flesh. O my evil will, which even the dumb animals do not follow! How canst thou look at me or approach me who am like a stinking god? With what eyes, O Angel of Christ, wilt thou look at me so badly snared in evil deeds? How can I ask forgiveness for my bitter, evil and wicked deeds, into which I fall every day and night, and every hour? But I fall down and pray, O my holy Guardian: pity me, thy sinful and unworthy servant (name). Be my helper and protector against my wicked enemy, by thy holy prayers, and make me a partaker of the Kingdom of God with all the Saints, always, now and ever, and to the ages of ages.

Hope and faith in a better situation stem from the deep conviction that Christ remains an everlasting Savior and Lord of history. What he did during his earthly ministry has everlasting significance. He is ever present, the helper and protector for each one and for all. His Gospel is rooted in the real past history of God's continuous care for Israel, His people, that is its truth and strength. But the cross and the Resurrection are supremely relevant both to the present and also the future. That is their abiding power. Christ lives now, in the present, and in the future, and unto all eternity. Death has no more dominion over him. So, the relationship of Christians with the Church of Christ is spared from becoming a mere ritualistic remembrance of things long ago. By virtue of the Resurrection, life becomes an experience of an ever-present companionship with the living Savior, a daily delight, a constant victory over sin, despair and corruptibility in the real presence of One who has broken the bonds of time and space.

As Christ transforms every present moment, so also he changes man's future. Apart from Christ, the future for any man who thinks at all, is full of anguish and fear. So it has always been. For in the future lies the certainty of death, with all the fear of the totally unknowable. But now, the sting of that fear is withdrawn. Christ who rose in the past, who lives in the present, will be on hand whenever the future brings men and women to the hour of their death. With death's conqueror at hand to save his own, death need not have any terror and certainly will have no victory. Man, after all, is a creature of time. Left to himself, the past for him is a prison, the present is a perplexity, and the future, a great fear. But Christ lives. The past now becomes a source of light and comfort, the present a joy of a living companionship, the future an expectation of ineffable bliss. Consequently, each one and all together are equipped to face the past, the present and the future with a confidence which nothing can ever destroy.

The old man in us is averse to the change that Christ requires. The old nature in us fights it. The flesh opposes it. That is the reason why the authentic life in Christ does not come with ever increasing ritualism. This does not reach the heart. It does not lead to the crucifixion of the flesh "with its affections and lusts." A closed mind spells stagnation and stems from self-righteousness, if at the same time there is no communion with the living and saving Christ. Symeon the New Theologian was right in saying:

> He that lacks awareness of his baptism and yet was baptised in infancy, who accepts it only by faith and already having effaced it by sins, but refuses the second one, I mean the baptism of the Spirit, given by God in his love to those who seek it in repentance, how can he ever be saved? Not in the least. When the Spirit descends upon you, it becomes like a radiant baptismal font to you, and, as he engulfs you, he gives you rebirth and he himself works within you (*Catecheses* 32,66).

Christ is not only alive evermore; he is also declared to be the possessor of the Name which is above every name, to his eternal Lordship as Lord (*Kyrios*) and Pantocrator. The fulfillment of the divine economy by Christ's victory over evil declares what is the goal of all the faithful. It is simply and solely and always the mission of love. For the victory, which was won at such bitter cost on the Cross and ratified with such glorious certainty in the Resurrection, was the victory of pure, unbounded, and unfailing love. The devil brought into action his whole armory of hatred and cruelty and falsehood. But the love of Christ conquered them all. Until the end of time, Christ entrusts to his believers the continuance of the perpetual mission of that divine love among and within all the loveless souls of men.

17. Fullness of Life

The description of the Orthodox Church's physiognomy in general, invites us, above all, to look into its spirituality. Whoever says spirituality must necessarily think of the "inner life," about which St. Paul speaks, referring to the inner man. Today we have become more conscious of the dynamism and fecundity of the notion "interior life." There is today throughout the world a widespread appetite for more transcendence and more inner life. Until recently, many thought that such a concern for inner peace was a pathological self-concentration, a mystification, an alibi to divert us from action. Thus, they identified it with deep introspection, examination of the conscience, meditation, contemplation, etc. Everything that brought people away from action, or from an agitated commitment, was seen as an asphyxiating turning into one's self, a terrible egoism and a self-imprisonment. Such an attitude has done a lot of harm, particularly as regards the development of thinking in Western societies. It has overfed an hypertrophied monotonous activism, which is often uncontrollable, to the detriment of peaceful judgment and reflection — which, nevertheless, remains the foundation of every authentic action.

But it is not enough, in these days of a certain spiritual awakening, to emphasize the existence of an inner life alone. The question remains: how does one live it? It is evident, that an inner life completely isolated, barricaded against any influence from the outside, will never have a witnessing effect or a shining capacity. Communication between inner lives as practiced by the people of God remains an absolute necessity within the life of the spirit, for spiritual men and women, who besides material joys feel immense thirst for sharing other-worldly pleasures. Since one is constantly seeking kindred spirits, inevitably he is going to meet others with the same concerns. Thus, Gregory of Nyssa expresses something about the joy of a redeemed Christian, manifesting in all directions the blessings of his new life:

> The kingdom of life has come and the power of death is no more. And there is a new birth, a living, a new kind of life, a transubstantiation even of our very nature. This birth comes about "not by blood, nor the will of man, nor the will of the flesh; but by God." How does it come about? I will give you a clear illustration of

grace by the use of words. This child-bearing is conceived through faith; it is borne towards the light by the rebirth of Baptism; the Church gives it suck, her teaching being breasts for it and the bread from on high its nourishment; noble conduct corresponds to the fullness of stature; marriage to a life lived in common with wisdom; children to hope, households to the kingdom; inheritance and riches to the delights of Paradise; and at the end, instead of death, life eternal is the beatitude prepared for the saints (*In Christi Resurrectionem orat.* 1; PG 46.604).

Because of our unique origins, as humans we have expectations for a more sublime existence than our present status which is plagued with imperfection. Through sin we fail to live up to the standards of the image within us. We fail to realize our true destiny as complete human beings, as god-like by grace. Instead of living in obedience to God's love and all that this encompasses, we often find ourselves in a vicious cycle of sin, despair, confusion, or hatred that characterizes the pain of living. If we do not nurture and cultivate the divine image within us, we become unable to respond to the divine call of communion with Christ. We become orphans who lose sight of God and become the bruised and battered children of the earth instead of his beloved and loving children. Through the virtue of obedience to our Lord we can nourish the divine spark within us, and continue to desire and long for the original beauty of our nature, which was revealed at the Transfiguration.

Although the Church has always preserved this anthropological viewpoint, it is only relatively recently, that is, within the last few decades, that modern psychology has come to acknowledge such a high calling in man. The humanistic branch of psychology, speaking of a Third Force, articulates these ideas when it states that man's ultimate need is that of "self-actualization." It also describes the phenomena of "peak-experiences," defined as moments when we become aware of our truer and higher, transcendent nature. Unlike earlier psychological interpretations of man which followed the models of Freudian determinism, of Skinnerian conditioning, it goes so far as to state that we have the potential for even becoming "god-like." This echoes closely the ancient patristic tradition regarding human destiny: "For he [Christ] became man that we might become divine" (St. Athanasios). Modern psychology indicates how modern man has become a victim of existential boredom and dread as a result of a valueless, affluent, and secular world. When all sense of the sacred and mystery are stripped away from us, we become insensitive to the divine beauty and to the transcendent quality of our own existence.

In celebrating the feasts, we are reminded of two essential facts. First, the dazzling brightness, shown forth from Christ which revealed to us his true identity as God Incarnate and, consequently, the magnitude of his love for us in taking on our nature. Secondly, hymns relate how in the Transfiguration, the Lord displayed the original glory of human existence that was intended for us before the Fall and which awaits us after the general resurrection. We are reminded by this to look beyond the mundane, to be attentive to our true calling, to achieve our true destiny — that is, to be truly human in the Image of God. We are to overcome the despair of our times and to accept the life-giving challenges that Christ sets before us. We are called to ascend the mount with him through faith, prayer, repentance and obedience to his will. In the apolytikion of the feast, we sing, "O Christ our God, showing thy glory to thy disciples as far as they were able to endure it." The time has come now to put our own endurance to the test.

Under whatever terms this ontological change is described in the New Testament, one thing is certain: human nature can overcome itself and, from the present state of corruptibility, enter into incorruptibility. For secular society, the concept of "theosis" disappeared about the time of the First World War. The guns and carnage tarnished the glory of the fatherland and the glory of dying for it. Universal cynicism, allied to Marxism and moral protest, undermined the glory that had been associated with royalty. Since then our mood has been matter-of-fact and suspicious of pretensions and extravagances, and that potential for its exploitation within the concept of glory.

The entrance into the divine glory contains a number of elements. It points to the sheer beauty of God, one of the most neglected aspects of twentieth century theology. But, as Augustine prayed: "O thou beauty most ancient and with all so fresh." This beauty is inseparable from God's perfection; it is the "beauty of holiness." Glory points to the royalty or the ultimate authority of God: an authority expressed in humble service but, nonetheless, royal as well. It expresses the final triumph of God's purpose of love for us. For these reasons, glory and theosis are ultimate constituents of the universe. We see this glory in Christ; this derives from God, whose glory he reveals. It is conveyed to us, whose glory it becomes through association with Christ.

In treating the aims of theology we often underestimate its Trinitarian character. Christian believing, as a way of being human in the world, is grounded, shaped and actualized by the mystery of God revealed in Christ whose life we share. Christian theology, as the critical reflection on Christian believing, as *fides quaerens intellectum*, operates in three fundamental perspectives: as reflection on the mystery of God, as reflection on the "epiphany" or appearing of God in Christ, and as reflection on the power and action of God's Spirit in history. One good test of the health of theological activity concerns the extent to which these three perspectives mutually illuminate and correct one another, for the dialectical relationship between them has to constantly be sought and is constantly in danger of being lost.

As for twentieth-century Western theology, the Christological perspective has tended to dominate — in Protestant theology — whereas, in the Orthodox tradition, the dominant perspective has been that of the ecclesiology and eucharistic liturgical life, the concrete form of the doctrine of the Holy Spirit, and pneumatology. Even today, there is often an abstractness, a poverty in Western Christological writings, and something "thin" in the Reformed theology of the Church.

Patristics see man as alienated in the life-process, suffering in his loneliness and self-withdrawal. Hence, he is subject to an anthropological determinism, which prevents self-fulfillment and which must be overcome by means of a radical metanoia and a reconciliation. Such a cool pessimism describing a world in which man, a rational creature of a disenchanted social order, contradicts "interdependence," must be countered by creating a new norm structure, in which human action can be directed towards self-fulfillment and away from the chaos of "anomie."

To put his faith into practice and to build up a healthy life, *zoe*, grounded on Jesus Christ, our Savior and Life-Giver, the Christian is immediately confronted by a fallen nature and an institutionalized evil. The magnitude of this disorder in human life may create in certain spirits a genuine pessimism, a frustration, and a doubt as to whether Christ remains the supreme Ruler - Pantokrator - the Lord - Kyrios - of the world and of history. But God is not passive. He intervenes but in his way which remains very often beyond our intelligence.

The major concern is the status of the world within the redemption that has been wrought in Christ. Even an untrained student of the Bible sees that the New Testament has more negative references to the world than positive ones. The problem is further complicated by the fact not only that the word "world" is used to translate three different Greek words: *oikoumene, aion,* and *kosmos,* but also that these Greek words have many nuances in themselves and as well, there are other derived meanings acquired through the usage of the Septuagint as parallels for the Hebrew words *erets* (2407 times in the Hebrew Old Testament), *tebel,* and *olam. Oikoumene* occurs fifteen times in the New Testament and means the inhabited earth, the civilized world, the Roman world, or the whole world (Heb 2.5) — parallel to the Hebrew *tebel.*

Aion is parallel to Hebrew *olam* and has the connotation more of time than of space as with oikoumene. The basic meaning is "age" or long duration, though it is often used synonymously with *kosmos.*

Kosmos is the most commonly used word for the world (188 times in the New Testament). 104 of these are in Johannine writings, and 46 in Pauline literature. Our Lord addressed his heavenly Father as "Father, Lord of heaven and earth," but he or the New Testament never calls God *Kyrios tou kosmou.* It is always Lord of heaven and earth (*Kyrios tou ouranou kai tes ges*).

The kerygma of the early Church never emphasized the doctrine of creation. The doctrine of creation ex nihilo is in the New Testament, but occupies no central place in its teaching, nor is it stated in explicit terms as directly relevant for the Gospel.

But as it is often stated in the New Testament, the "world lieth in the evil one" (2 Jn 5.19). For Paul, the wisdom of this world is folly with God (1 Cor 3.19; 1.20-21, 26-28); certainly this does not give a positive reference to the world. None of the rulers of this age understands the wisdom of God, and the prince of the power of the air is still exercising authority over the world. "The world has been crucified to me, and I to the world" (Gal 6.14) affirms the apostle. Is this a positive evaluation of the world? Perhaps we can write off James, who claims that "religion pure and undefiled before God is to keep oneself unstained from the world" — but then we tend to hate "religion" and love the "world," and so James does not make sense to us.

The Christian outlook on life is not Manichean — seeing only the negative side. Of course, we are fallen beings. But in general, life is a gift which God entrusts to us. It requires a personal crisis, some painful suffering to remind us of this gift nature of life. Such as Hezekiah after his deliverance from the threat of destruction at the hands of Sennacherib. Only when mortal sickness had visited him, was he reminded that he had again received his life anew from God, graciously, mysteriously. "The living man, the living man, he thanks you as I do this day," sang Hezekiah.

During the Palamite controversy of the fourteenth century, the transfiguration theme was central to St. Gregory's distinction between the essence and energies of God. However, from the hymns which comprise the Vespers and Orthros for this feast, we learn something about Christian anthropology and divine economy.

In the *aposticha* of the Vespers, we hear that when Christ was transfigured "in his own person he showed them the nature of man, arrayed in the original beauty of the Image." At once we think of the Genesis account of our creation (1.27) when mankind was created in the image of God. It is this divine spark that graces the human species with dignity and nobility. In the Transfiguration, a two-fold revelation occurs; that of the true divinity of the person of Christ and that of the original, pristine beauty and status of our human nature. With the fall of Adam, the divine image in man became distorted or tarnished. Through the Incarnation, however, Christ restores our nature by joining his divinity to that of his assumed humanity. This theme of the Redemption is also heard during the Orthros of the feast when we sing the third ode: "Thou hast put Adam on entirely, O Christ, and changing the nature grown dark in past times, thou hast filled it with glory and made it godlike by the alteration of thy form."

The splendor and radiance that emanated through Christ's human nature at the Transfiguration reveals the majesty that was from its very conception intended for mankind. To be truly human is to be in the image of God. This endowment, however, goes along with a responsibility — that we have to always progress, in order to achieve the likeness with God.

This theme of divine light is expressed in the prologue to St. John's Gospel (1.1-7). What we read there is not, in the strict sense, an account of the Resurrection, but it is the gospel of light. Christ is the light that enlightens all.

The joy permeating all the hymns is the outstanding characteristic of the service of Easter, both in liturgical texts and in the attitudes of those who are present.

> This is the day which the Lord has made.
> Let us rejoice and be glad in it.
> Let us embrace each other joyously.

> Let us be illuminated by the feast.
> Let us embrace each other.
> Let us call "brothers" even those who
> hate us, and let us forgive all by the
> Resurrection.

Yet even during this most joyous of all feasts the cross of Christ is not forgotten. In one of the hymns of the Resurrection (sung also every Saturday evening of the year), the cross and the Resurrection are combined:

> Having beheld the resurrection of Christ, let us worship the holy Lord Jesus, the only sinless One. We venerate thy cross, O Christ, and thy holy resurrection we praise and glorify; for thou art our God, and we know no other than thee; we call on thy name. Come, all you faithful, let us venerate Christ's holy resurrection. By enduring the cross, joy has come into all the world. Ever blessing the Lord, let us praise his resurrection. By enduring the cross for us, he destroyed death by death.

The veneration of the cross is prominent in Orthodox worship and spirituality. By the cross, as John of Damascus summarizes the teachings of the Fathers, all things are set aright. Sin is destroyed, death is overcome, and resurrection is bestowed. The cross, as the services exclaim, is the "lifebearing cross," "the banner of joy," "divine glory of Christ," "the power which raises us from corruption." There is no resurrection without the cross. The cross and the resurrection are one whole.

With his resurrection, in the words of the liturgical texts, Christ has transformed the corruptible to incorruption, and revealed a fountain of incorruptible life. He has crushed the bars of Hades, driven away its darkness, released Adam, and brought joy to the world.

> When thou, the Redeemer of all, wast placed in a tomb, all Hell's powers quaked in fear. Its bars were broken, its gates were smashed! Its mighty reign was brought to an end, for the dead came forth alive from their tombs, casting off the bonds of their captivity. Adam was filled with joy! He gratefully cried out to thee, O Christ: Glory to thy condescension, O Lover of man!

The cross and the resurrection — their power and joy are the foundation of our faith and the source of our life.

Christ by his resurrection conquered evil and death. At the same time, he transmitted to his disciples qualities quite beyond man himself, an *epektasis* as it is referred to by Gregory of Nyssa (*Comm. On Cant.* 12; PG 44.1025 and *On the Soul*, PG 46.105). This march never ends. This growth never stops, because it is beyond both measures, time and human conditions. Man thus surpasses himself and his own limitations. Since Christ is a living person, the image of him — this *ikon*, i.e., the human being — also is a living entity. An existential divine *koinonia* and presence take possession of man. A long process of sanctification is involved; moreover, the potential for such sanctification is present and available, provided that man freely accepts it and cooperates with God's soteriological plan. In short, *theosis* becomes a reality, insofar as this may be possible in human terms (John of Damascus: *De Imag.* 1, 9; PG 94.1240). Man's thirst for the "Other," for the "thou," becomes an empirical experience.

It is in the light of this that the Greek Fathers understood Colossians 3.10 and its reference to baptism which maintained that "the neophyte, dead and clothed anew in Christ, has cast off the old man." As a result he is the "new man." This gradual renewal, constitutes the foundation of ascetic spirituality (2 Cor 4.16). In this context, flesh and body take on another meaning. Athanasios of Alexandria in his treatise on the Incarnation says that Christ appropriated the human body, he took upon himself the senses of all men, thus sanctifying the human body. Ten centuries later, Gregory Palamas asserts that Christ became incarnate in order to honor mortal flesh. He raised up the human body through his resurrection, so that our body co-resurrected with his might enter into incorruptibility. This explains why in the Orthodox services the body plays the role of a companion, of a partner to the soul, actively participating in worship: it kneels, it raises its hands, it makes the sign of the cross, etc.

Far from a narrow approach of man, as an isolated being, the Orthodox Church considers man in the midst of the redemption of the whole universe. All the earth, all the cosmos, must be delivered from vanity and be divinized. Christ is the Savior of all mankind, the "first-born" of the coming *aion*, constantly working to bring the universe to its original dignity. The body is not to be despised or treated as hybris, but disciplined and governed according to God's will. Both the body and the soul are in need of redemption and of deliverance from the dominion of evil. John Chrysostom advises us "to possess the body and not allow ourselves to be possessed by it" (*Homily 2 Statutes*; PG 49.41).

Sophokles centuries earlier had said about man: "he is the strangest creature," in the sense of something mighty, overpowering. Man is strange. He casts himself outside the familiar, he departs from the customary, overstepping his boundaries. Patristics conceived the same characteristics in man but in a different way. While respecting his being and his liberty, Orthodoxy sees God's intervention as a liberation of man from himself. Man needs redemption. He was incomplete, imperfect, empty, waiting to be completed and perfected. This is realized by a divine meeting between God as person and man as person, which was inaugurated by Christ's incarnation — manifesting thus the ontology of the created in his relationship with the uncreated. In such a way, man finds his most profound advancement, spiritual development, expansion, and elevation — from being a receiver to becoming indeed a partner and a co-worker with Christ for working out his will.

18. Images of God

Christian anthropology's task is in main lines to convey that man without God, or God without man, cannot exist; this is inconceivable. The task of all human beings, regardless of their class, color, language, race, and religion, is to be in relationship with God, whose image they are. Our relation to God constitutes part of our human condition. We are reminded that we are mirrors, reflections, certainly disfigured, of God. But anyhow, whatever happened, even in the most wicked case, we remain his images. Are we always conscious of this unique sonship of the creation, of this most precious heritage? Because it is indeed heritage: a free gift, as life is, of which we have to be shown worthy.

Many have dealt with this theology of the image of God: Origen, Athanasios, Gregory of Nyssa, Cyril of Alexandria, Hilary of Poitiers, either with an analytic or synthetic method. But all the Fathers never lose sight of the essential point in their research: that man is created according to the image of God. There exists a profound cleavage in this respect between the thought of St. Augustine and that of the Greek Fathers. The bishop of Hippo occupies unique place in the history of image and similitude. He has written a theology of history. Being influenced greatly by Plato, the neo-Platonics and Plotinos, even to a certain degree by the Manicheans and Pelagianism, he starts with the empirical man, of this earthly being in daily reality, in order to attain God. Proceeding in such a way, he follows a quite opposite method than that of the Greek Fathers who, being inspired by the Bible, start rather from God in order afterwards to attain man.

What makes innovation a remarkable asset in Augustine is that he was seeking and he found in the structure even of man, in his *mens*, in his soul, in his spiritual eye, in his spirit, the nature and even the life of God. Consequently, the image of God makes an integral part of the whole structure of every man, as it is the expression of the similarity. Thus faith in God and religious feeling must be included in human nature itself in terms of essential, ontological propriety. For him, as for St. Paul, man being the temple of God becomes in his body the image of God, expressing then the Resurrection and the Transfiguration. Augustine describes, in an extraordinary grandiose vision, the likeness of all the saved persons; he sees them in Christ, thus defining *totus Christus*. Four times he had commented on the book of Genesis on the subject of man created in the image and likeness of God. Unfortunately, it is admitted by many theologians that this capital theme was neglected in the Latin writings of the Middle Ages. But when one seeks to know better, starting from man created in God's image, or seeks a better definition of man, starting from the notion of God, the conclusion remains the same: both, man, as God, are a mystery. Consequently, both these subjects were studied and will always become subjects of studies.

The Alexandrians, Clement, Athanasios, and Cyril have been profoundly nourished by the writings of Pythagoras, Plato, and the Stoics, and profiting from the translation of the Septuagint into Greek, place the Incarnation in the very heart of history and thus affirm the theology of the Logos-Image. For them, man is not image, but "according to the image"; man is the image of the Image, the Logos being the only true image, an authentic intermediary between God and the creation. Neither Basil of Caesarea, nor Gregory the Theologian were occupied so much on the theme of the image and the likeness. Gregory of Nyssa makes an exception, having given enough thought on it.

Hilary, bishop of Poitiers, has also reflected on the nature and on the structure of man. But contrary to Athanasios, he lacks philological precision, resulting inevitably in a very poor anthropology. Due to the absence of elaborated concepts and structured frames, he was unable to express his thought with rigor. For him, the word *imago* is synonymous with *figura, forma, similitudo, species*. He places the Incarnation in the center of the economy of salvation.

Only Christ allows us to pierce the mystery of man and of that of humanity. What interests him is the destiny of man, the future of the image in the future city; his doctrine on the image turns rather to the eschatology. Being inspired by Origen and Philo, Hilary remains a personal thinker. Only Christ explains and clarifies history. It is in Christ also that the true nature of man is clarified. Christ is the true Adam, the Incarnate Word who realizes the perfect man. Hilary accords priority to the soul rather than to the body. Often he culpabilizes the body considering it as if it were the prison of the soul. In the book of the Psalms he sees a continuous tension between history and the spiritual life, oriented to the life to come, toward the new Jerusalem.

Gregory of Nyssa remains one of the greatest mystics. His thinking is extremely beautiful although sometimes eclectic, nurtured abundantly by the Greek culture. He has reflected in length on the theme of image and likeness. It is to him that we owe the most elaborated theology of ancient Christianity. A theology of the body, whose capital role is to glorify the Creator, as it is prefigured in the resurrection of Christ. He conceives the image in us as a vocation for communion. Evil is the alienation of this communion with that One who within us is not possible to uproot, being ever endless, incommunicable, unchangeable. The image is the mirror of the mystery of God. It ensues then that man himself is mystery. For Gregory of Nyssa, Paradise is God himself, and the Beatitudes are identified with him. It is neither a place, nor a time. As Irenaios before him, he enables the liberty, a royal gift, to come out. As theologian of history, Gregory regards Christ as the key of the universal history.

In general, contrary to the Latin authors, the Greek Church Fathers knew widely ancient philosophy, expressing the very human aspirations throughout human history; consequently, it is impossible to ignore them. They knew perfectly well the pre-Socratic thinkers, Plato, and Aristotle, the Stoics, Epikurios, Cicero, Seneca, Lucretios and Posidonios, without forgetting the philosphers of their times.

Now, the idea of God as holy and the attribute holiness are regarded differently between East and West. While Greek patristics sees this holiness as the person of God, identified with his being, in the West there exists a tendency to isolate such holiness, as the eerie feeling, the feeling one has at night, alone; it is the shudder of holy awe. For this feeling the German Otto invented the word *numinous*. Not wishing to prejudice the argument, he takes the word *numen*, from which to form the adjective *numinous*. *Numen*, in Latin, is the word for the most primitive, general, and unreasoned conception of the supernatural. So a numinous feeling is any feeling of awe in the presence of the supernatural. We must recognize the religious feeling — a feeling of something more than mere dependence. We might call this an utter sense of abasement and worthlessness in the awful presence of God. Even as Jacob said: "How dreadful is this place! This is none other but the house of God" (Gen 28.17).

In fact, the numinous feeling, or the realization of the supernatural, is always accompanied by dread and awe. On the lowest plane, where there is no trust or obedience or love, but only the sensation, it is rightly grisly, uncanny, eerie. The flesh creeps, the hair stands on end, and the blood runs cold. This is a debased, a degenerate form of experience. It is not the whole, but a part of reality. It is as real and as distinctive a thing by itself as the fragrance of violets, the taste of wine, the light of day, or the roll of thunder. It is not due to any illusion or sign of primitive mythology.

Rising to higher planes of religious thought, the experience is due not to the presence of ghosts, but to the presence of God. The experience, however, is not due to a belief in God. It is of itself like another experience. It antedated the higher conceptions of God. Yet, now, with higher conceptions, comes a much nobler and loftier interpretation of the experience. So we read in the book of Job: "Shall not his excellency make you afraid? And his dread fall upon you?" (Job 13.11). "Let not your dread make me afraid" (Job 13.21). Compare with this also: "Procul a mea tuus sit furor omnis domo" (Catullus 63-92). This creature-consciousness, this dread of the supernatural, this fear of God, this simple experience, however it may be interpreted, is an essential part of the conception of holiness, known also as *Mysterium tremendum*.

The Fathers treat this subject rather from a perspective of personal relationship. There is a spirit of community between the Creator and his creature, since it is his image and as such he is called to follow the course to become Godlike, like him. This feeling: I belong, therefore I am, expresses the strongest sense of sonship, security, and love. This feeling embodies the whole incarnational theology, where oneness, participation in Christ's divinity are stressed. Let us see even the substance of his body, the Church, where the spirit of *koinonia* prevails. People as members of the same body are happiest and most secure and most creative when they depend on the goodwill and helpfulness of their neighbors and know that their neighbors depend on them, so that each person's contribution is needed and valued and each is able to feel in some sense responsible for the other.

But the same Incarnation stresses the otherness of God, his difference from us. He is the holy one: infinite, immortal, encompassing this vast universe in himself, beyond what the human mind can conceive or understand. The idea of this transcendent mysterium becoming a human is literally inconceivable. The Fathers are not talking about the kind of divine manifestation with which the Greek and Roman myths abound: a god not all that different from us appearing on earth, as when Paul and Barnabas were taken for gods. We believe in the same God as the monotheists, the one infinite and eternal Creator of all things.

But the Fathers want to say much more: that God not only uses the divine reason and moral sense that he has implanted in each one of us, but that this logos took human flesh — "So the Word became flesh; he came down to dwell among us, and we saw his glory" (Jn 1.14). Theology works by making, breaking, and remaking images.

We will never be able fully to understand the Incarnation. What we can do is what the New Testament does: take some metaphor, push it to the limit, and say that, in the end, more than that is indicated. We want to say that, in the Incarnation, God's very being is involved and put at risk in a way that goes beyond the inspiration of good men. God, through his Son, has become part of the flux of events. But we can never fully grasp what it is we are trying to say, for as Maximos the Confessor by his apophaticism reminds us, we are dealing not with a human being writ large but with God.

The sense of security for a Christian during these contradictions and dangers comes from his deep conviction that in spite of all these there exists a clear and evident divine pedagogy. This is due to God's very character, namely, that he, as Pantokrator and Lord of all, is continuously active. God is not abandoning us or waiting to be discovered by his creatures. He, first, takes the first step. Thus, he first, by one way or another, proceeds and advances, comes forth to meet and to reveal himself. He does not desire for a single moment to be absent from our existence, out of reach, or ignored. Without revelation, and his continuous epiphanies, man would have been searching for him and seeking him in vain. Man would have been left by himself, unable to meet his creator. Never had man, relying only on himself alone, succeeded in completely reaching the truth without risking the danger of confusing or distorting it. Only God alone can speak for himself, thus revealing his presence.

On the other hand, when God speaks, he affirms and reaffirms his faithfulness to his promises. He does not try to demonstrate sophisticated arguments and unnecessary proofs, since he is not the God of the philosophers and scholars. That which he affirms, in fact, exceeds all human demonstration. Only his word is enough. The Prophets, in order to show his authority, did not cease to say again and again: "Thus says God the Lord. . .The word of the Lord . . . Oracle of the Lord." But it is equally true, that God highly respects our autonomy, never forcing or crushing human liberty. On the contrary, he highly esteems our freedom. "If you want to enter into real life," Christ proposes to the wealthy man, thus placing his appeal at his disposal for free choice (Mt 19.21). What really enables man to accept God's appeal is the fact that he carries with him, as God's image, the presence of the creating Spirit. The Holy Spirit in reality is to every one of us the more intimate feeling than we really are. This Spirit extends the affirmation of the Logos which "teaches us all, reminding us all that Christ has said" (Jn 14.26).

Thus by the repeated suggestion of the Spirit, freely accepted by each of us, is faith born. In this context, we must be precise: God's pedagogy is progressive, following a certain rhythm of growth. He is arranging the steps and the speed of his interventions, either in the history of peoples or of each individual, according to his wise plan. This very character of process and advancement go from implicit to an explicit action. This is why the disciples said to Christ at the end of his earthly mission: "Finally you speak clearly and without images," (Jn 16.29). Taking this as a model and solid departure, we can establish what could be our human pedagogy as God's ministers engaged in pastoral activity to reach others and to help them in their steps on their way to truth.

Our method must faithfully copy and implement God's practiced pedagogy. And in order to do this successfully, one must not change the order, starting from the opposite end, namely, to bring man forth to God, and not inversely substituting a subjective action: of man to God. Instead he must show God to man. This is so because human effort, sinful and polluted, can never reach a transcendent God: Jesus after all said clearly: "Nobody goes to the Father except through me" (Jn 14.16). In this earthly sinful life, there can be no possible theoretic postulation of God.

Of course this does not signify that human pedagogy must be confined or restricted to a literal repetition of the word of God. The indispensable role of a human pedagogy consists in translating, adapting, interpreting, and faithfully applying the proclaimed word first and above all, and then carefully examining whatever language is better fitted to the people in question. It is good to remind ourselves of the wise method of articulating the faith used for his catechumens, by Clement of Alexandria, most of whom were coming from pagan intellectual backgrounds.

Clement often refers to the ancient classical world by displaying quotations from philosophers and poets in order to strengthen his methodology and to inform his listeners of the continuity and consistency of God's action in human history. This is why he calls his instructions *pedagogue*, having in mind that the first such pedagogos is Christ. The use of the most proper method, the nearest possible language and the most successful message in order to reach the people has a tremendous impact.

In rendering this both to human and spiritual service, the affirmative character of God's word must be fully respected, showing the coherence of his various and unusual steps. Namely, that this progressive process implies interventions, difficult for our mind to explain and to be fully understood. God in all his contacts with us, while meeting our present situation, looks more and more to the end of time, to the eschaton of creation. If this point is not sufficiently explained beforehand, God's pedagogy could be seen as a scandal, as an indifference by God to all human tears, sufferings, and outcry. Even, unable to see the "whys" before the sufferings, the illness, the human disorder, the cynical behavior, the offending moral values, and the contradictions one might be led to the idea that God is either absent from the world's scene, or unable to show his sovereignty by intervening in timely manner.

19. The Sacredness of Human Life

To understand the fullness of life, we must bear in mind the biblical teaching that the human being is created in the image of God, that each human life is sacred and of infinite worth. Consequently, a human being cannot be treated as chattel, or an object to be disposed of for someone's program or project or ideology, but must be treated as a personality. Every human being is the possessor of the right-to-life, of dignity and honor, and of the fruits of his or her labor.

However, justice is more than a mere abstention from injuring our fellow human beings. "The work of justice is peace, and the effect thereof quietness and confidence forever" (Is 32.17). It is a positive conception, and includes economic well-being, intellectual and spiritual growth, philanthropy, and every endeavor that will enable human beings to realize the highest and the best in their natures.

Nothing is more fundamental in biblical and Rabbinic ethics than the moral obligation of *tzedakah*, a Hebrew term which means both "charity" and "to do justice." The rabbinic sages of the Talmud declared that "almsgiving — i.e., aiding the poor and feeding the hungry — weighs as heavily as all the other commandments of the Torah" (Talmud Baba Batra 9a).

In proclaiming the jubilee year, which like the Ten Commandments, was ascribed to divinely-inspired legislation revealed on Mount Sinai, Holy Scriptures ordained: "And if your brother waxes poor, and his means fail with you, then you shall uphold him: as a stranger and a settler shall he live with you" (Lev 25.35). The rabbis observe that the expression that "Your brother may *live* with you" means that it is our personal and communal duty to see to it that our fellow human beings do not die of starvation. Though the person be a "stranger" or "an alien settler" he (or she) is to be included in the term "your brother" and is to be treated in a brotherly and compassionate manner.

The rabbinic sages regarded such compassionate care of man as an act worthy of association with Divinity itself: "God says to Israel, "My sons, whenever you give sustenance to the poor, I impute it to you as though you gave sustenance to me, for it says, 'Command the children of Israel . . .*my* bread for *my* sacrifices . . . shall ye observe unto me.' Does, then, God eat and drink? No, but whenever you give food to the poor, God accounts it to you as if you gave food to him" (Numbers Rabbah 28.2).

The virtue of such care for the poor and hungry is depicted in Jewish tradition as the salient attribute of the "founding father" of Judaism, the Patriarch Abraham, who is called the archetype of the "Pharisee of love." In a midrashic commentary that begins with the phrases, "Let your house be open; let the poor be members of your household. Let a man's house be open to the north and the south, and to the east and to the west," the rabbis describe the humanitarianism of Abraham:

> He went out and wandered about, and when he found wayfarers, he brought them to his house, and he gave wheaten bread to him whose wont it was not to eat wheaten bread, and so with meat and wine. And *not* only this, but he built large inns on the roads, and put food and drink within them, and all came and ate and drank and blessed God. Therefore, quiet of spirit was granted to him, and all that the mouth of man can ask for was found in his house (Abot de Rabbi Nathan, 7.17a,b).

Elsewhere the Talmud admonishes: "He who has no pity upon his fellow creatures is assuredly not of the seed of Abraham our father" (Bezah 32b).

From biblical times through the present, there was much free and generous giving of alms to all who asked — even to deceivers! — and there was also much systematic and caring relief through established institutions. Each Jewish community boasted of a *tamhui* (public kitchen) from which the poor received two meals daily. There was also the *kupah* (alms box) for the disbursement of benevolent funds on the Sabbath eve to provide three meals for the Sabbath (Mishnah Peah 8.7). Additional care was exercised with respect to the itinerant poor, who were provided with a loaf of bread which sufficed for two meals, and who were also entitled to the cost of lodging.

Thus, there arose the charitable traditions and institutions of the Jewish people which have remained a religious-communal characteristic ever since. These customs of charity, which were foreign to the pagan mentality of the Greeks and Romans, also had an abiding impact on the nature of the Christian "charitas."

Our Christian faith should clearly assert what is God's message in Jesus Christ for the contemporary world. We shall probably not express it in the same way as the questions dealt with by Ecumenical Councils of the past. For instance, questions regarding the human and divine nature in Jesus Christ (adoptianism, docetism, ebionism, monophysitism, diophysitism or monotheletism), which were discussed at the Council of Constantinople thirteen centuries ago, may still be attractive for theological thought, since the mystery of God's sonship in Jesus Christ is too profound to be entirely grasped by the human mind. But the Christological theme of today must be correlated with the entire broad and complicated context of our present life. We find ourselves in the midst of some very serious threats. They are manifold, conditioned by their deep historical roots, and influenced by their social, spiritual, and moral context. In such a situation, we search first of all for the life-giving strength of the Gospel, extending our longing hands towards the saving power of Jesus Christ, the living Lord of the Church and of history.

The abundant world resources are being wasted on destructive purposes while poverty continues to assume alarming proportions. Indeed creation itself mourns over the irresponsible and sinful acts towards nature and its resources. The frightened people all over the world yearn for peace while political structures defiantly ask, "Am I my brother's keeper?"

The great Indian sage and poet Tagore says:

> Thou art the Brother amongst my brothers, but I heed them not, I divided not my earnings with them, thus sharing my all with thee. In pleasure and in pain I stand not by the side of men, and thus stand by thee. I shrink to give up my life, and thus do not plunge into the great waters of life.

On 4 September 1224, the feast of the Holy Cross, St. Francis of Assisi prayed thus in a prayer vigil:

> Who art thou, my god most sweet? And what am I, that unprofitable servant and vilest of worms? O, my Lord Jesus Christ, two graces do I pray thee to grant unto me before I die. The first that while I live I may feel in my body and in my soul that sorrow, sweet Lord, that thou didst suffer in the hours of thy most bitter passion. The second that I may feel in my heart that exceeding love wherewith, O, Son of God, thou wast enkindled to endure willingly for us sinners agony so great.

It is this love says Ignatios of Antioch which abolishes death, the love of God's Suffering Servant, the truth of Christ's humanity which he calls "a mystery of shouting accomplished in the silence of God"

(Eph 19.1), "God in man, true life in death" (ibid. 1.2). This love is a passionate intensity, a freedom from restraint, which surmounts all barriers and holds nothing back in order "that all human beings might be gathered unto it."

God is ever incarnate in the very flesh of human history. He is crucified in human pain and agony. To put it in the words of St. John of Damascus, "Just as charcoal burns not of itself but through the fire with which it is impregnated . . . I am but black, cold charcoal. In order to be set ablaze by the fire of Pentecost I want the bread of God which is the flesh of Christ of the seed of David, and I want as drink his blood which is love incorruptible" (*The Orthodox Faith* 4.3), the mystery of shouting accomplished in the silence of God, the truth of Christ's humanity, a passionate intensity, a freedom from restraint, God in man, true life in death. In him only are we more than conquerors. "In him is our focal point . . . in him is our meeting place in which we may live our peace" (St. Maximos the Confessor, *Mystagogy* 1-PG 91.665-68). He is in us an offering of peace, the "Offering as well as him who offers, the interpreter as well as the interpreted" (Liturgy of St. John Chrysostom).

Life — A Gift of God
(Masuo Nezu)

Buddhism affirms the sanctity of all life. Its goal is to free all living beings from the miseries of life, so that they may attain the "joy of peace." This peace and liberation are the right of all beings; they are equal before the *dharma*; the message of liberation therefore falls on all, like rain, that their lives may blossom and bear fruit. This is best expresssed in the following Lotus Sutra:

> I appear in the world just like a great crowd, to our enrichment on all parched living beings, to free them all from misery and so attain the joy of peace, joy in the world, and the joy of nirvana.

> To give peace to all creatures, I appear in the world and, for the hosts of the living, preaching the law, pure as sweet dew; the one and the only law of emancipation and the nirvana.

> I preach the law equally; as I preach to one person, so I preach to all. This is the law preached by the Buddha. It is just like a great cloud which with the same kind of rain and which is men and blossoms, so that each bears fruit." (Lotus Sutra, mainly from chapter 5 but also from 3 and 4).

20. Some Consequences of Perverted Views

Certain fundamental beliefs and values have considerably influenced human behavior in history. Primitive societies, monotheistic or polytheistic, remembering the shame resulting from disobedience to God's will, tried through expiatory sacrifices to bridge the gap between God and man and in so doing to find reconciliation and peace. We do not intend to enter into controversial issues as to whether such conceptions contain elements of a mythical nature or are exaggerated. One fact remains beyond any doubt, i.e., that in whatever culture he lives, man feels more or less guilty, this notion being nurtured by religious conceptions. Of course, such a question is related to the whole problem of sin, and the sinfulness of human nature after the Fall. Sin, fear, culpability, are therefore interrelated notions, which if exceeding their proper measure, may poison creativity, the joy of this life and create unhealthy, neurotic manifestations.

Western Christians, led by theologians such as Pelagius and doctors such as St. Augustine, were deeply involved in this delicate debate to such an extent that a whole theology of grace, redemption, free will versus determinism, and of human degradation was produced, exercising an impact on a wide scale within Western thought and culture. Man began to despise himself due to the damaging effect of original sin. This overstatement of sinfulness largely contributed to the creation of an erroneous evaluation in a variety of areas: namely, those of existence and human potentialities, of creation, of the ultimate purpose of life, and of adequate capacities for overcoming the omnipresent attractiveness of evil and the aggressiveness of carnal passions. Even the whole question of human liberty becomes uncertain and problematic if such a pessimistic view prevails concerning the effects of the original fall on Adam's descendents. There are even further consequences of such an approach to our fallen nature, as for example, death, the effectiveness of human resistance and the assurance of human recovery from the throes of evil.

There have been two opposite attitudes to the place of our body in this earthly life, either extreme ill-treatment or exaltation, degradation or glorification, unmerciful, cruel inhuman treatment or idolatry. These extremist views became an "hybris," a slander on the body which is much more than a prison. Christ never considered this present life to be a hell. On the contrary, in the presence of God, it is a great blessing; it might, in very real measure be enjoyed. Such views are foreign intruders which were not from within the Church but rather penetrated from non-Christian sources. The theory that the body is a prison is not Christian but pagan. It did not come from Jerusalem but from Greece. And not from the old Greece of Homer and the Olympic gods but from a later period of decline, the later Orphic cults. *Soma sema*, "the body a tomb" was the Orphic teaching: that bodily frame is the great hindrance to the enjoyment of God's presence and of eternal life, so that the longing for release from the body was at the very center of hope for immortality. This concept of identifying the body with prison had long influence in Western thought mainly through Platonic philosophy. Plotinos seemed ashamed of being in the body. For the Gospel, the body is not a tomb but a temple (1 Cor 6.19). Christians do not hope for release from embodiment as such, but rather of the revivification of the whole man, soul and body, unto life eternal. Man is a single, united whole: not only man's mind but his whole being was created in the image of God, the body standing as partner and collaborator with his soul. In this present life, the glory of the saints is, as a rule, an inward splendor, but in the life hereafter it will be clothed as the soul, with splendor, says Makarios the Egyptian (*Homilies* 5,9). Only extremists, like Manicheans with a pseudo-ascetic cover considered the body and the things of the body as evil.

Without idealizing this issue, we must not forget another factor in such a debate: that our body is not the same as when it was created. It bears the consequences, a kind of stigma of the fall. Since the flesh revolts against the spirit, it disobeys the voice of the spirit, and it needs watchful care, stewardship and self-discipline. In such a perspective one should understand the admonitions by Christ or by St. Paul on the body's mistrust, subordination, continuous *askesis*. In fact, it became a difficult partner. The flesh pushes us to do that which is against its own interest.

A saint, or a committed Christian, while in communion with God, is compelled to also be involved in worldly affairs. But he does not see them with a Manichean eye. In everything he finds Gods mandate for responsible stewardship. Man is seen as a commissioned co-worker, to lead this creation in revolt back, with Gods help, to the pre-Adamic state, to order (*taxis*) from disorder (*ataxia*). Thus, there is nothing clean or unclean. It is our use which determines the quality and the value of things. They become meaningful if they are put to the service of God and his creatures. Two movements characterize the saints: attachment and detachment. Time and eternity, here and there. Only these together can yield the full blossom, the richest fruit and fascination of healthy spirituality. Over and beyond life in Christ, every saint lives and has to live various other lives. Indeed, such a soul cannot attain its fullest possible growth without witness (*martyria*) in the midst of the world, during the term of this earthly sojourn. Admittedly, it is not easy to keep the interests of time and eternity in proper balance one with the other. Thus, there is a constant need of prayer for guidance and appropriate action, a need of God's presence through eucharistic communion, sustaining and protecting us. Such a life is, of course, full of tension between the perishable and other worldliness. Such tension required alternations in daily life, moving successively from earth to heaven and from heaven back again to earth.

It is rather difficult to define the boundaries between first and last things, those visible here and those invisible there. We need the key — the gift of discernment (*diakrisis*). Our destiny in God inevitably implies a certain way of living, in between "here and now," exactly Jesus' way, during his earthly life, dwelling among us. Jesus showed us not only what God is like, but also, in practical terms of loving service, what man can be like, because he is both God's image and child. It is unfair to divert our attention to doubtful engagements, suggesting that eternity is somewhere else inhabited by someone else, at the expense of the common ground of daily life. Often we must seek eternity within the "here and now," i.e., to discern and perceive the deeper moral significance of temporal concerns. To apprehend the point of intersection of the timeless with time: this is the prerogative of the saint. Moreover, his self-examination will be balanced, thus avoiding the extremes of scrupulosity, which is the breeder of anxiety, and also of nonchalance, and the refusal to assume any form of responsibility, either for oneself or for others.

In the light of the above reflections, one may ask: is it right to blame those scholastic theologians who preferred a legalistic interpretation of penitence? The answer to such a vital question must be linked with the paradox of recent times: while we are facing a strong and manipulated movement from all quarters for *decriminalization*, at the same time, as never before seen in history, there is a criminalization of the "other" person or social structure. We have even reached the point of blaming, for every present evil, the "other," our body as such, our fragile nerves, our heredity, our natural environment, the established system of our society, history, supernatural forces . . . everything but our own selves.

The trouble nowadays is that culpabilization is directed not just to persons, tangible and concrete, but to structures, to social categories, even to sex. There even prevails a distinction between the dominating and the dominated. In these worldly affairs people fall into other kinds of traps, namely, as they tend to be deculpabilized of one thing, they become culpabilized of another. This dual error is a paradox because while they should escape from one kind of guilt, in reality, they fall into another one, precisely because of belonging to a specific category — political, sex, economic class, etc., where there is no stability and total security. Every category is unreliable. On the contary, when God deculpabilizes this world, his forgiveness is true in every sense. He pardons. A pardon proceeds from one person — from the Father — to another person (see Lk 15.11-32).

If culpability is not directed properly, it can lead to aggressiveness, polluting cultures and even moral institutions. Beyond all such frustrations which are wrought with evil and guilt, the Gospel seeks to liberate man in his totality. This constitutes the entire mystery of redemption for a world imprisoned in an endless circle of repressive culpability. On the other hand, since the ongoing secularization provokes a loss of the sense of sin, relativizing transgressions by evacuating this distinctive sense of evil, people are at the same time deserting the ways of hope. If a personal relationship with the transcendent does not take place, evil strengthens its dominion, and the perversion acquires suicidal proportions with falsified therapies, pseudo-scientific theories, and confidential advice by radio. All these result in the banalizing of faults and justifying of evil behavior.

The Fathers reminded their contemporaries how difficult it was to understand the true spirit of the Gospel. Often one-sidedness leads to the denunciation of inoffensive pleasures, which in turn produces a feeling of culpability. Christ was not negative in assessing earthly goods and pleasures. A Christian cannot see around him only satanic forces and stark judgments condemning all as sinful. We are asked rather to see God's love, his redeeming action upon creation. A Christian, conscious of his responsibility, shapes his daily behavior according to the dignity of beings created by God. Condemnation of persons disturbs, wounds, and irritates. Culpability imprisons us in a bad conscience. But this is not a positive or a creative process. As Christians, we expect to be freed from the dominion of evil.

In this connection, self-accusation is not the same as Christian contrition. Oral confession of evils is not effective outside a personal relation to God, whose transcending love removes the weight of culpability. To pass from the guilty state to that of a sinner and consequently to that of a penitent, is nothing other than to pass through the experience of reconciliation with one's self, with others and with the world in the light of God's mercy. Without this active presence of the mystery of salvation by Christ, culpability, whether social or individual, will be distorted into a foolish idea, backed by violence. On the contrary, the assurance that we are really forgiven by God gives us the power to soar and to hope more and more regarding man's future and progress.

There is a tendency to displace the real causes of the sixteenth century separations into other factors and grounds. And the question reappears: Where does the real responsibility lie? Is it only the corruption of the leading clergy, as is assumed? Are the abuses of the then existing institutions, ecclesiastical and religious orders mainly to blame? The first element, humanly speaking, in any period of history, is unavoidable, even if a more rigorous discipline existed. At the same time, nobody can deny the honest intentions of the Reformers. We rather detect as principal causes of the degradation and cataclysm the philosophical and theological streams prevailing in the Middle Ages, and above all, the very unbalanced, strange doctrine of salvation which was developed in all kinds of theological schools during the previous two centuries, from John Duns Scotus to Gabriel Biel. Here the responsibility of medieval theological thinking is immense, because its protagonists contributed to the elaboration of a soteriology obtainable by the natural forces of man (Pelagianism) on the one hand, and on the other by the growth of another parallel stream of thinking that God intervenes arbitrarily to accept a soul for salvation. The confrontation of these streams leads to all kinds of excesses, as, for instance, the use of indulgences, while at the other extreme is found the most radical and incomprehensible anti-Pelagianism, namely, that advocated by the polemist William of Occam (1285-1347), claiming as possible the beatific vision of God by a damned soul. For him nothing can limit God's freedom. He makes a subtle distinction between the absolute power of God and his ordained power. This position, relying on a metaphysics of the absolute liberty and unmeasurable potentialities of man and of the absolute omnipotence of God, inevitably leads to the alienation of the one from the other. But such considerations were in radical contradiction with the traditional spirituality either of the Eastern Fathers or even of St. Augustine and St. Thomas. In particular, Gregory Palamas made it very clear that only God's energies reach us, not his essence. The curious thing in this context is that the initiators of the above eschatology, Scotus and Occam, belonged to a Franciscan order and contended that they borrowed such views from a literal reading of Augustinian writings.

It is precisely this existing conflict of widely circulating distorted theological views which provoked the reactions of Luther. Honestly speaking, he was a deeply religious soul of an exceptional strength. His anguished temperament could not resist becoming totally inflamed by divine fire as he stood before Almighty God, full of love and awe. It was a *deus nudus*, partial, subjective and at the same time hostile to all kinds of evil, that Luther discovered in Occam's writings and saw propagated as if they were the authentic teachings of the Church, and not simply as one theological pure opinion and nothing more, *modo disputandi.* As far as Luther was concerned, though he escaped from the trap of falling into despair, nevertheless, in reality he did not deny his attachment to what he called the *"factio occanica,"* a confused and perplexed theological acrobatics. In fact, we have to admit that the main theses of Luther were shaped in accordance with the established structure and tradition of Scot and Occam. Thus, Luther arrives at extremely anti-pelagian positions, by making his own the doctrine of Christian justice *extra nos.*

Today, we can see more clearly the positions and the efforts to fight errors in certain instances by balanced means. We also realize to what extent extremist arguments were often used, due to the existing tension and psychologically heavy climate between the opponents. Today, the most urgent theological and metaphysical problem which theologians have to face in this period of ecumenical encounter is how to re-establish and elaborate a sound theology of grace, how to arrive at a true and balanced interior perfection of the soul, exactly such as that which was formulated by the Cappadocian Fathers or the school of Alexandrians, who never, it is true, had before them the thorny question of Pelagianism. It is on the basis of this spirituality and metaphysics that an eventual reconciliation can be produced in the future and that the unity of the broken bonds of the churches can be re-established.

The above introductory reflections lead us to study the following issue: what are the relations between man and God? In this ontological comparison and confrontation, what image men or women make of themselves and of God as well? At certain historical stages, like the thirteenth to eigthteenth centuries, deeply immersed in Augustinian reflections of sin and redemption, a devastating pessimism massively enveloped all expressions of human thought. Overcome by a shameful assumption of human nature on the whole and a fear of the distorted self, reinforced by overculpabilization — unique in the history of civilizations — humanity began to feel completely disarmed and inferior. Such views totally paralyzed the leading representatives of theology and philosophy before the aggressiveness of the universe and evil forces in revolt. By also attributing a disproportionate weight to evil in the framework of the penitential practice of forgiveness of sins, certain overscrupulous theologians, preaching contrition for faults committed rather than the joy resulting from liberation and divine mercy as expressed by God's pardon, produced a variety of ill-conceived ideas: confusing views on penance, on the amount of required expiatory meritorial works, and the measure of divine forgiveness administrated by the clergy. By insisting rather on the punitive and expiatory character of the Christ's penitential discipline, by overstating the juridical or strict canonical nature of the sacrament of confessing sins, unintentionally a kind of melancholic contrition, of overculpabilization, a heavily depressive piety was cultivated. People were approaching God, especially when coming for the remission of their committed sins, no longer with "a holy fear, reverend and filial feelings," so legitimate and normal, but with an obsessive fear of a vindictive God. What in this respect is forgotten is the true nature of the relationship between God the Father on the one hand, and sinners as his children on the other. Like the father in the parable, God is awaiting the return home of his children.

Suffering from such a bad frustrated conscience, the Western type of man and woman, in penetrating more and more to the depths of their selves, developed an exaggerated sensibility.

Today the Christian faith's impact has been diminished. God's transcendence in the setting of the present Western society, has much less effect on our attitude towards the present world. The ultimate roots of this change are to be sought much deeper in the soil of the West than in the thin topmost layer, which has been contributed in the intellectual stratum of the Renaissance. While until then all amenities of culture were drawn into the service of religion, a tendency arose to find in all terrestrial occupations a rather serious importance of their own. There appeared a strange phenomenon: the pursuit of knowledge simply for the sake of knowing and the pursuit of beauty simply for the sake of enjoyment. Those humanists became more and more humanistic. The earthly interest became all-absorbing, while the interests of eternity receded into the background. Italy's advances in painting traces this revolution. Here in the place of the Byzantine gilt and azure, bright natural colors began to be used, and instead of the stylized Byzantine symmetry, the flowing natural lines of homely human garments appeared. Here for the first time are real men and women, often sensual, not as they could have been in Palestine, but as they were in Florence that day. Plato had defined wisdom or *philosophia* as "a meditation upon death; those who philosophize aright study nothing but dying and being dead" (*Phaedo*, 64). But as a reaction to this, there now appears an opposite stream: Free man thinks of nothing less than of death; his wisdom is a meditation not upon death but upon life. The two contrasted sayings typify the change that has taken place.

Consequently, intellectuals begin to underestimate the past. Even intentionally they completely forget the roots and the sources of the Western progress. They become amnesiac. Being thus forgetful all these foundations of our culture, education, keeping spiritual values on the top, suddenly are undervalued, are pulled down, and instead replacing them, are proposing a man-centered culture. How urgent, therefore, becomes this kind of *anamnesis*, reminding this frustrated and forgetful generation that in every human there exists certain elements which are more than human and which cannot be ignored.

Chronologically, signs of moral confusion and pessimism can already be found in the period before and after the Renaissance. Especially in the fields of art, poetry, and music, we find an open contradiction, greatly discrediting the Church in general. On one side we are witnessing a promising renewal in the letters and sciences, but on the other hand, and at the same time, a sense of perilous insecurity, agonizing frustration and uneasiness in view of the future. While without any doubt, the glory of ancient classical literature was revived, simultaneously a pseudo-piety, steeped in despair and melancholy, is introduced. This society one day acknowledging its faults and sinfulness, the next day becomes perversive and foolish, fragile, superstitious, relying more on all sorts of esoteric, apocryphal messages, the caprices of fortune rather than on a living, evangelical faith. Instead of educating people to receive God's love through Christ's victory over death, so that *theosis* is already provided here and now through eucharistic communion and a living spirituality, a paroxystic "pedagogy of fear" was systematically promoted. This aspect was linked with an excessive underestimation of and contempt for the present world and followed a complete resignation and devaluation of all earthly commitments. By an erroneous confusion between the two opposite terms of the biblical term "world" or *cosmos* — namely, either the domain of Satan or the earthly space where human beings have to live — theologians in the West violently attacked the "present time," and even the very nature of man, his binding stewardship and duty.

Faithful to this line of thought, earthly life cannot be viewed other than in a dark perspective, as a preparation for our ultimate death — a death richly dramatized and described in horrible detail. The corruption of the dead body is nothing else than an analogy, an image of the decomposition of the soul, which is expected for the impenitent who is eaten away by evil. It is true that a certain hatred of the body and of the world, the urge to escape human realities, and the challenges of time was practised within reason by ascetics both in the East and in the West. But from then on, it was manipulated and falsified, and was even imposed on a whole civilization during so many centuries.

We need a sounder analysis of the Christian doctrine of sin, with all its direct and indirect implications of original sin. Humanity as a whole remains one with Adam, sharing his responsibility, even in the case of newly born children. If this doctrine is not understood in the right way, we may be led to a terrifying and disappointing view of the actual nature of the Church and its salutary mission to the progeny of Adam. A perverted view is that it is rather a communion of only a "few chosen." Such an overestimation of original sin and its effects on our will and dignity after baptism is misleading and associated with an approach of God as judge, rather than as father. His justice from then on is identified as a horrible vengeance, while his mercy and ineffable clemency is now reserved for a small minority of the chosen. All these elements, taken together, create a hopeless view of evangelical action. Full of despair, Christians suffer from a neurosis and a collective dissatisfaction, expressing itself in an inner aggressiveness.

Such a religious malaise or disease is even more violent and dangerous than other evils of the body. In its aberrant search for absolute purity, one falls into the trap of obsessive scrupulosity and willingly imposes inhuman punishments; he undergoes the most tyrannizing and exhausting mortifications of the body, through unreasonable hardships, cruel fastings and excessive penitential acts. Finally, terrified by the vision of ultimate death, a Christian is neither at peace nor secure for the "hereafter voyage," but suffers feelings which disquiet even the most pious of souls.

Must we say, therefore, that the redemptive mission of Jesus, sent by God to save his creatures from damnation, has failed? In one sense, yes, if we take this distorted and wrongly applied religious life and the perverted image of God's attitude to us. But such a God is unknown to the New Testament. God is the *Philanthropos*, the lover of mankind who is near to us, constantly longing for our salvation. Only God seeks our cooperation for our salvation. He attaches such immense value to us and to the potential he has bestowed upon us, that he invites us to become co-builders of a new world, working with him, and sustained by him. We are also so close to him, that he makes us members of his body. We are children of his family, the Church. Man becomes a bearer of the Spirit (*pneumatophoros*), because he remains, in spite of his shortcomings, the *imago Dei* a distinctive element which never will abandon him whatever may happen. Against any defeatist attitude towards evil and the adversities of this life, patristics develops a pastoral treatment. For them God is infinitely good, one who suffers for man's disobedience more than the sinner himself, one who continuously envelops him with his affection in order to restore him and bring him back "home." Of course, he is also a God of justice, but even when he allows sufferings, they must be understood as pedagogical and reformative means, and not as punitive, stemming from a sense of vengeance. His mercy is more operational than his justice.

God is most sensitive to our precarious state and faithful to his promises regarding his relationship to the created world. Because he loves us, he does not want anything which might intervene, hurting or damaging this harmony of communion.

Another phenomenon connected with Western religious upheavals was the apparition of the Cathari, especially in France. Many historians find a close parallel in that both the Cathari and Reformers were aiming to purify the Church from an inner pollution and to restore purity. Catharism claimed to be a biblical movement, with a faith founded only upon the Bible. The oldest text about their history, found in Florence, had 400 scriptural references in the space of 135 pages! The Cathari recognized Christ alone, ignoring any saint and any other mediator, excluding even the Virgin Mary. But in reality, there were differences among them. As early as the twelfth century, the Vaudois, the precursors of the Reformation in the Rhine Valley, began to distance themselves from them. On various occasions the Vaudois declared that they were not identical with them. During the crusade of 1208 the Cathari persecuted the Vaudois, and one of the Cathari communities later became a Franciscan Order.

Because they believed salvation is not offered by Christ from the cross alone, the Cathari affirmed that this would be given by the transmission of the Holy Spirit, through the *consolamentum*. This Spirit could be transmitted only by the members of the Cathari hierarchy itself, through the laying on of hands. All those who received this unique "sacrament" became true disciples, or "Perfects," thus having access to God. As far as the non-Cathari were concerned, they were condemned to a kind of "metempsychosis" or transmigration of the soul, until the time that their soul would find a Cathari body, thus breaking the inexorable chain of reincarnations. For the Cathari, the human soul, once departed from a dead body, ought to be incarnated into another living being, which could even be a horse, a chicken, or a mouse, but never a fish. For this reason, the eating of meat, eggs, and cheese were strictly forbidden to the Cathari believers. Another excessive belief — about sex — namely, the formal prohibition of "corporal" marriage for procreation, led gradually to sexual asceticism.

In short, their doctrine was rather Manichean and dualistic, thus denying the Incarnation, the Redemption, and the Resurrection. For them, the world was created not by a unique God, but by two distinct divinities, the good principal and the bad. The visible world — bad and sinful — created by the evil principle, could not escape its corruptibility, while the spiritual world belonged to the realm of the good principle. Such an error, as we know, was already condemned by the early Church in 272, when Manes was circulating his ideas. But this Cathari Manicheism contained many other inconsistencies as well, namely, that the human body was part of the "bad" creation. The Cathari could not accept that Christ, the Logos of God the Father, could be united with a body belonging to a bad principle. For them, the real birth of Christ could not be accomplished on earth, but only in heaven, in a state of utmost bliss. Therefore, Christ's nature, which appeared upon the earth, was not a real one at all. Jesus never ate or drank material food with his disciples. From this fact, Jesus could not die on the cross. He was replaced at the last moment by Simeon the Cyrenian or by a bandit. Such a Christ who did not know any death consequently could not experience any Resurrection. In other words, Manicheism eliminates, in one radical swoop, all the basic Christian affirmations concerning Christ. This is really a distorted Christology.

And yet, the cultural and economic influence of Manicheism during the Middle-Ages was considerable. The Cathari were powerful bankowners in Florence in the twelfth, thirteenth, and fourteenth centuries, after the abolition of the professional lending of money by the Council of Lateran in 1097. Claiming that lending money is not a sinful act, the Cathari in Florence became the promoters of the new economic order beginning in the twelfth century. So the Cathari of Arras in France financed the construction of certain Gothic churches, according to a letter of Pope Innocent III. Indirectly, they had a considerable influence upon the Renaissance. Painting, too, was considerably influenced especially with regard to picturing Hell. All kinds of representations of the bad creation — the damned, who merit a *dies irae* of an unmerciful judgment — are found. This wealthy community in Florence succeeded, through its famous painters, to articulate their basic beliefs in frescoes, thus challenging the authority of the republic and of the pope.

The origin of the Cathari lay with the Bogomils who probably appeared around 950 in the Balkans. Their influence invaded France through southern Italy. The first reference to a systematic organization of a Cathari community is around the year 1000 in Toulouse. Although persecuted and burned by the Church and civil authorities, their theories spread to other regions as Foix in Carcassonne. It is very strange that although their theory had already been known as neo-Manichean ever since the third century, there were many adherents who were willing to leave the Catholic Church and join it. For the Cathari, the Creator in the Old Testament is an evil spirit. The material world is nothing other than a prison for the soul which must seek liberation and salvation by an *askesis* through rational knowledge and a kind of total self-denial. Only the Gospels, and above all St. John's, were accepted by them. They systematically refused to venerate the cross, which was a symbol for them of cruelty, or of Satan. To achieve an integral liberation by spirituality, a considerable number of earthly incarnations were necessary for each Cathari and for this reason they accepted the theory of metempsychosis. Thus, the soul passing through different degrees of evolution, goes into or out of other human or animal bodies. This is why the Cathari remained pure vegetarians. Great emphasis was placed on the domination of the senses and over every kind of attachment to the body. Even marriage was despised, at least for the "Pure" and the "Perfect," that is, for the preachers. The simple, faithful lived rather in concubinage. But such disorderly groups could not but be persecuted as subversive anarchists, illegal and even heretical, in the context of the established feudal system of the eleventh century. Neither the pope nor the king could tolerate such a threat to an orderly society, but, nevertheless, this movement succeeded to prosper in one third of France. Small groups of Cathari can be traced in other parts of Europe, but in the French Languedoc, it became the official religion, the Albigenses being some of the bravest martyrs ever in a famous holocaust during the medieval crusades.

What then characterizes such religious writers is a dark description, horribly pessimistic of man. He is not only a miserable sinner but sin itself. It follows from this that fallen man has no real freedom of choice at all. He invariably wills what is evil. His will is completely paralyzed and mortally wounded. He is not free. Writing asgainst the humanist Erasmus, Martin Luther speaks *de servo arbitrio*, on the slave will, a phrase he had certainly borrowed from his master St. Augustine (*Contra 2. Pel.* 11,8,23). The moral impotence of unregenerate man is expressed in the celebrated dictum: "In spiritual and divine matters which pertain to the salvation of the soul, man is like the statue of salt into which the wife of the patriarch Lot was turned, nay rather he is like to a log, a stone, a statue lacking life which has the use neither of eyes nor of mouth nor of any other senses nor yet of heart" (*In Genes.* Chap. 19).

From this unqualified determinism, there follows a passive attitude, pure passivity. Synergism, cooperation, is thus ruled out. A monergistic view of grace is substituted, namely, that every initiative comes from God regardless of human reaction. The inevitable corollary of such a position is the doctrine of absolute predestination. Grace is not considered communication with God, but the benevolent disposition with which God regards his elect. God does everything, man is only recipient. John Chrysostom in his comment on St. John 6.44: "No man can come to me, except the Father which sent me draw him," refutes such a view by putting things in order: "Now he that draws him is who with his consent wishes to be drawn."

It is usual to think of the Reformation as being the result of several factors: 1) Disgust for the corruption on all levels of the clergy and the superstitious laity and the consequent demand for an urgent purification. 2) The revolt against the domination of a clerical imperialism seated south of the Alps. These and other causes, accumulated over several decades, produced the great cataclysm. But it is vital, in addition to all the above, to remember the perspective of religious psychology and temperament against a piety adapted to the spirit and the needs of the once-born man. What was needed was the uprising of the *twice-born* genius.

Before such accumulated deviations, instead of attacking the evil in its very source, they with bitterness began the attack upon the mechanical daily Mass, spectacular pilgrimages, indulgences of all kinds, rosary, and adoration and processions of the reserved sacrament and other external observances which they thought encouraged man to acquire a purely mechanical holiness without any inward change of heart. The *twice-born* man's experience, translated into intellectual terms, leads to Augustinianism. Hence arose a colossal resurgence of Augustinianism and an opposition to so-called semi-Pelagianism. So Luther designates as a triptych: Bible, *Theologia Germanica*, and the writings of Augustine. Quite the opposite, the Fathers of the Church look upon this from a different perspective. Thus, John Chrysostom refuting the errors of Manicheism against the free determination of human will, underlines the complete freedom of choice without any pressure whatever exercised by God: Man is a person and as such has his own free will which is highly respected by his Creator:

> God does not want human beings to become good by force and constraint. His choice of us as called or chosen beings is not imposed but rather proposed. Calling does not tolerate imposition from outside. It depends entirely upon our own choice as free persons to be saved or to be lost . . . (*In Johannem hom.* 47,4: 59.268)

The philosophical pattern of the Puritans is, in turn, rooted in the images, principles, and laws of the Old Testament. America's European roots lie deep in biblical soil, planted there from the country's very beginning. John Calvin and other Reformers held the Bible to be their main theological authority. Like the Hebrews, Protestants, too, looked upon themselves as God's chosen people, comparing their situation to that of the ancient Israelites. The central theme of Protestant identity was the covenant between God and man. They sought to obey the Bible's commandment of concern for the poor, the orphaned, and the mistreated, and took it as the basis of their view of the equality of all people before God, especially where the brotherhood of the elected saints was concerned.

God for them was the only true monarch. No man could be more than his chosen agent. In the sight of God the humblest slave equaled the mightiest prince. They saw their defiance to the ruling system by monarchy in terms of Moses' defiance of Pharaoh and Nathan's rebuke of King David. For modern Socialism, the Exodus from Egypt served as the classic model of liberation from tyranny. Revolutionary doctrine became crystallized in the slogan: "Rebellion against tyrants is obedience to God." No less potent was the influence of the Old Testament in determining the basic political system of the new emergent industrial society. The rise and influence of rationalism in Western Europe is visible in the various structures concerning family, pedagogical methods, and intellectual trends of writers.

It is well known that for John Calvin wealth, earning power, and progress in the field of trade were signs of special divine grace and favor. On the contrary, economic stagnation and inability to improve one's financial situation were viewed as signs of an inadequate relationship with God, or as signs of God's disfavor. For this reason, early Protestant families were distinguished for their cleverness in creating new industries and developing banking, as over against Roman Catholic citizens. The richer one was, the more one showed that divine love was bestowed upon oneself and one's family.

There is no doubt that religion, according to its kind, shapes society. Among Christian nations, too, belonging to a specific confessional family influences the temperament, culture, and whole ethos of the citizens. This is visible on all continents. Modern democracy, with its affluent and liberal trends, is a child of the Protestant Reformation because overstatement of individualistic theology of the Reformation largely owed its origin to the enunciation of two intellectual principles: the rightful duty of free inquiry and the priesthood of all believers.

Free inquiry meant nothing more to the Reformers in the sixteenth century than the right of each person to read the Bible for himself, and that principle led straight from theological to socio-political criticism. It became, in fact, the foundation of political liberty and the creation of political parties based on similar ideas. The theory of the universal priesthood of all believers became an argument in support and justification of human equality, the abolition of sexism, the acceptance of female ministry, etc. These central ideals of liberty and equality were transported by the Puritans to the Americas. Much of what is recognized as distinctively American in thought, culture and tradition is derived essentially from four very distinct sets of values. These begin with seventeenth century Puritanism and go on to the eighteenth century fusion of liberalism, federalism, and the southern aristocratic code. Then follows nineteenth-century transcendentalism, and finally the Western frontier's rugged individualism. Most historians agree that of all these influences, Puritanism has proved to be the most stable. Not to understand Puritanism is not to understand America.

Puritan piety relying exclusively on Scripture, overstating the experience of conversion, of daily scrupulous examination, and imposing a heavy and sophisticated moral code, with emphasis on austerity and secular industry, far from becoming the final moulder and shaper of an authentic spirituality, for a long time fostered only dissent. General distaste for the bleaker aspects of Puritanism and also for the fanatic and sometimes neurotic distrust by State and people alike of Latins (often the victims of crude and cruel psychological warfare) reflected a general antipathy to extremes and enthusiasms. However ramshackled the establishment might be, and however worldly and money-grubbing many of its prelates, yet moderation and tolerance dominated the thinking of some of the great divines of the Reformation.

These two centuries witnessed an intellectual questioning of the traditional claims of Christianity of unequalled intensity; but they were also a period of dedicated and literate apologists. Some were engaged in a desperate evangelistic mission to persuade people that the Gospel is a self-revealed truth, about which nobody must ask questions, scrutinize, or even contest. But without the recourse of appeal to revelation in religion, the conscience itself could assure man that, in the long run, his true self-interest coincided with his true duty to others. Such an approach stands out against the scepticism of the time by its firm grasp of principle, sustained reasoning, and moral force. Such reasoning set the tone for much of the better natural theology and ethics from which the future Church of England, after some arid decades, was to draw its strength. It was a strength that came into its own in the revivals of the next century.

A general review of the sacramental popular piety and elements of superstition in everyday religion will reveal many deviations. Renaissance humanism and rhetoric, easing out medieval patterns of scholastic theology, largely contributed to this state of things. The maturing of the Age of Reason during the first four decades of the eighteenth century, and the shaping of the intellectual forces which led to that most convulsive of upheavals in human history, the French Revolution, are a few of the sad consequences. This whole period was the threshold to our own, with the emphasis shifting from the supernatural to the rational and from the rational to the secular. Secularism was readily identifiable by the twelfth century. Our inquiry about elements in the complex pattern of religious attitudes under the later Tudors and early Stuarts, during the Commonwealth, and into the early decades of the Hanoverians, is extremely valuable in analyzing what came afterward.

Present-day attitudes in our ecumenical encounters need a corrective, careful assessment of Puritanism, for the spirit of this many-stranded movement remains a certain strength within the Western churches. Puritanism was the yeast in the soggy and ill-formed dough of the post-Reformation Church. It reflected more than anything else an urge, an impetus to remedy the immoralities of the late-medieval Church and State. Puritans were, by and large, idealists touched with what the more easy going saw as bigotry — especially over such things as the wearing of the surplice. But the Church needed such idealists, for it gave a dismaying impression of being a ramshackle department of the State, riddled with abuses, incoherent in its spiritual life, and unable to command men's deepest loyalties. By the very force of its convictions and the heroism of its leaders, Puritanism should have hammered the Church into its own shape. But it was not to be so. Where the Puritan idea can be found at its most distinctive form was within Calvinism, but the essence of Calvinist teaching was absolute predestination. The idea that God, even before the Creation, predestined some of his creatures to salvation and others to eternal damnation was hard for many to stomach.

An overemphasis on human autonomy, instead of making man a really free and emancipated being, created rather a vicious circle where he became more enslaved. Herein lies the human drama. Freedom under such conditions really means arbitrary choice and utter disregard of another's equal rights and dignity. But true liberty cannot exist outside the communion of love, and we mean love in this context not as a pure sentimental expression but as a concrete attitude, full of relevant commitment and a high respect before God's own image. There is a relationship, but it is framed and exists under certain appropriate conditions. On the opposite side, there is an autonomous being who is self-reliant and egocentric, who is not ready to recognize the other's rights and give due respect. He may even refuse to give to God the right to intervene in human affairs, and such giving of priority to one's own exclusive logic, reduces love to its lowest state and version. But logic is unreliable; it often counsels momentary pleasure, instant profit and satisfaction, and a certain isolation from other equally important challenges within our existence. Such cold logic, in assessing the world's realities, makes relations impersonal, without linking one item to the other, and is totally independent from the mystery of Creation. Such, often, is the approach of certain scientists, who overlook or disregard the inner invisible links in human psychic manifestations.

21. Diverted Artistic Streams

Recent complaints from various quarters about the horrible decline in art, and particularly in painting in certain countries, have deeper causes than meet the eye. One has to go into the principles and motivations of so many artists, educated in a less spiritual milieu, animated by a disrespect for tradition and sacredness and dissociated from the essential roots of culture and historical continuity. We must repeat in this context the ancient wisdom formulated by the Greek philosophers: "that everything modern is not always new and original, and even every new thing is not edifying." There are legions of voices to denounce the horror of every arbitrary innovation at whatever price, at the expense of certain values, which encourage and consequently authorize the excessive. Of course, such criticisms, for many may seem to be cruel or fanatic, while for others passionately onesided and theoretical. Whenever an honest diagnosis and cathartic reflection appear, they may create enthusiasm in a few quarters on the one hand, while they are a source of irritation or ill-disposed reactions on the other. The idea is not at all to accuse globally contemporary art as such, but to proceed to an objective analysis of the malaise which seems to affect it more generally during this dying century.

One disquieting remark: art is deprived of memory. During the seventeenth century new trends and relations were taking the place of man and of history. Both have tried to complete the damage by ruining the entire body of painting, reducing it to nothing more than an assembly of incoherent pieces. Every artist begins to illustrate a derisory technique. Until that date, every artistic work was judged in relation to the nearest surrounding immediate and tangible world and prevailing values. In other words, the artist was measuring his production and the quality of his work only in contrast to that of his contemporaries. But later on another element enters into the scene: the giving up of any relation to other factors and the alienation from the very roots. Each was consulting his own self and articulating it in art. Such a rupture resulted in the overthrowing of esthetic sensibility in a radical way. A particular taste was absolutized, systematically ignoring any other consideration. There is no concrete or stable reference. While neo-classicism refused all future dimensions, the futurists, suprematists, and other progressist utopians, reflecting a confused amalgam of rival schools, were seeking refuge in a golden age to come, thus inventing non-conformist, deviationist heterodoxies, and a new iconoclasm. By doing this they were establishing as a permanent feature the rupture with ancient models and sources of inspiration. But an art without a real perspective, without passion for the future on the one hand, and on the other being cut off from the memory of the past, is inevitably bound to follow a road leading to nowhere. Here, indeed, lies the absurdity.

This excessive confidence in what is new, original, unusual, novel, obtained at whatever price, over-estimating the new, simply because it is new, and promoting the unknown to an absolute, while absolutizing the realities of time, in reality places the aesthetic criterion in an embarrassing situation where it cannot function properly. Meanwhile, scandals and aberrations result and attack all expressions of art. The way lies open to incompetent critics and strange ideologists, each driven from different motivations. The result has been the apparition of all those controversial, fragmented, historical classes of the famous "isms," growing more and more narrow and forming special wings in museums reflecting the agony and frustration of the times. One can see such paintings, sculptures, and other arts isolated in their identity, vague and unprecise in their objectives. Only a few initiated can catch glimpses of their message and their implied meaning. But they witness in fact to a state of radical separation from life.

Of course, many may find an excuse, pretending that by launching extravagant works they were looking for an expression of their own creative genius. After all, art cannot remain static or petrified. It needs expansion, newness and change. But if creativity, moved by a strong illusion, seeks to produce a work of art relying only on intention, it risks falling into the trap of an unhealthy subjectivism, closing all its senses to the upward and external dimensions. That a work be artistic is, in a real sense, a primary condition of "bearing fruit" in its own time and being able to overcome the material conditions. This means to elevate minds, to inspire, to feed, and to edify. Such an example, known for his eccentricities, is Giovan Francesco del Cairo (born in Milan in 1607). He is considered the last of the great Lombard painters of the seventeenth century. If in Rome the anti-Reformation movement produced spectacular victories and the triumph of the Baroque, in Lombardy it seems, on the contrary, to be delayed due to various extremist, intellectualized explosions. Here are produced the more obscure and sombre mortifications of the Tridentine Reformation, depending both on pietism and ecstatic morbidity, in the degeneration of a certain religious spirit of the century.

seventeenth Francesco del Cairo is the most representative of such a pathological state, which went so far as to be qualified by some as cataleptic. He passes the limits of the reasonable, preferring that strange style of his predecessors, as for instance the violent pathetic spirit of Morazzone, and the dolorism of Cerano.

It is true with regard to iconography itself, St. Francis of Assizi in ecstasy, Lucretia, St. Agnes, Cleopatra, St. Catherine, Salome, and Herodias plunged in meditation, offer many themes, biblical or otherwise. Each particular theme expresses all states of the prevailing macabre psychology. All these human feelings are mixed in a languid, sensual atmosphere. Saints, men or woman, are always ready for martyrdom. One may object, after all, that this was the spirit of that time and the favorite of the century. Certainly, but the tragic hero killers painted by Cairo, namely, Salome or Herodias, heads bent, eyes closed, mouths half-opened in an expression of pleasure, awaiting a caress, a hand of perverted tenderness, outstretched towards the cut head, all these have nothing in common with their homonyms, namely, the Salome of a Battistell, which really directs to you a penetrating look of serenity, or even the Judith of an Artemisi Gentileschi, engaged to cull energetically the head of Holophernes. This trembling hand painted by Cairo, expressing at the same time hate and love, paralyzed, it seems, by the horror of contact with the head cut yet warm is a spectacle which is neither edifying, nor to be considered sacred art. In general, in spite of their vivid colors, most of the paintings are judged by competent critics as mediocre. They are unable to widen their horizons, to go beyond human tragedy. They are even boring, a distinctive mark which flooded all the palaces, grand or small, of Italy, during this period. An honest admirer of art will search time and again, but will find only meagre and disappointing presentations, where suffering prevails over hope and the light streaming from the risen Lord, "conqueror of death by his own death," as the Paschal service sings. While Byzantine iconography is plunged into an uplifting effort towards the blessed Trinity, the West cannot escape the weight of death, earthly bondage, darkness, frustration, and thus is unable to detach the spirit from the corruptibility of the world and the flesh. The latter less and less refers to spiritual sources, mainly of artistic inspiration.

Many critics of medieval western iconography, after a thorough analysis, come to the conclusion that, except for its impressionism and figurative qualities, very little helps people in their spiritual meditation and meeting the Absolute and Supreme Being. Thus, it is less "sacred" iconography than human, rather, anthropocentric "art." While it could easily detach people from the attractiveness of the flesh and the material world, it generates feelings of an esthetic nature, purely as *ars gratia artis*, but not with the ultimate goal of conversion or a change of mind and soul. Let us not forget that architecture, painting, religious poetry, and art are channels for the articulation of the Christian message, serving the liturgical life. They possess, therefore, a didactic and educative purpose, retaining their own proper rules.

Such an art beckoned incessantly and resolutely, because it looked away from the social ills of its period and concentrated instead on the more ethereal delights of fantasy and dreams. Even certain enthusiastic followers were declaring that the more materialistic the scenes become, the more angelic the scenes will be painted. Yet, this art was more than mere escapism: it had a positive and constructive message, and it also endeavoured to capture a universal language that spoke of new and very valid sensibilities and moral values.

22. Morbidity in Arts during the Renaissance

Myths are deformed into tragedies. The most famous and most moving scene of Monteverdi's (1567-1643) *Arianna*, Ariadne's lament when abandoned by Theseus, is one of the culminating points of musical tragedy. It was the beginning of a long tradition of heroines who wept for the torments of abandonment in long and passionate monologues. In Ovid's text few words are lost on Ariadne. She certainly does not sing a lament; but the Italian translation has a long and dolorous lament, inserted by the translator, who says in his commentary that he took as a model the lament of Olympia in the Orlando Furioso of Ludovico Ariosto, the most widely read of all sixteenth-century Italian poems. And Ariosto in his turn borrowed the model of his weeping Olympia from Ovid, not from the Metamorphoses but from the Heroides, and in fact from Ariadne's admonishment of Theseus. The subjects of the first operas are, in fact, drawn from the cultural heritage, noble enough in origin but very middle-brow in practice. Every spectator had easy access to the knowledge he needed to make sense of the gorgeous and outlandish spectacle that was enacted before his eyes.

Theatre and operas are flooded with singing sorceresses in flying chariots calling forth the celestial spirits and the Furies from the fiery mouth of Hell. Spectacular plays, truly splendid phantasmagories! Apollo's combat with the serpent Python; the lyre-player Arion who charmed the dolphins with his song; and finally the divine gift of harmony to man. All these relate to music and its supremacy in the world of men and gods, themes alluding to Plato's concept of harmony (of body, feelings, politics, and society) and to the *effectus musicae*.

The scenes and the costumes illustrate the splendor of the empyrean, the horror of the mouth of Hell, and the grace of the supernatural beings that dazzled the eyes of the spectators. Opera was to be full of such deities and allegories, of terrific infernal scenes and of miraculous celestial apotheoses. The question of how much the public understood of these allegories and symbols remains.

The themes in principle were drawn from classical mythology which was more or less identical with Ovid's Metamorphoses, at that time familiar even to people of average education. But the myths involved were less the heroic ones of tragedy, Oedipus, Elektra, Orestes,

132

Iphigenia, Herakles and Alkestis, than the metamorphic ones of Ovid: Orpheus and Eurydike, Narkissos and Echo, Perseus and Andromeda, Pluto and Proserpine, Venus and Adonis, Amor and Psyche. The contradiction between this Ovidian preponderance and the declared intent of restoring classical tragedy was manifest; in the prologue to Euridike, the personification of tragedy appears on the stage to announce that from now on she will renounce "sad and tearful scenes," and will awake "softer feelings in the heart." And, in fact, the convention of the happy end was accepted in opera from the first. We see depressive traces of such melancholic piety from the very start of what is known as post-Reformed theology. All kinds of art illustrate it and try to make it tangible: the departed souls who are in the "intermediate" stage *in transit*, so to say, awaiting the meritorial effects of the good works or indulgences by their relatives on earth, are presented as being devoured by worms and toads. It suffices for a researcher to go through the amazing literature and paintings of that period to discover the application of the dictum: namely, of the discussion between the three dead and the three alive: "What you are now, we were already. What we are now, you will be too." The "dance of death" experienced a tremendous success from the fourteenth to the seventeenth century, in all its variety of forms: dances as such, frescoes, and engravings. All these artistic products have one common feature: the determination to act as a salutary mirror to the vanity of this visible world. We have to await the beginning of the sixteenth century for radical changes, in terms of replacing the obsesses principle of the famous *memento mori* to the other extreme dictum *memento vivere*, a self-centered epicurism. Then we find ourselves in a state of arrogance and drunkenness for sensual life, for pleasures of all kinds, for worshiping the bodily attitudes and all of these marking the artistic and literal production of that period.

The abundant literature and artistic works on death are not at all accidental. They reflect the continuous fear, anguish, and terrifying uncertainty of Christians about their fate, although earlier Fathers of the undivided Church had pronounced many wholesome and comforting words. We should mention here the terrible spread of the plague, as a source of fear and melancholy, and the feeling that "God has abandoned us." One must say that, in spite of their merits, all such writings constitute a challenge before which any kind of speech or book vanishes and falls down in ruin. They rather "prepare" all of us for the unavoidable inquiry: death. But what mainly was terrifying people was rather the utterly inadequate weak preparation of Christians before all kinds of sufferings: natural disasters, earthquakes, epidemic sickness, wars, calamities, revolutions, the paroxysm of religious conflicts resulting even in open wars. And above all, there reigned the image of the Four Horsemen of the Apocalypse, triumphantly trampling on humanity shrinking from them in defeat and horror.

In such confusion the weight of Christ's death and its soteriological impact on the life of Christians was forgotten. Life and death for us is inseparably linked with the name of Jesus Christ. When we ask how it was that martyrs and confessors succeeded in attaining to that triumphant faith, we can only give the answer that it was and will remain forever the same, that it was not by simple contemplation of their own souls or by thought of their own death, but by being in a living, ontological communion with another who had died for them and who was ever-living, and thus enabling them to die with him. Christ's resurrection was their own too. He whom they loved had risen, and they were caught up into his immortality. To live with him, that was the essence of their hope. The Evangelium of the first generation had nothing to quote to one another for their mutual fortification but a few "trusty words," which had gradually crystallized into epigrammatic form (2 Tim 2.11; Rom 6.5). This faith, well grounded in the early hymnography and patristics, is formulated by Athanasios of Alexandria:

> For us when a tyrant has been utterly vanquished by a true emperor, and is bound hand and foot, all who pass by jeer at him, smiting and abusing him, no longer fearing his rage and cruelty, because of the victorious emperor; so also death, having been conquered and branded as infamous by the Savior on the Cross, and bound hand and foot, all in Christ who pass through trample on it, and as witnesses to Christ deride death, scoffing at it, and saying the words written against it above: "Where, Death, is thy victory? Where, Hades, thy sting?" (*The Incarnation of the Word of God*, 27).

23. Implications of True Iconography

Orthodox hymnography and iconography have these factors in mind when they evoke our Savior and his saints. Theological sensitivity inspires the poet and artist to such an extent that the material and fleshly are seen as essentially transformed (1 Cor 15.52), having "put on immortality." The worshiper feels the sacred persons to be more familiar through their similarity to them, and at the same time, they can understand the element of transcendence which constitutes their essential characteristic. They strive to express through an idealized realism the belief of the Church that the saints, while living in the natural world, were through their noble struggle against evil made worthy of theosis, which exalted and spiritualized their earthly life. One can discern the presence of redeeming grace upon their physiognomies, since Christ through his incarnation offered in his redemptive work the possibility for man to be united with God, as Dionysios the Areopagite states: "Theosis is the assimilation and union with God, as much as possible" (*theosis estin he pros Theon, os ephicton, aphomoiosis te kai enosis*) (*The Ecclesiastical Heirarchy* 1,3; PG 3.376). John Damascene explains how the grace of God is spread over all the material elements of worship: "The Saints were filled with the Holy Spirit even when they died; the grace of the Holy Spirit is permanently descended upon their souls and upon their bodies in the grave, and in their characters and in their holy icons, *not in essence but in grace and energy* (*ou kat' ousian, alla chariti kai energeia*) (*The Orthodox Faith* 3, 15; PG 94.1249).

If we wanted to define the purpose and the place of icons in the liturgical life of the church, they should rightly be described as "windows of eternity." Indeed, through them we have access to unseen realities. They are visual aids helping, in a simple and comprehensive way, even little children to understand doctrines and truths otherwise unapproachable.

If the early Church advocated the use of icons, it is because Christ, the Logos, is manifested in the flesh. The Son of God became visible in order to shorten the distance separating the divine from the human world. One of the greatest Fathers and exponents of this teaching on icons is John Damascene. He refutes their opponents by referring to their educational use. Just as books are essential for educating children in abstract ideas, he says, so icons help Christians to a

135

better understanding of celestial concepts.

Iconography was put into the service of theology, and especially of the Holy Trinity. And yet, the question was often put forward: Is any attempt whatever legitimate for the visible representation of this invisible, beyond our eyes, mystery? Is it even possible to give any kind of pictorial representation of the divine persons? The inherent and apparently insuperable difficulties of any such attempt at once become evident if one begins to reflect on the question.

In the New Testament, we can find some kind of Trinitarian representation, i.e., the Annunciation of the Virgin Mary and the scene of the Baptism of Christ in the Jordan. But the real problem is that of the possibility of representing the three divine persons in their eternal being, as John speaks of them in his Gospel or as they are confessed in the Nicaean Creed or venerated in the liturgical texts. Christians have been faced with the same impossible choice: One or Three? Ought one, bearing in mind Christ's own words: "He that has seen me has seen the Father" (John 14.9), to express the Trinitarian mystery in a single figure. Or should one rather, as has in fact most often occurred, in some way lay the emphasis upon the Trinity?

Even when the decision has been made in favor of the latter alternative, there remain several important problems. What visible form is to be given to the first and the third persons, who alone possess the divine nature? And in what way is expression to be given to the real distinction between the three persons and the hypostases: how can it be indicated that the Father, himself who is without a primary source or origin, is the principle of the other persons; that the Son is begotten by the Father, and that the Holy Spirit proceeds from the Father as from one principle; and that at the same time this order and hierarchy of origin in the three persons implies absolutely no inequality whatsoever with regards to perfection or to eternity, nor does it in any way impair the perfect unity of the divine nature?

Numerous are the representations which show the Trinity drawn from the Old Testament. In Genesis there are three passages in which God speaks of the Trinitarian reality when he uses the plural instead of singular (Gen 1.26; 3.22; 2.7). Others derive from the Psalms (Ps 2.7; Ps 109.1). The eighteenth chapter of Genesis gives an account of how Abraham gave hospitality to the three men in whose shape Jahweh appeared to him by the oak of Mamre:

And Jahweh appeared to him in the vale of Mamre as he was sitting at the door of his tent, in the very heat of the day. And when he had lifted up his eyes, there appeared to him three men standing near him; and as soon as he saw them he ran to meet them from the door of his tent, and adored down to the ground. And he said: Lord, if I have found favor in thy sight, pass not away from thy servant: But I will fetch a little water and wash ye your feet, and rest ye under the tree. And I will set a morsel of bread, and strengthen ye your heart, afterwards you shall pass on: for therefore are you aside to your servant. And they said: Do as thou hast spoken (Gen 18.1-5).

After describing the meal, consisting of cakes made of flour and a boiled calf, the sacred writer continues his account, thus, in some detail and not without humor:

And when they had eaten, they said to him: where is Sara thy wife? He answered: Lo, she is in the tent. And he said to him: I will return and come to thee, life accompanying, and Sara thy wife shall have a son. Which when Sara heard, she laughed behind the door of the tent. Now they were both old, and far advanced in years, and it had ceased to be with Sara after the manner of women.

And she laughed secretly, saying: After I am grown old, and my lord is an old man, shall I give myself to pleasure? And Jahweh said to Abraham: Why did Sara laugh, saying: shall I whom am an old woman bear a child indeed? Is there anything heard to God? according to appointment I will return to thee at this same time, life accompanying, and Sara shall have a son. Sara denied, saying: I did not laugh: for she was afraid. But he said, Nay: but thou didst laugh. (Gen 18.9-15).

This appearance of Jahweh to Abraham, with the announcement of the birth of Isaak, was one of the great landmarks in the history of Israel, for it was not only a solemn confirmation of the eternal covenant between Jahweh and Abraham's descendants which runs like a silver thread through the entire Old Testament, but it was also the beginning of its fulfillment. And even in the New Testament, it is still the "God of Abraham, of Isaak, and of Jacob" who is glorified in his redeeming acts; and here, too, this theme of the covenant retains its profound significance, as we can see by reading the Epistle to the Hebrews or the ninth chapter of Romans.

This episode of Abraham's hospitality, the so-called *philoxenia of Abraham* was interpreted by the Fathers in a variety of ways. Cyril of Alexandria (*Lib. I adversus Jul. Apost.* PG 76.532-33), St. Augustine and others consider that it was in fact an account of the appearance of the three persons of the Trinity to Abraham. Augustine explains how it was that Abraham, in speaking to the three men together, says "Lord: Were not Abraham's visitors one single guest? As guest, table-companion, and friend, all gifts were offered to him in three-fold hospitality and thus the whole event shines with the glory of the blessed Trinity" (*Sermo* 85,2). Justin, however, and also John Chrysostom (PG 54.387), as also John Damascene (*Third Discourse in Defence of Icons*) following Eusebios of Caesaria (*Demonstratio Evangelica,* 5), ascribe this Old Testament theophany to the Word only, explaining that on this occasion the divine Logos was accompanied by the two angels. Subsequently, it was the exegesis of Augustine that triumphed. For him, the theophany given to Abraham was nothing less than a revelation of the three divine persons. His reasoning was of the greatest evidence in the current struggle against the Arians, and he expressed it time and again in lapidary as carved in stone phrases: "Deus illi apparuit, et tres aspexit. Cui Deus refulget, Trinitatem vidit . . . " (*De Abraham*, lib. 1; PL 14.435), or: "*Tres vidit, unum adoravit*" (*Contra Maximinum Arianum Episc.* PL 42.809, also see: *De Trinitate* 3,2 (21-22).

On the other hand, Augustine was well aware that this and other Old Testament theophanies could not have gone beyond the nature of a vision: that in other words, it was not the three persons as such who were revealed to Abraham, but some form of a created image or appearance. It is also Augustine's interpretation which would appear to be implied in the well known mosaic of Abraham in the Church of San Vitale at Ravenna (fourth century). Once it is admitted that the meaning of the scene is not so much to depict an historical occurrence as to describe Abraham's vision of the three divine persons, then it is, theologically speaking, fully justified, expressing clearly as it does the teaching of the great figure who is known as Dionysios the pseudo-Areopagite. The latter, in his *The Divine Names* (4,22), describes the angels as "images of God, visible revelations of God's immaterial glory, pure mirrors, bright and unspotted, the full impression of the divine goodness." In other words, he teaches that the angels are the visible form of appearance, by means of which the Godhead reveals himself in a manner adapted to the weakness of human nature.

Thus it is, on the basis of a mystical interpretation of the story in Genesis that the theme of Abraham's hospitality has developed in the West, no doubt, too. Especially and above all in the East, art was developed as the sole form of representation which, while justified scriptually and theologically, can provide a satisfactory expression of the sublime mystery of the Holy Trinity. The angels become the three persons; the very landscape takes on a deeper significance: the patriarch's tent is now both palace and temple, and the oak of Mamre stands for the tree of life. In a world now completely transformed, every detail takes on a new meaning. The whole divine event which is being represented takes place in a world which transcends every possible scene which man could ever gaze upon. It is thus indicated that the true dimension in which the Godhead lives has its origin and intelligibility not in the point of view of the onlooker, but in a point which transcends every possible earthly representation.

Christ himself precisely came down from heaven and united himself forever with our human nature to redeem us and to restore us to God, a truth so brilliantly formulated by St. Irenaios: "The Son of God became the Son of Man, that man also might become the son of God" (*Contra Haeres.* 3, 10, 2). As Christians continue to ponder in awe the abiding mystery of the Incarnation, they chant the wonderful scene of this unique event, looking on the icon's representation: "I see a strange and paradoxical mystery; the cave is heaven; the Virgin is the throne of the Cherubim; the manger is a cradle for the uncontainable God — Christ — whom we praise and glorify" (ninth ode, Christmas Katavasiai).

If iconography frequently appears in such reflections upon Christ's incarnation, does this mean that we worship the icons? Then, what correlation exists when icons represent various episodes from Christ's life? John of Damascus draws a distinction: Adoration is directed uniquely to God, while veneration and respect are given to icons. John of Damascus felt that this veneration is closely related to that which happens in human affairs. In ancient times, for example, when an emperor was not present, his likeness would be set up and those who revered the likeness were understood, thus, to also revere the person of the emperor. On the other hand, those who refused to revere the likeness would not revere the emperor himself. Also, when we show veneration to an icon, this veneration is then passed on to the prototype represented on the icon:

The icon is a hymn of triumph, a manifestation, a memorial

inscribed for those who have fought and conquered, humbling demons and putting them to flight (*Apology* 2-11).

You see what strength and divine power is given to him who accepts the images of the saints with faith and a pure conscience. Therefore . . . let us stand on the rock of faith and on the tradition of the Church, not removing the ancient landmarks which our holy fathers have set, nor allowing any room for those who would decree innovations and destroy the structure of the holy Catholic and apostolic Church of God" (*Apology* 3-41).

The entire mystery of Christ's crucifixion became an important event for artists and iconographers. Already from early times, Christians were trying by figurative works to describe the saving action of the cross. In Rome, in a significative formula, was placed an inscription, conveying that this sign was a source of strength and liberation from the bond of tyranny: *Hoc salutari signo, vero fortitudinis indicio*. In the palaces of Constantinople, above the halls, hung a cross fashioned in gold. But later, the crucifix appears rather as the *servile supplicium* showing forth the triumph of the crucified Lord. Christ's dying on the cross as painted art comes, without any doubt, from Syria at the end of the sixth century. A Syrian artist named Rabula in 586 made an evangeliarium, now located in the Laurentiana of Florence for the convent of St. John of Zagba in Mesopotamia. Here, Christ is not totally naked, but partly dressed with a long tunic. The eyes are open, the head turning to the right, and the open arms extended in a horizontal manner. On both sides are crucified the two criminals. As we look at it, nothing is very depressing in such a presentation. Only the persons assisting around give it a dramatic character. Thus, for the first time, the Crucifixion is really offering a scene of sorrow. Longinus' brutality, the indifference of the soldiers playing instead of sharing in the agony, in contradiction to the anguish of the Mother of God, the holy women, and the consternation of John the evangelist. Only Christ remains a stranger to all the emotion and grief coming out of this scene. His attitude is neither that of a dead one, nor of one in pain. We shall find again in the coming centuries, even until the thirteenth this same living Christ, if one can use this expression, in some way indifferent to the sufferings of the cross. In order to prevent any stylistic deviation and safeguard the classical form, against a dolorous style, the Council of Trullo in Constantinople, 692 (Can. 82), stated the following:

In some of the paintings of the venerable icons, a lamb is inscribed as being shown or pointed at by the Precursor's finger, which was taken to be a type of grace, suggesting beforehand through the law the true lamb to us Christ our God. Therefore, eagerly embracing the old types and the shadows as symbols of the truth and preindications handed down to the Church, we prefer the grace, and accept it as the truth in fulfillment of the Law. Since, therefore, that which is perfect even though it be but painted is imprinted in the faces of all, the Lamb who taketh away the sin of the world Christ our God, with respect to his human character, we decree that henceforth he shall be inscribed even in the icons instead of the ancient lamb: through him being enabled to comprehend the reason for the humiliation of the God Logos, and in memory of his life in the flesh and of his passion and of his salvific death being led by the hand, as it were, and of the redemption of the world which thence acrues.

Interpretation

Since some painters paint Christ as a sheep and lamb, with the Forerunner pointing his finger at him saying, "Behold the Lamb of God that taketh away the sin of the world," therefore and on this account the present Canon commands that hereafter in the future this shall not be done, but instead Christ himself shall be painted a full-grown man, with respect to his human character, in order that by means of the human aspect we may be enabled to recall to memory his life in the flesh and his passion and his death, and the salvation of the world resulting therefrom. For, as regarding those old types of the Law, we honor and value them, out of consideration for the fact that they prefigured the truth of the Gospel and of grace, among which one was that of the lamb slaughtered on the occasion of the Passover (or Easter), taken in the image of Christ, the true Lamb which taketh away the sin of the world. But now that this truth and the realities themselves have come, we prefer it and accept it rather than the types.

A curious artistic originality appears only at the beginning of the fourteenth century, first in Reims, then in Amiens and Strasbourg in France. Taking this subject of Crucifixion, all begin to exalt the dark side more than the victorious. The Roman style in Rhenania is that of a violent expression, underlining above all the weakness of the body. At the same time, the body extends, goes out, as something

detached from the wood, thus becoming a subject of special veneration. They sacrificed the exactitude of the proportions while the
idealism of the face gave way to a sorrowful realism. All of the fifteenth century becomes shaken with a certain religious sensibility,
leading more or less to the pathetic, with the climax being the expansion of the Passion drama in different forms. From now on, the
representation of Calvary becomes more and more dramatic. In-
novative streams and trends, started in Renaissance times, and mostly
by the Italian artists, are mobilized to add their most melancholic
genius in painting Christ's sufferings. His face loses its individual
character and all marks of conventional art supersede. The Byzantine anatomy, mixed with that of Gothic, almost always makes a
pathetic synthesis.

But other artists seek different models. They return to the ancient, classical models trying to apply this style to Christ's sufferings. Thus, we discover in Rome, the Tors of Belvedere, the Apollo
the Laocoön around 1516. No longer do we see a Christ exhausted,
despised, or suffering because of the crucifixion. Instead, only strong
muscles and the rosy face of a healthy, virile, and pleasant Jesus
prevails now. All members of the body seem as if they belong to a
sporting athlete, corresponding to the concepts of the new art. A kind
of Prometheus replaces on the cross a Christ weak and bloody. To
this rising of the Renaissance in Italy is added the Reformation whose
criticisms obliged Rome to think seriously about the content and the
deeper significance of religious art. This is the end of the liberties
of which the Renaissance abused. It is also the end of the traditions
and the legends.

24. The Urgent Need to Restore a Global Approach to Art and Science

While men for centuries were seeing events of history and things in a theocentric way, i.e., that God is the very center of the universe, and science and the arts have reference to him, a revolutionary anthropocentric movement developed during the Renaissance in which knowledge and human activity have an independent importance of their own. This emancipation resulted in an explosion of their inner coherence and interdependence. We find ourselves before a departmentalization of each discipline. From a unified personality, we pass on to a divided one. Instead of a synthetic view, an analytical atomization enters all fields of research. Autonomy is claimed as if each field is self-ordained and exists by itself without reference to another. From now on different attitudes prevail: life versus death, the here is sharply distinctive from the there, the body from the spirit, the Church from the world, faith from works, etc. We mean by this the abandoning of the wholistic, global or "catholic" approach by hypertrophying the one aspect at the expense of the other. This sharp dichotomy between the profane and the secular on one side and the sacred on the other has produced an opposition, as if two rival entities ruled life. The separation of the secular from the eternal has resulted in a far fuller understanding of secular detail, but it has robbed life of much of its meaning. Thus, many today are searching for meaning in science; in gaining its freedom it has lost its *raison d'être*, its sense of direction. In gaining its self-reliance, it lost its unity. Life is seen in a narrow sense; hence, fear and anguish become daily realities. Those who truly knew the dimensions of life, as the saints, looked upon daily activities without loosing sight of the prospect of death and eternity. All these godly men and women were fully conscious of the fact that our existence belongs to the Lord.

Without this relationship to the Logos and their intimate unity of existence with and for each other, all products of culture inevitably isolated themselves from each other; conflicting with one another they became absolutized, idols, ends in themselves, and ended by tyrannizing mankind like a Moloch. Human beings became mere ciphers— *numeri sumus*—self-complacent, impersonal entities rather than persons. We have forgotten the meaning of cosmic redemption, i.e., that since Christ's Incarnation all human activities, even the smallest gestures, are called to serve God's overall *oikonomia*, God's plan. John of Damascus said: "The Logos made flesh has deified the flesh. God has deified matter, making it spirit-bearing" (*On Icons* 1,21; PG 94.1253b).

Certainly, we must recognize the autonomy of earthly things such as art, science, and technology under the condition that they are rightly measured, namely, as relative and not absolute. Respect for the human being must be a law unto itself, but in the last resort it must take its law from beyond itself. How empty is art turned inwards upon itself instead of outwards upon the real eternal world. It is a self-conscious art, a subjective art, and a bad art, in a single word. The greatest works of art have been produced in the service of an end (*telos*) not merely artistic, within the framework of a definitely other-wordly reality. It is as if the beauties of eternity, as evoked in the *Philokalia,* proved to be the greatest beauties of all. "There is no other beauty like unto the beauty of holiness," as Gregory of Nyssa testifies.

One of the main, distinctive differences of such an approach to life and art is the following: a thinker of the Renaissance period starts below, from earthly realities moving out to assess and to understand the various phenomena of history as well as all the other manifestations of our existence. His basic presupposition is anthropocentric and geocentric. He is wrestling to solve first, and before everything else, the problems of the here and now, the nearby, the immediate of this particular moment. After having solved all these, he then proceeds step by step to higher horizons, widening his perspective and trying to find reference from the already established conclusions to the Christian faith. This method betrays an excessive confidence upon his achievements, and equally shows an unbalanced dependence upon his analysis of the socio-political problems emerging from our human existence. The art of the Renaissance period is influenced very much by such considerations. Even the Renaissance religious painting is characterized by an anxiety of how to deal with pressing realities — faith being seen as a far distant solution.

The inverse of the picture is seen in the Orthodox approach. The Byzantine thinker starts his investigation from already given principles. He is already a believer not in an abstract way, but his whole being is merged and plunged into his firm conviction about God's ever-present reality in human history. God shows the divine Epiphany in the smallest details of our life, being the *kybernetes* of the whole world (This kind of "cybernetics" of God was developed by the Fathers as expressing the continuous concern of the Creator for his creation.). Such a view is reflected in the confidence, hope, and joy about the conquest of evil, the trust in diverse ways about the triumph of God's lordship over dark forces, injustice, and disorder. One can see this approach in most of Byzantine iconography, where there is no rupture or complete division between the celestial and earthly realities. A martyr or saint, although earthly, at the same time is attached to the non-perishable world and in his daily dealings meets at every step the Lord of heaven and earth. This uninterrupted *koinonia* is the key to optimism and to courage in the darkest moments. Even more, through this light of the risen Christ, he is able to overcome the obstacles, seeing beyond and above all the finality of all and the fact never being imprisoned within the limitations of present imperfections, short-comings, and relativity.

In the Renaissance, man became isolated from that necessary complement of his life with all of nature and of Truth. He became isolated and cut off. Thus, he would look at everything from his own particular standpoint, and would not take responsibility as a part of a "whole." This is a "Western" phenomenon. In the East the old idea of a totality survived, especially in the Greek and Byzantine tradition. Thus, the Western cultural situation should be positively criticized from the Eastern point of view, where the idea of "totality" persists.

How, then, can the West be brought back to some understanding of this? The mutual understanding of Eastern and Western Churches might facilitate it. Where is the point of contact? There the Western Church senses its lost unity and the fact that it has lost its cultural and intellectual unity and seeks once again to regain it. The Orthodox theological tradition is one way of helping the West to recover the wholeness of its intellectual standpoint. But the West is more interested in "results," in logical and pragmatically tangible fruits, than in wholeness of life and understanding. And it is probably true that this impulse for "results" originated in the loneliness of man after the Renaissance and in Cartesianism.

How is the mutual understanding of Churches related to this cultural crisis? The Western and Eastern Churches have entered into bilateral theological dialogues but have not as yet descended into the realm of bilateral dialogues about the results of their theological positions upon their various cultures. This is the problem which we are urgently challenged to deal with, together, in the coming years.

It is perhaps the next stage in the bilateral dialogues. People who have lost hope in their own culture might be encouraged if they knew something of the many Church Fathers who had already worked on this problem. Not only should Orthodox be brought into ecclesiological and theological dialogue with West, but also the cultural results of different theological stances should be carefully evaluated. This reflection is related to the Faith and Order study on: "The Unity of Church and the Renewal of Humanity." Because the renewal of humanity requires new "cultural" points upon which to build, why not study such topics as the belief in angels, for example. It would be an important topic, especially in its relationship to psychology and cosmology. But the basic point upon which to build is the need for a *unity* of thought, in sense of one totality having many aspects and sides. This is what the Western cultural tradition lacks and needs to regain.

Most of Byzantine iconographers and ascetics have escaped the aesthetic danger inherent in the use of beauty as an end. They sought instead to recover a spiritual consciousness embodied in the heroic actions of the martyrs and the anchorites. Although living hidden from the eyes of the world, they have recalled for us those tense regions of life where meditation and prayer are sovereign, and the timeless invades and overrules the narrow world of time. They did it to free themselves as best they could from a profound need, to deliver themselves of a great incubus of living matter, *opus non factum*. For the moment one has faith, and from that very moment one has the omnipresent conviction that either Christ is everything, or that if other activities require faith, faith does not require them.

Since the advent of post-Renaissance humanism, we have faced a new kind of approach to the human body. Eulogies of it, an overemphasis upon it, as a new discovery, and angelic glorifications of it were attributed with a kind of unreliable romantic mysticism. Certainly, the body had been given considerable attention, and had been studied by the Church Fathers, and there exists a clear and concise Christian sexual ethics. In antiquity the Fathers were opposed to pagan laxism, and stressed the sanctity of discipline over bodily appetites. Since the body is the temple of the Holy Spirit, it should not be absolutized or sacramentalized. Baptism consecrates it to Christ's service, and, therefore, it must be kept as pure and clean as possible. St. Paul clearly states: "Those controlled by sinful nature cannot please God" (Rom 8.8).

This has remained ever since the evangelical ideal about the body's function in the realm of Redemption. But in practice we see a risky compromise between this ideal and the demands of the flesh intensified up to the commitment of a sin. After the Renaissance an excessive attachment — a kind of quasi-pagan view — prevailed throughout the arts. Since then, what is new is to see the "glorious body" magnified not to its deepest or highest meaning, serving our growth in Christ, but to its lowest, earthly meaning of which the Roman poet Lucretius (95 B.C.) in his poem *"De Rerum Natura"* said: *"At Venus in silvis jungebat corpora amantum,"* that is, "Desire in the woods was joining the bodies of the lovers." Because Venus is nothing else than divinized desire.

As humans we are neither angels nor animals. Angels, by nature, are not exposed to dangers, but the "animal" is not a sleepy or inactive thing. It is watching, present always and everywhere not only the dirty, well-known, ill-famed places, but in each one of us, and in all kinds of temptations of the flesh. All efforts to fight an idolatry of sex and to purify art from polluted ideas about the human body will remain void unless, first, we see where the enemy really is, as the Fathers and the spiritual men of the desert have seen and detected it with their warnings that the human body can become either the best of servants or the worst of masters.

The exposition of nudity in Western iconography is a significant departure from the traditional style. The idea motivating the presentation of the whole body was originally to stress its beauty and the role it plays in human relationships. Thus, we see Sebastian the martyr's whole naked body, that of John the Baptist, King David, etc. But it has become a widespread rule today to present a religious theme with the various persons presented in their robust well-constructed bodily features, just as if there were no care at all for guarding against revolting desires. The Byzantine, Ethiopian, Coptic, and Armenian styles are quite the opposite. The painters of the Eastern tradition hesitated to reveal the carnal side of the human body, obviously preferring, with discretion, an ascetic discipline, a prudent *prophylaxia* regarding dangerous games. Behind this stylistic approach is hidden a whole theology about the body which is not considered to be evil as such, but rather an unreliable companion, something to be mistrusted, which must be subject to a continuous control, since the disobedience of the first couple.

25. The Problem of Language in Dialogues

We must always bear in mind that the Church lives in history and in time. Theology, consequently, is greatly influenced by the language of a given cultural context. This creates a certain difficulty in fully understanding another denomination's use and application of terminology, which have been shaped in a specific historical context. We sense, therefore, much difficulty in all the types of ongoing ecumenical dialogues.

There is much in man's life, and still more in the mystery of God, which is obscured to man's reason, and which can, indeed, only be understood, through "a mirror" as St. Paul says, or as enigmas, or as contained in the "mysteries" of faith. The Bible speaks, by choice, in the language of poetic imagery, and many Fathers are known for the fervor of their thoughts. Whenever their thoughts touch upon the mysterious reality of the Holy Trinity, they renounce the dogmatic expressions which are customary for its description. It is no longer a reasoned, logical theology. The key changes, and the Fathers begin to speak another language, as if their whole being was responding to a contact with the most intimate, the most personal kind of mystery, one filled with a limitless wonder, a falling into a sort of intoxication. In fact, one might say that in patristic writings there are more than a few traces of such sober drunkenness, such divine *eros, ekstasis,* and so forth.

No adequate study of the apophatic and "negative theology" exists to help us clarify the many delicate issues which have emerged concerning Eastern and Western theologies. St. Gregory Palamas may be quoted in this respect (*Capita physica et theologica* 34; PG 150.1141):

The supreme mind, the ultimate good, the nature more than life and most divine, which is in every way absolutely incapable of including certain elements within itself, manifestly does not possess goodness as a quality, but as essense (*ousia*); therefore, what may be conceived as good, is already in it. Nay, rather, the good is that (what is in God) and it is even more than that. Again, whatever we might think about the good that he possesses, it is indeed the essence of good (*agathon*) and even more, the fullness of good, a certain goodness which surpasses any of good's measure

148

— *yperagathos, agathotis.*"

When theologians and mystics were endeavoring to speak of God, being conscious of the inadequacy of language, they were soon using negative rather than positive terms: *gnosis-epignosis, epinoia, theoprepos, theopoios,* etc. Conveying and translating a certain knowledge for the benefit of our intelligence and receptivity — which have their limits of space and time — they realized that human language was unable directly to attain the infinite, to embrace it, or to "understand" it. Thus, they arrived at the conclusion that God remains and is ineffable, indecipherable, beyond any definition. This negative form of expression is called "apophatic theology."

In the context of spiritual life, this theology speaks of the "mystical depth" or "mystical night," the *gnosis*-darkness and *agnosia*-ignorance. The early Fathers tell of a saintly soul marching through a particular living, inner experience. Having left behind all external, conspicuous appearances, not only those which the senses perceive but also what the intelligence believes it sees, the mystic continually goes deeper and deeper into the innermost part of our inner world. He proceeds gradually until that stage where he can reach and penetrate — by an intensive effort of the spirit, sustained by prayer — to the invisible and unknowable, and there he sees God. The true knowledge of what he is seeking and its true vision consists in perceiving what is invisible, separated in all its parts by a great incomprehensibility, as if in a deep cloud.

The "apophatic way" allows us to transcend all the different kinds of concepts and thus the soul of a mystic, at the end, enters into the "great space of contemplation," through which God is present for him.

Many in the West are perplexed about the words "apophatism" and its opposite, "kataphatism." Apophasis and kataphasis derive from the Greek *apophasis* which means negation and *kataphasis* meaning affirmation. Aristotle and Plato used the adjective and adverb which are derived from these substantives, i.e., "apophatic" and "apophatically," in order to explain a procedure of logic and rhetoric. Later on, other thinkers spoke of the "infinite" as if it were only a broken mirror of a world whose dimensions escape our measurement. This sphere assumes this where the sphere is everywhere and the circumference nowhere. This was their apophatic description and illustration. In short, there exists certain thought without language, and even behind words lie things more hidden than what is being expressed and revealed through them.

If we do not want our ecumenical dialogue to become a dialectic between or among deaf people, it is necessary that we use an acceptable and intelligent language. Orthodox theology has shaped and formulated the faith using patristic and ecclesiastic vocabulary, and this is not always easily followed by others. It contains idioms which are not easily digested. The West, unfamiliar with such patristic style and forms, uses more rational definitions, departmentalizations, and a particular style of clear-cut analysis with detailed categories. Now, how is each side able to understand the other language? How many Orthodox have gone beyond the ninety-five articles and indulgences dispute, and have seriously studied the complexity of the causes behind Luther's reformation, the hidden problems involved and his polemic style, with the favorite: *sola?*

Either by alienation from a common culture and language, or by antipathy and mistrust, most of us do not want to go beyond generalities and the classical statements. We are not even disposed to accept the other's opinion, because it is not familiar, or seemingly orthodox, or because it is strange and unusual. But this is no reason for refusing to proceed further and to put ourselves in this position or to take steps to better understand the other's way of thinking. Others, too, like to put far too much weight on their terminology, on their morphology, to play with words *quid pro quo,* for example with the categories nature-surnature, venial-mortal sins, order jurisdiction, etc. Others restrict themselves to well known typical, currently employed words, using them again and again through snobbism or just in order to show that they know how to master technical terms, Latin terminology or language, etc.

Written or spoken words exercise a tremendous influence. Language is a vehicle, an instrument of feelings and attitudes: love or hate, rebuke or praise, anger or calm. All these rely on well chosen words which articulate the prevailing feelings. In time, typified expressions become inseparably identical with inner dispositions, like the body and spirit.

In current language we face manipulated systematic efforts to eliminate certain words because they displease and disturb modern man. By attacking such "archaic" or "traditional" words in our daily vocabulary, such efforts attack the spiritual values which these words imply and express; thus, the infrequent rare usage of such terminology not only in the secular but even in the modern sermons preached. How seldom we hear such words: duty, responsibility, self-respect, guilt, sin; instead we hear their polished alternatives: weakness, bad habit, social evil, unavoidable. These old words, meaningful and inclusive, almost are condemned to an eclipse from our spoken vocabulary. However, they are rich in content. Each one lifts, serving animation, further courage. Words are reminders, accusers, serving a great salutary task: the *anamnesis.*

Language today enters into the battlefield against falsifiers distorting what originally was meant. This fraudulence is not an accidental phenomenon. It is a departure and rupture from words weighty and binding which express meanings systematically avoided by our generation, simply because they commit and morally engage. This alienation from such vital important words entails at the same time an alienation from our very roots and sources of our civilization, our culture, and spiritual values. It means further to take distance from the Tradition which sustained a society throughout history from so many vicissitudes. It means also suffication and isolation of our soul. Is this progress, simplification of a language, as it is claimed, or rather is it a betrayal of our culture?

In the actual fever for replacement of words with superficial ones taken from the lowest sectors, we are losing essential elements supporting our spiritual health. This replacement with alternative expressions has reached a paroxysm and undermines a correct assessment of values and persons. We live, therefore, during a crisis both of substantial things, but also of forms of which language is a most important agent.

There is a Latin phrase: *rem tene, verba sequuntur* (hold to the matter, the words will follow). This is excellent advice to anyone who engages in public speaking, but it is also a useful reminder that words are only a means to an end. They are never ends in themselves. It is, of course, the legitimate business of the critic, having noticed that the end has not been achieved, to comment on the use of words, which lay behind the failure; but the end must be considered first.

For it is with words, as it is with virtuous people — their business is to be self-effacing. Words should be like windows which open up to a new experience of life. If the window is clean, you do not notice that it is there. So, too, it is with words and their usage.

We would suggest, therefore, that the test of an act of worship should not lie in the question: "What did you think of the words?"; instead the test lies in the question: "Did the particular act of worship bring you an effective experience of God?" If it did not, something is wrong. But the fault may not necesssarily be with the usage of words. There might have been something wrong with the individual's state of mind; there might have been something wrong with the way in which the words were presented, etc.

If a person goes to church intent on worshiping God and is not predisposed to being put off by the use of out-of-date prose, I suspect that he may even share my attitude, which is that I find myself comfortable equally in the use of all kinds in my worship. In our personal experience all types of usages can succeed as vehicles of worship, and all can fail; and the reason for the failure or the success is often to be found in the presentation of the service and the attitude of the congregation rather than in the words of the liturgy.

I often wonder if those who claim to be put off by archaic language are not in fact put off by the particular dreary incantation of prayers which they have heard, or by the apathy and isolationism of a congregation whose members seem to wish to have as little as possible to do with each other. This is only a plea that an act of worship should be judged in its whole context and not by an evaluation of the words alone.

If one is interested in understanding the development of theological language as a vehicle of our common faith, one must look into the very origin of the formulation of dogmas and of their reception by the *Ekklesia,* the assembly of the faithful.

As we are aware, dogmas have their own history. The Seven Ecumenical Councils were held in the East, within the context of many burning issues about which the Oriental spirit was passionately interested. Everything that touched upon the after-life, eschatology, or metaphysics became the very core of theological disputes. Thus, conflicts about Trinitarian doctrines and Christologies remained current issues for several centuries. A temperament of researching into the profundities, a certain genius, or the mere fact of having been forced to make definitions since the Donatist controversy, greatly contributed to certain issues becoming priorities. The West was more absorbed with questions concerning sacramental theology and ecclesiology. This preoccupation greatly influenced most of the thinking in the West from the time of St. Augustine until the Council of Trent. Inversely, Orthodoxy never officially defined the nature or the number of the sacraments, nor the generic notion of a sacrament.

In addition, the iconoclastic controversy took place exclusively in the East and primarily concerned the one essential question: Was Jesus really the Christ incarnate or not? The struggle was against an aggressive Docetism concerning which the West not only was ignorant but in some ways was even surprised by the raising of such an issue — namely, the veneration of icons — which it considered as completely unnecessary. Further, many Western theologians found that the establishment of such piety of icons in worship might provoke extremist religious manifestations.

Embarrassment with regard to ambiguous terms used and difficulties for correct translation occurred also during the Iconoclastic period. The Second Ecumenical Council of Nicaea (787), as is well known, although it reaffirmed the legitimacy of the veneration of icons, by using, for the Latins' ears, the most unusual and strange expression *proskynesis* against *latreia,* introduced a language familiar to the Easterners but not easily understood by all in the West. Immediately after this Synod, Pope Adrian I dispatched the proceedings of this Council to Emperor Charlemagne. The Emperor instead of being satisfied with the orthodoxy of the restoration of icons, and by the clear exposition of the whole issue, strangely becomes more dissatisfied and hostile to the conciliar resolutions.

The translation from Greek into Latin of these proceedings which arrived in 788, although made with good intention, was very deficient and unfortunate. It said in the Latin version completely the contrary from what was meant in the original. The poverty of ideas rendered from the original text into Latin was so disappointing that later in the ninth century even the famous Anastasios the Librarian in Rome, would rightly confess that it was unintelligible and almost unreadable (Anastasii Bibliothecari . . . *Mansi* 12,981). The linguistic mistakes were serious, completely distorting the original meaning. One of the conciliar fathers, namely Constant of Cyprus, confirmed that the translation was hasty and by an unskilled person and admitted the linguistic mistakes of the unhappy translation (*Mansi* 12,1147).

The consequence of such poor translation had subsequent painful consequences. Charlemagne, a great authoritarian, in his indignation at once relying on the mistranslation, convoked a Synod in 790, while at the same time asking a competent theologian, Alquin, to compose as refutation, the famous "Libri Carolini" (full text in PL 98.999). From the first page one sees the biased intention of the author to discredit the Second Ecumenical Council, and at the same time to seek to humiliate both the Empress of Constantinople Irene and to attack Pope Adrian I. The most controversial term *proskynesis, adoratio,* in the eyes of many Westerners, did not favor the spirit of the Nicaean Council. The views of Charlemagne were approved by a local synod of Frankfurt (794) with 300 participants.

While this controversy raged in the East, as far as the West was concerned, all the seeds of the Reformation had already begun silently to be sown; thus, both England and Bohemia contested a centralized Roman Church and demanded not only liberty and conciliarity, but also a recognition of religious liberties and ecclesiastical autonomy, especially after the councils of Basel and Constance. In Germany, the mysticism of Rhenania sought a spirituality relating to the divine essence which would be able to deify the soul. In Florence, a platonizing Renaissance was born in opposition to substantialism and certain reformers tried to destroy the ecclesial mystery, and for them conciliarity was confused with congregationalism and secular liberty with individualism. It would not have been such a disintegration and alarming situation in the West, if Western Christendom had been more familiar at that time with the spirituality and the source of worship of the Eastern Church. The Hussites in Czechoslovakia already in revolt demanded that their cause be discussed in an Ecumenical Council, in the presence even of the Orientals. Florentine Platonism sought its inspiration from Byzantium. The Rhenans began reading John of the Ladder and discovered forgotton links to the past by means of a thirteenth-century translation made by Franciscan monks living at Meteora. Here and there one glimpses a form of nostalgia for the common roots and the well-springs of the East and West, but meanwhile, theological language unfortunately crystalized in less than precise Latin terms, thus alienating more and more the West from the East and creating a deep chasm along with a lasting mutual mistrust.

From the earliest times, theologians were confronted with language difficulties in their quest to render, in intelligent terms, the meaning of the Christian faith. Arriving at God's existence, emerging difficulties increased for the formulation of our common faith. Origen, for example, refusing any rational approach, preferred the "enoptic" (*Comm. in Gen. 3*) or "mystical inspection" (*Comm. in Lam.* frg. 14). Now the *enoptic* approach is neither contemplative nor theoretic, because the contemplative suggests looking at God, as far as it may be possible without any intervening images, and the theoretic lost its original idea of beholding the divine and carried with it an almost wholly intellectual meaning. What Origen calls *enoptic science* is concerned with the unseen realities behind those that can be seen. Others might prefer spiritual love and mysticism. The inner man has his own logic. When one neglects to cultivate his ability to understand because of idleness, the functioning of his thinking becomes atrophied and he loses heart. Origen often links the heart and the mind together (*De Princ.* 1,1,9). In this manner the term *mysterion* prevails ultimately having its origin in the verb *muo,* which means to close or to be shut, as in "closed eyes" and "closed flowers."

Consequently, the Eastern theologians of the third century formulating statements of faith were often embarrassed by the lack of comprehension of the West. In fact, the Latins were unable to understand the peculiarities of the Neoplatonic terminology plunged in a philosophical context. Such being the obstacle, a sense of malaise occurs, accompanied by an uneasiness to endorse any such theological statements, or even conciliary pronouncements emanating from the East. We mention one significant case with regard to the Trinitarian dogma. The classical doctrine of the Holy Spirit, summarized in the formula issued by the Council of Constantinople in 381, was partly the result of the emergence of the Pneumatomachoi in the latter half of the fourth century. An open conflict developed between the adversaries of the *Homoiousian* and *Homoousian* parties. A memorandum issued by Bishop George of Laodicea which provided the most comprehensive description of the *Homoiousian* position of the Holy Spirit (359). This was sent to the bishops of the West requesting their fraternal support of a joint declaration issued by him with other bishops. In the common letter he attempted to explain the position of the Orthodox in the East in such a way that the Western Church would be able to understand the depth of the problem and what was at stake.

> Let no one be disturbed by the term "hypostases." For the communities of the east speak about hypostases in order that they might make known the real, subsisting properties of the persons. For though the Father is spirit, as also is the Son and the Holy Spirit, the Father is not considered the Son. Moreover, the Spirit, who is not considered the Son, has his own subsistence . . . For the Holy Spirit is neither the Father nor the Son, but the Holy Spirit, who is given to believers by the Father through the Son . . .

As we have said before, the communities of the East call the properties of the subsistent persons "hypostases," but this does not mean that they maintain that the three hypostases are three sources or three gods. For they anathematize anyone who says that there are three gods. Nor do they maintain that the Father and the Son are two gods. For they confess that there is one God-head, which, through the Son in the Holy Spirit, encompasses everything . . . (Preserved by Epiphanios: *Haer.* 73,16; PG 42.432-33).

George of Laodicea desired to assert the reality of the distinct hypostases of the Godhead, his use of Mt 28:19 to support this belief, as well as his concern to avoid the charge of tritheism are common features of the Eastern theologicasl tradition. There is an effort at the same time apart from the emphasis on the distinctions between the hypostases to move on to a discussion of their unity. This attempt is revealed in the confession that there is one Godhead, one sovereignty and one source.

A better understanding of the ethos of the East and as well as of the eastern way of thinking, compelled the Latins to undertake painful efforts to acquaint themselves with its particularities. Their language with all its technical implications had to be carefully read. The *symphonia* of faith dictated the use of a common language, which was difficult to bring to reality. Thus, Tertullian the African jurist, while at first resisting, finally adopted a corresponding Greek terminology because of his contact with the Valentinians or Gnostics, whom he was refuting. In fact, the Valentinians in Carthage spoke Latin, whereas their co-religionists in Rome spoke Greek. They were the first to use the terms: *infinitus, consubstantialis, trinitas, substantia, persona, natura,* etc., borrowed from Greek (*Adversus Praxeam*). Moreover, in Carthage at the same time there were Encratites, Monarchianists, Gnostics, the Valentinians, the Marcionites, the Cainites. The authentic catholic faith, which was centered in Rome, and a latecomer, respected the towns of the undivided Church. But the Church in Carthage may have created such typical words as: *satisfactio, propitiatio, placatio, regula, meritum,* etc. In Rome the liturgical language remained Greek until the fourth century. There is no evidence that any Christian in Rome spoke or wrote Latin before the Novatian Schism (250 A.D.) It took a long time for the acceptance of any of the doctrinal terms which were used by the Orthodox, which were accepted in a Latinized form since there were no corresponding words in Latin.

Later the Trinitarian conflict produced particular language. In 365 a delegation from Asia Minor was commissioned to go to the West in order to seek support in the Church's struggle against the Homoeans. The Homoiousians especially desired aid from the Emperor Valentinian and from Bishop of Rome Liberius. Liberius accepted a written confession of faith, which in turn was ratified by a synod of Sicilian bishops (Socrat. H.E.4,12; PG 67.484-96. See Basil *Epist.* 67; PG 32.425). This agreement between Liberius and the Homoiousian delegates was greeted with enthusiasm by a Synod of Eastern bishops at Tyana (Sozomen H.E.6,12.2-3; PG 67.1321-24).

One can easily understand the alarming situation of the danger from heretics in the East, and the Church's concern for solidarity and moral help from the West. After the death of the Orthodox Bishop Silvanos, Basil of Caesarea deplores the installation of a Homoean bishop in the see of Tarsus. In 369 he wrote about his grief to Eusebios of Samosata:

> Tarsus has been lost to us. This loss is not the only calamity, although it is unbearable. Even more distressing than this loss is the fact that such a city, which has the good fortune to unite within itself the Isaurians, Cilicians, Cappadocians, and Syrians, has been given over to destruction through the folly of one or two men, while you hesitated, and gazed at one another (*Epist.* 34; PG 32,320).

Basil continued to write letters to the West seeking their help, their supporting signs of concord and appropriate action in order to show the oneness of the faith.

26. The Wholistic Approach

Another area where the Orthodox might contribute in theological research is in the entire methodology, namely, by taking into account not just one particular issue but several doctrinal elements which can be considered interrelated and interdependent. How can one, for example, speak about birth control if at the same time one does not give any thought to the whole theology of the body, the purpose of the marital relationship, of sexuality, of personal responsibility, of stewardship, of the doctrine of the image of God, etc.? Space and time often transcend any thinking. Equally, the perspective of the Christian is by far wider than any merely human point of view. At the very moment I am here just now, I also feel the presence of the past, of my predecessors in the history of the faith — which raises my eyes to other worldly realities beyond the temporal and material restrictions that surround me. I am a child of tradition, of history, of God's *oikonomia*, and thus, I transcend all limitations of human nature — seeing and experiencing more than my existential being dictates me to do. I overcome the biological condition, discovering other kinds of "*biotopes*" where my spiritual thirst finds what is most appropriate, and for which it was created. Past, present, and future surround my very being, and in this tridimensional world I think, I move along my path, and I feel my identity as a creature.

From our human point of view, there were three factors (enumerated here without further elaboration) which converged and brought us to the foot of the cross. First, a continuous, critical and thinking search for a coherent meaning and purpose in life. Second, and simultaneously, an ever-increasing personal awareness and experience of the captivity of man within his own egocentric and sinful nature, as well as a realization — in frustration — that ideals and reality do not match, and that desires and abilities were miles apart. The self-sufficient humanist fails because of his bondage to his sinful self, which is in need of liberation. And then, thirdly, the most decisive element: a loving and praying father who lived his life and expressed his faith as a new man in Christ — who was a witness to answered prayers in transformed lives, restored marriages, and occasional physical healings.

Such are the three streams which are often providentially used by God to bring about a complete turning point from the self to Christ.

When I put my trust in God, the old rebellious and unbelieving creature suddenly and completely is overwhelmed by the redeeming love of the God-Creator whom I then find myself addressing as Abba-Father. A burden is lifted, the search is ended, and the soul is set free. Jesus Christ becomes so central and so real that an unshakable inner assurance replaces all doubts. An exultant sense of joy and power accompanies the emergence of a new man, experiencing, for the first time, the fullness of life brought about by the Holy Spirit.

Behind each crisis of identity and theological confusion lies the more basic and potentially destructive notion, that the various constituent elements of the Christian faith can be compartmentalized. This means that the theologian to be can freely pick and choose which of these elements he will accept while discarding the rest as irrelevant. Essential to the quest for truth is a commitment to accept this truth in universal fashion, with full and unqualified respect for its dogmatic, liturgical, and ascetic content. Of course, this does not imply absolute and uncritical acceptance of every controversial element or *theologoumenon*. But it does mean that the pursuit of a real theology requires the acceptance of an integrated world-view, a unified vision of the divine-human reality which can resist every attempt at an arbitrary determining of the content of faith and the spiritual life in Christ.

It is very easy to say that theology is an eternal wellspring of living water. This affirmation implies a living reality, and not a dead word, contrary to what the Church sometimes has held. Each teacher of theology, who is called to guide and instruct persons in their spiritual pilgrimage, bears a grave responsibility. He is called to lead them not merely into an "external" commitment to a new tradition, but also into the eternal communion of the Body of Christ. For people and the Church as a whole, we are obliged to insure, as far as we possibly can, that theology is grounded upon a living reality and a daily experience. For commitment to theology is something to be tested by fire. A theology emanating from the Incarnation is urgently needed if we want to correctly understand the needs of all those who constitute the *polis* and *koinonia*. Both, and especially "politics," mean not only the "art of administering a city or polis," (see the *Politike Techne* of Aristotle), but also the art (*politike arete*) of developing right personal, human, and social relations based on the Trinitarian inter-personal life. Therefore, "politics" is not just a superficial social relationship, but a problem of true behavior. This problem determines the very meaning of life and existence, its spiritual and cultural goals that transform time and matter and make perfect man's humanity as God's creation. "Economy" and earthly matters, going hand in hand, are the instruments for the development of the inner man.

Frustrated by disagreements over the meaning of words, theologians involved in dialogue, decide that a common language must be found in theological discussions if they are to succeed. It is only then that we realize how vast is the area of the non-theological factors. Even if all the participants speak the same language, this language may also become a foreign one to them if the meaning attached to it by some differs from the meaning assigned to it by others. To some, certain words assume an "exotic" character and exercise a fascination precisely because they are so remote from us in time and space. There are also words which the French call "false friends"; that is, words which though so familiar and in such common daily use are, nevertheless at the same time, alienated one from the other. Latin words similar in form to words in modern European languages can be misleading: the Latin *fama,* for example, does not mean *"faim"* (French) or "famine" (English). The Latin *irritus* does not mean "irritated" but "vain or useless." Words are encountered in current texts which have come to have a completely different meaning in the course of a long history.

Consider the word *"tropos,"* for example. When it is said that the sacramental nature of the mystery of the Christ is the *tropos* through which the unique person of Christ exists, then the meaning of the word *tropos* is quite clear to an Orthodox Christian, because it is an every day expression; however, it is less familiar to the Western (Catholic) Christian. *Tropos* connotes a "turning," i.e., we speak of the "tropism" of plants (the tendency of a plant to move or to turn in response to an external stimulus) or of a "troparion" (a technical hymnographic term meaning a poetical stanza or a musical *tournure* in liturgical singing). In a wider sense the word *tropos* means a "condition" — the human condition, a human way of being or a modality. In brief, the mystery of Christ remains to this present time in the condition of a sacrament. Behind this usage of the term *tropos* there is obviously a certain nuance. The old Latin terminology sought to distinguish between "mystery" and "sacrament." The Eastern terminology in theology uses the same term without changing it to indicate a singular or plural number, i.e., the mystery and the mysteries.

A good deal of work is still to be done if we are to rediscover the original meaning of words that are used in theological texts and to arrive at an agreed understanding of them. While the Orthodox used the term *mysterion* to indicate either singular or plural, the Latin tradition used the term in the plural, too, yet still keeping the term *mysterium* in its wider soteriological connotation to mean the whole mystery of the Incarnation. Classical Latin scholasticism sees in this term a *signum* a way, a mode, a means of Christ's condescension for our human redemption. Again, *signum* seems to Orthodox Christians a very weak term, suggesting merely a "sign" of a far richer totality and fullness of God's action in history. The Church is the *mysterion* (in Aramaic *raz* and in Arabic *sirr*). This is the mystery of Christ, i.e., himself, according to the familiar Semitic genitive. This dispensation of the mystery is revealed in the Spirit (Eph 3.5) and is preserved by the Church (Eph 3.10). St. Ambrose said: "By his ascension Christ passed into his Mysteries."

There are limits, of course, with regard to the precise meaning of words. *Antonomasia*, the use of an epithet or title instead of a proper name, opened up to us a new field of research in the history of words. In recent centuries outstanding linguists succeeded in establishing the special science of historical semantics. The origin and evolution of words has always exercised an extraordinary fascination on the human mind. We have here a way of discovering the original primary meaning of words, lacking which we cannot express ourselves with precision and exactitude. In addition, it helps us to observe even more easily the influence of a particular culture, the traces of human history and the features of the human spirit in formulating particular expressions colored and tailored according to the traditional setting.

Thinkers and philosophers often dig down into the etymological sense of a given word in order to discover an image which will more expressively and even more accurately represent their thoughts. For example, many authors use the word "solemn" (derived from *solemnis = solus + annus*) when they want to emphasize a certain happening or event. Precisely because it happens only once a year, an event becomes exceptional, important, as distinguished from the many other ordinary events in our daily life.

The neglect of "fullness" and "wholeness" in theological research and spiritual investigation has had deplorable effects on human life. Nowadays much effort is given toward improving the earthly aspects of life. Prosperity and higher industrial output have heralded optimistic hopes for the unity of humanity. But it has been a one-dimensional progress with much emphasis placed on eudemonism and hedonism — on anthropocentric, and geocentric happiness. Everything for the temporal, for the attractive pleasures. As a result of forgetting the dual nature, man has been, the vacuum, the anguish, and the general pessimism with a concomitant erosion of God's fatherhood.

This is an era which is dominated by what we could call urban industrial culture. This kind of culture grew out of the use of the "scientific method" and the technological development which followed. Science and technology were seen by very many to be sources for the discovery of the ultimate answers to human aspirations. This type of culture came to be expressed in two major, competing ideologies — capitalism and communism. While there are many differences between these ideologies, there are also some very great similarities. Both, in practice, if not in theory, are materialistic, and both tend to limit their focus of achievement to what happens in space and time, concentrating upon people and things. Both are very concerned about the production and delivery of goods and services, and both tend to emphasize persons as units of production and consumption, and they measure progress, in a country or universally, in terms of the gross national product. The material achievements of such a culture, in both its ideological expressions, has been and continues to be quite incredible.

Yet, neither of these ideological expressions of culture adequately responds to the challenges of our day. These ideologies no longer satisfy the deepest human aspirations, and neither display "the power to galvanize adherents and so provide unity, direction, standards, and courage to their respective communities." Both are on the defensive, and in the present struggle between them (involving power of magnitude previously unknown in human history) there lie the possibilities of destruction not only of our civilization, as we know it, but also of all life on this planet. Both these ideologies, however powerful they remain, no longer adequately respond to the challenges which confront mankind.

Where has the Church been in this cultural process? It has remained in a kind of cultural captivity and a slave to a monastic stand which disregards the deepest needs of human nature. Far too often it has retreated from criticizing culture by means of its own faith affirmations and has, instead, accommodated itself to the cultural values of the world. If it had remained truly faithful, it would have much more positively affirmed that human beings are not mere units of production or consumption, but "relationship-beings": beings made in the image of the Creator and called, not to seek the meaning of life in the abundance of things possessed, but in the quality of relationships with God, with each other, and with nature.

The undivided Church of the ages, has never separated the function of theology from the particularities of its pastoral application. *Praxis* and dogmatic faith go together. The Church always saw its clergy-priests as theologians; and at the same time, saw its theologians as pastors. Ministry, in other words, is a diaconal theology, and theology is a ministerial service given for the benefit of the liturgical life of the Church. In this way, the deepest needs of human beings are served. What promotes the real mission of the Church on earth is this double service, where man is met and served in his totality and fullness. Thus, Gregory of Nyssa, describes those engaged in the ecclesiastical ministry as "higher than those who work in ordinary human functions and measure" (*Enkomion 2 to the Forty Martyrs*; PG 46.761). Not that they are supermen, but they formed in themselves the antitype of Christ, his *kenosis*, his human-divine *philanthropia*, which goes beyond what is expected of temporal activities.

The radical differentiation of elements in the Church as either practical or theoretical leads to a dangerous isolation of both and to a false approach to man. Moreover, it leads to a misconception about the role of the Church. In fact, theological and ecclesiastical problems do not exist separately. The burning problems of theology are at the same time real problems for the Church; consequently, the problems of the Church are also acute problems for theology. Otherwise, where and in what direction should theology go, if it has no reference to the Church? And where could the Church or ecclesiology go without using theology as its partner and helper?

Christian truth is not abstract speculation, a quantity of doctrines, but a living reality centered upon the person of Christ incarnate, a Savior who is continuously saving. In Jesus' person, we see God, and we have the Gospel as wisdom and power and a means leading to real life — *zoe* — and to salvation. In the persons of the saints we have models to follow, the actualization of authentic discipleship following Christ. Faith-words, or *theoria-praxis*, are indivisible and inseparable. The Church Fathers have often been accused of neglecting action, as if they were rather absorbed by contemplation, and of ignoring practical needs. In fact, they penetrated into the endangering roots of social evil, and proceeded to a curative, remedial diagnosis, not stopping at the level of phenomenological symptoms. Let us hear remedial diagnosis, not stopping at the level of phenomenological symptoms. Let us hear Gregory the Theologian:

> Every true philosophy is divided into two parts, namely: theory and *praxis*. Theory (contemplation) is higher and unattainable. *Praxis* (action) is more modest and more tangible, utilitarian. For us, as Christians, only when they come together can they bear fruit. We penetrate by contemplation into the realm of the saving truths, thus making the theory our companion now, but immediately after we make the *praxis* too, which confirms the theory (*Contra Julian* 1,113; PG 35.649-52).

Every baptized person lives the past in the present. All the *theophanies*, throughout the history of salvation, come anew before each Christian and are actualized, as if the events were happening at the present moment. Syrian hymnography eloquently conveys this permanence of the divine presence when it sings, not "at that time" but "Now, behold, today, now we see before us . . ." Stones, water, trees and nature are not strangers to God's redeeming action. After all, in the Old Testament and particularly in Christ's incarnation, God used the material world to communicate spiritual messages. This faith, deeply rooted in God's omnipresence and the inner relationship between body-soul, material-spiritual, earth-heaven, and secular-eternal, is seen in the veneration of sacred sites, most often in the Holy Land, for example, of caves, hills, and places of pilgrimage, not for their own sake, but because they were used by God to impart grace to articulate divine revelation to Israel throughout history.

Christians do not divide human nature. They are not pantheists. For them, bodily needs also concern spiritual needs. Man is taken as a whole — in his completeness — undivided, living under the pressure of both elements which complement each other. Not only is the worship of these Christians rich in ceremonial signs, but in their devotions they speak to the beasts or to the stones as if they take part in a "cosmic doxology". . . In fact, these objects reflect God's providence and cosmic fatherhood. The poems of Isaac the Syrian, who is renowned for the austerity and sanctity of his life (306-73), are characterized by an accumulation of metaphors giving us a masterpiece of such combinations. Isaac asks: "What is a merciful heart?'' He answers:

> "It is a heart burning for all creation — for men, for birds, for
> animals, for demons and for every creature. Seeing and con-
> templating all of these, tears come from his eyes. Because of his
> great compassion, he cannot forebear hearing of, or seeing, the
> least damage or ill treatment towards nature. For this reason
> precisely he weeps and offers supplications and prayers, that God
> might take pity upon and protect the unreasonable, the enemies
> of the truth, and oppressors. Similarly, he shows immeasurable
> goodness to the reptiles, thus showing, as a human being, his
> likeness to God'' (*Homily* 81).

This degree of goodness — very important for the protection of
the environment and for ecology today — reminds us of the
apophthegm of Abba Paul: "If one has acquired purity, then all are
submitted to him, as was the case in paradise with Adam before his
fall'' (*Apophthegma*, PG 65).

Such a theological background enables us to look upon nature not
as an enemy or alien, but as a friendly field which has been redeemed,
since God remains, even after the fall of man, the *Kyrios*, the *Pantokrator*.
Christ worked out not a partial salvation for only one race or only for
humanity, but a cosmic one — for the whole universe. Consequently,
one can believe that he already provides a foretaste of incorruptibility
and other-worldly reality. Oppression, suffering, ill-treatment, humiliation, poverty, and death, therefore, are seen in the light of Christ's victory, and they can be overcome. A Christian does not feel alone, abandoned to adversity or surrounded by inhospitable nature. In everything
which surrounds him he can find God's grace, an educating *paidagogia*
and also a *philanthropia*. Thus, in the darkest moments of history, over-
run by Asiatic invaders, pagan races or pirates, suffering persecutions
and atrocities, Christians never yielded, betrayed their faith, or became
discouraged. The Middle East is the part of the globe *par excellence*
which offered to the undivided Church the most martyrs and confessors.
Thanks to their faith, Christians can resist all kinds of aggressive power,
trusting that God will not abandon his people. Indeed, this is the people of a continuous "*Kyrie eleison!*'' The following acclamation, part
of the Divine Liturgy, is said repeatedly by the celebrant, thus expressing the innermost feelings of the worshiping assembly: "Help us, save
us, comfort and protect us, o God, by thy grace.''

If one wishes to study the character of this people he should read
the liturgical books, for these books express joy and trust, hope and

faith, as, for example, in the following troparion of Lent: "Christ, the joy of all, the truth, the light, the life, the resurrection of the world, did through his goodness manifest himself to those on earth, and he became a pledge of the Resurrection and grants to all divine forgiveness."

27. Learning from the Past

The craze for change has manifested itself widely, even in religious circles. More and more books flood the market, incoherently proposing changes in all sectors of religious life. Unfortunately, these proposals are no more beneficial than were the frogs of Egypt which overran that land. Self-reliance, self-confidence, new approaches, new evaluations are the frequent cries of today. These ideals are surely worthy but their ramifications have led to confusion, disrespect, chaos, and even anarchy — between tradition and innovation, yesterday and today, past and present. There are obvious dangers as well as obvious advantages in the changes cited above and also in others not listed. But change is not necessarily good because it is new, nor are old criteria bad simply because they are old. In the clamor for change merely for the sake of change, we should remember that some unchangeables exist, that some principles have proved their worth in the past and now command respect and demonstrate a certain wisdom. While religious instruction by its nature seeks to make difficult things simpler — to elucidate, to clarify — there, nevertheless, remains a necessity, a conscious act upon the part of a Christian to subdue his rebellious passions, to take up a hard *askesis,* and to bend his energies in order to penetrate into the mystery of the faith.

There is an unchangeable something which affects every believer. Christian example incarnates and manifests what we believe. In a machine age where automation reigns as king, people must never forget that religion does not come in pre-packaged bundles to be dispensed by a soulless pastor. It is still something to be "caught," not taught — from the pastoral relationship of the father in God and child in God. The Christian leader's attitude towards the vicissitudes of life, the continuous challenge to aspire to the high virtues which he has set as his own personal goal, will fire laypeople to do likewise. This attitude is a bulwark against selfishness and hypocrisy. In a world where standards are slipping, where values are variable, let the spiritual father perpetuate these essential unchangeables.

Where does the Christian stand in the tumult of historical changes, especially in these modern times when the faithful are flooded by many challenging events and the acceleration of revolution in all fields? Critically analyzing our return to the "event," not as a historian but as a person, is significant because it influences our march. Today man, not external factors, are required as the chief author of every event in human history. Whatever happens in the natural sphere — earthquakes, accidents, death, thunderstorms — all these and others as well, are not considered "determining" events as long as man does not participate in them. In its essence, an "event" means that constitutive moment of a sharing and willing participation in the life of an individual or a group — the expression of the meeting between deeds, the outside, and ourselves. In other words, the event is man himself. In general, an event is not so much that which arrives or what changes, but what we do with that which arrives before us.

Every analysis of history and of philosophical views about man is written with regard to the present prevailing views. And yet, these analyses cannot ignore the past. Even if much of these analyses are rejected, as expressing views of dark ages in decline, we cannot avoid seeing their relationship to the actual trends. Since the field of the past is vast, we need guides. Historians are always searching in their own way, claiming that their field is an autonomous discipline. What, nevertheless, is most important is the objectivity of observation. Xenophon, in his memoirs, spent much energy and material in order to give us a record of the main ideas of his master Sokrates. Plato, we must admit, realized a certain progress, although in doing so he also interjected his own ideas into the Socratic teachings. We have to wait for Aristotle, considered as the "father of the history of philosophy," who contributed to the promotion of human faculties for proper reasoning by providing us with a full account of human thinking. From Aristotle's time on, four axes of reference have been established: doxography, that is the history of philosophical *doxa* (doctrines), the study of sects, the biographies, and the lists of outstanding persons.

Diogenes Laërtios (2nd c. AD), author of the *Lives of the Philosophers* (a valuable but uncritical work), and the most eminent of ancient anthologists, fluctuated between the quest of knowledge and exterior erudition on one hand, and on the other a more thorough discussion of doctrines expressed concerning the vital sectors of human life. Christianity helped this legitimate research by opening up new dimensions and by giving priority to the basic criteria of human existence and life after death. Even in the patristic period we encounter a confrontation between faith and philosophy. Some claimed that any kind of philosophy was pure foolishness in the eyes of God and of their own as well, thus despising and underestimating the value of philosophy. Others, more reasonable, look upon philosophy as having a propaedeutic value. This cleavage will remain well beyond the patristic period. Thus, two major approaches appeared before the division of Christendom which again produced two parallel models of study. For the one model, everything that is included and defined as the past, heresies, paganism, schisms, errors, will be considered as *historia stultitiae,* that is a history of error. The other model, a healthy and sound research of truth, will consider this study as a *historia sapientiae,* a history of knowledge, all that human wisdom can produce. These two antithetic models will prevail until the eighteenth century. The first group, somehow prejudiced with a case of myopia, reads the past as pure error, i.e., Tertullian, Lactantius. Consequently, for these authors human knowledge holds no interest whatsoever. The other approach, on the contrary, finds useful elements by using a type of scrutinizing, testing, and filtering method, arriving at the conclusion that everything which the human mind, in searching in this world, brings about is not bad, but rather should be considered as a *preparatio evangelica.* There are many thinkers in this camp who will even say openly that God in his divine economy did not leave philosophers, thinkers, or non-Christian religions without any degree of wisdom or revealed truths inspired by the Holy Spirit, even if they were only "small grains" of the *spermatikos logos.* Thus, Justin, martyr and philosopher, said: "All that in the past has been said to be good and positive by all who preceded is Christian." His balanced reflection will be followed by Clement of Alexandria, Eusebios of Caesarea, Basil of Caesarea, and other Cappadocian Fathers. We see then that from this moment starts the theme, so familiar and so widely expounded upon in the Middle Ages, that, in reality, philosophy is and should be considered a most "useful servant of theology."

Hesitantly St. Augustine acknowledged these two models. He recognized the part of truth already contained in philosophy. His genius made him embrace the past as an indivisible totality, stating that all history, past and present, is oriented towards the triumph of Christianity as the fullness of the revealed truth. He saw a humanity *in via* continuously marching, crossing successive ages, in order to rise up from earthly time (*chronos*) to eternity, from the finite to the infinite. This schema of successive ages of humanity will be taken up later by more thinkers. But by admitting the usefulness of the past and finding its heritage to be so important, Christianity introduces

a new question, namely, that of its own particular value and importance for the well being of men and women. In other words, it is not
enough for a historian to record past events without at the same time
penetrating into their causes and their consequences. This inquiry
leads yet to another question, namely, is it enough to study human
phenomena with only human criteria both subjective and relative?
We have, on the contrary, to enlarge the goals to be attained by using yet another criterion which reflects on the finality of human life,
consisting not just in the gaining of earthly success, in dominating,
or in building up temporal achievements. Something more is miss-
ing, and so here the Gospel introduces another measure which encompasses the various needs of the body as well of the spirit.

After the Middle Ages, when the balance was realized between
the approaches, a divorce appeared on the horizon which even harmed
the philosophical tradition. Since the tradition was identified with
the thought of Aristotle, it became a synonym for a free culture.
Gradually, philosophical reflection became undervalued because it
made any progress unfruitful. Faith was totally isolated from the process. Reason from now on turned to the school of social struggle and
daily experience — empiricism, working only under the guidance of
a strict mathematic reasoning. Both faith and past tradition were ignored. Despite a certain rebirth during the Renaissance, tradition
still lost its two arms of great help, namely, faith and reason. Descartes
considered the history of philosophy as an obstacle that hinders learning true philosophy. Malebranche even said that one learns
philosophy, going beyond phenomenal approach, by meditating rather
than by relying on pure, external knowledge. Many other philosophers
followed this way, pretending to liberate philosophy from its roots.
Thus, these philosophers succeeded in detaching it completely from
its history, from its proper grounding and its roots in the past, as
it had already been liberated from the faith. Many others attempted
to heal the gap by trying to reconcile the current thinking with that
of the past. But the real return to the history of philosophy has been
made during the last three centuries.

The task for today's reader is not an easy one. He has to go through
all these oscillations between a sharp refusal of the past and of its
true assessment. Human beings in the course of time and humanity's vicissitudes have gathered an immense amount of wisdom which
can be enormously helpful. Present day human beings especially need
the lessons and the wisdom of the past more than ever before, in view

of man's catastrophic alienation from all those uplifting and redeeming elements which produced our civilization, our spiritual sense of life, values transmitted through blood and sacrifice by past generations of martyrs and confessors. We are facing in fact an alarming flood of anti-values, anti-humanistic slogans, a dry unidimentional technology at the expense of the inner life, human affection, relationship, and family unity. All are sacrificed at the altar of instant comfort, profit, pleasure, the temporal, and selfish satisfaction. Thus, we find dissatisfaction, vacuum, loneliness, and frustration appearing everywhere. Real culture is not only a pursuit of what attracts the lower nature of our existence, but a look far beyond, looking into the light of eternity and permanent values, to the life of the afterlife. Only then does man become a real man, provided that he returns to his real self. Disrespect for all that constitutes the past deprives us of the natural background on which we can stand. We are not creating *ex nihilo*; rather we profit from what has been created, adding only additional elements. I believe in the tremendous strength of the roots. It does not matter if I do not see them. They are invisible, hidden. But I can look on the stem; I can contemplate and gaze upon the flower in admiration, all these existing, thanks to the invisible roots. Likewise, we cannot neglect the past, the Law, the Prophets; we are not allowed to ignore all that has preceded us. There is an intellectual as well as a religious process in human history. The Gospel dilutes the Law not by abolishing it but by perfecting it. So, also, in other fields of human knowledge, we take advantage of all the positive accomplishments that were made and proclaimed by previous generations.

Cicero said that history is "opus maxime oratoricum," a work above all of eloquent speeches. That definition means that oratory has as its task to instruct, to put idle feelings into motion to incite for imitation. Similarly, Titus Livy, a Roman historian (59 BC-c.17 AD) stated "that history offers what is most salutary and creative, the instructive examples for the benefit of all models for copying them and horrible misdeeds for their causes and for their consequences which we have to avoid." History, therefore, is not a simple parade of events but a lesson lived by human beings like us, to enable us to love our country and virtues. For Livy, therefore, history is an epic and a drama as well; it is a living reality of human beings who succeeded in overcoming difficult conditions and reached success. Like a representation in a theater, or like a fresco, the history of Rome is described like an epic in prose, celebrated by the Roman people just as Virgil the Roman poet (70-19 BC) did in his *Aeneid.* In tragic situations, each tries to save his own life, forgetting his duty to the mother land. But for Livy what counts more and has priority is the love for the whole community, how to preserve religion, the worship of the gods and above all morality. Through his *History of Rome* (*Ab urbe condita libri*), he incites the citizens to live for higher causes.

28. Gospel's Hidden Success

If one attempts to understand human problems and the whole inconsistent march of history, he will arrive at an impass. There is a certain logic, but there is a lot of inexplicable developments and events which our reason cannot explain. Rationalism always insisted on using a narrow method of approach, and inevitably it forced diagnosis and produced wrong conclusions. A good historian, an honest philosopher is forced to admit that there are many other unseen factors emanating from the mystery of human existence, that determine life and universal history.

Blaise Pascal had already rightly remarked while meditating on the mystery of the Incarnation: "It was not right that God could appear in a totally divine way, thus absolutely convincing all men. Equally, it would not be just if he came in a way so hidden that it was unknowable to those who would seek him sincerely. There is enough light for those who really desire to see him. But equally, there is enough obscurity for those who have an opposite disposition."

If we extend this reflection into today's realities, we can see that, undoubtedly, there is enough progress in human history so that optimists can maintain their confidence in man. But also, there is enough instability so that the pessimists can subordinate *homo sapiens* to *homo demens*. Thus, the complex development of Christianity led both materialists and rationalists to see only its negative aspect. While more spiritual, the believers see the positive elements worldwide. Consequently, charity and love are often despised as marginal elements by all those who no longer believe in it. At the same time, there are so many others for whom love is what keeps them alive. The press, the mass-media tell us very little about this aspect of life. But it exists, real and incarnate in the daily activities of many. This aspect is a continuity of the past. It is the past which, with all martyrs and confessors, encourages and sustains them. This aspect is also history, written with blood and self-emptiness, enough to inspire and sustain our present generation, in spite of any opposite forces and fatalistic slogans.

One factor escapes the attention of many students of human phenomena, namely, that human nature is fallen and, therefore, distorted, resisting the challenge to do things, i.e., to seek the real, the permanent, the absolute, the authentic. Without a personal reaction, a regeneration, man will continue to follow the impulses of his alienated nature. He, therefore, needs help to overcome this weakness and enter into a new relationship with his own true self and with his fellow-men. Life, after all, is not a ready-made gift. From this imperfect state and also from these rebellious elements within us and outside of us, we are called to create a new kind of existence. Here exactly lies the supremacy of the human being, in comparison with the animal world. Thus, the important question remains: why do I live? For what purpose are all these resources given to me?

Man has a finality. Real life is conquered, after labor, self-denial, struggle, *askesis*, pain and sufferings. All these sufferings and so many others, constitute a kind of school wherein, as a pedagogical instrument, we are called upon to work out our perfection and to complete our real progress and the ascending process. If we do not struggle to move higher up the ladder of perfection but rather are fascinated instead by earthly pleasures, life becomes monotonous, an emptiness and a dissatisfaction which flood our existence. We are invited to make use of our free choice to choose between what seems attractive, easy, comfortable and what is in reality useful, uplifting, improving our very being in many more dimensions and compelling us onto higher horizons. Since the time of Hercules, the son of Zeus, man is called upon to choose between two ways of life, one ascending and difficult, the other descending and, therefore, very easy. The first is of the gods, while the second of evil. Most of us have experienced the first to one degree or another, and experience the second more and more; with horror we see its ruins, deceptions, and we are disillusioned with the sad feeling of a vacuum.

Without energetic resistance to our passions, we are at the mercy of evil forces, resulting in a type of spiritual slavery. Spiritual health and real liberty imply a discernment of our enemy, what undermines our very vitality and dignity. Christ was referring to such a situation when he said: "Know the truth and it will free you" (John 4.32). True faith keeps away any threat of such slavery because it puts reason into the service of our authentic freedom. This is how John Damascene saw it: "The possession of free will always joins reason. The nonreasonable beings do not have free will; they are led by their nature. This is why they never can resist their natural appetites, but once they are drawn by it, they rush into action. On the contrary, man being a reasonable being leads nature, which follows him. This is why, even if he likes something, he has all the power to resist or to follow after it" (*The Orthodox Faith* 2,27; PG 94.960-61).

Now this march towards our finality has no limits or end. Isaac the Syrian said: "There is not a point of perfection. Because perfection even with regards to those who reached it, remains incomplete, unaccomplished" (*Ascetic sermon 55, On Passions*). We now enter into a vast field of questions. Being weak and fallen, how then can man achieve his ultimate goal? Since Christ's incarnation, man is no longer alone or by himself. God is with him, in a permanent way not simply near him but in him. This activity of Christ does not imply any reduction of his divinity, neither does it imply a removal from his divinity to humanity, or a transfer from heaven to earth. The incarnation is a *parousia,* a real presence without any displacement, or a "presence without absence." Redemption of the human condition implied, according to Gregory the Theologian, "that the similar could be purified by a similar" (*Oration* 38,9; PG 36.633). This means that since man is fallen, man again ought to undertake the mission of liberation from evil, but not an ordinary man because then we would treat him as god, but we needed a God who would become man, as we are, in order to save us from the yoke of evil.

Christians, while realistically facing evil in all its forms in the world, i.e., corruption, injustice, sensuality, one half dominating the other half, do not have the tendency to fall into a selfish attitude, relying exclusively on their own strengths and abilities. In contrast to others in such a pressing situation, they feel that they are not alone or abandoned. They recognize their proper strengths as being insufficient and relative. If they remain confident and full of hope in their striving to renew themselves and society, it is because they have found the source of endless energy and the source of "living water." Christ is our everlasting companion, our co-fighter, and our Father, always ready at any moment to go before us, opening up the way for us. This conviction of security fires up each fighter with confidence for the final victory. Thus, man is strengthened and enabled to transform fear into joy and to continue this revolution of renewal.

This quest for Christ is due to yet another reason, namely, that human beings are continuously irritated by an incurable wound, a longing or a nostalgia that is of the other thou, the other-worldly space. In moments of spiritual drought, when loneliness finds no happiness within or without, neither from earthly prosperity nor from glorious achievements or careers, man then turns his soul towards that eternal God. The divine chases him. The infinite follows his paths day and night. The eternal attracts him. We know from daily experience, that even if we have succeeded in putting into effect a new economic order or an improvement in international relationships, even if we have succeeded in establishing a better type of society or a political system, our very heart still is not filled with what it really desires. And why? Because man is made for yet another kind of life which never dies. In his innermost being man looks for "new heavens and a new earth" (2 Pet 3.13).

The problem then remains: how to help modern man to build this new society not on hate and competition, but on love? God is present only where love exists; and inversely, love exists only where God is manifestly living and ever present.

29. Worshiping in a Secular Age

Ever since the Uppsala Assembly of the World Council of Churches in 1967, the crisis of worshiping the Triune God has been underlined in the sharpest manner. Proposals concerning projects for alternative services, for substantial changes in, and the renewal, reshaping, and restructuring of the traditional patterns of worship have invaded the WCC. Experimental types of worship, taking newly-formulated models from the Third World and other models, are being used in the process of finding the ideal service which could meet modern needs. As Orthodox, we fully understand the problem and all that is hidden behind it. Modern man prays less and less. As a result, he believes less. The crisis of faith is actually the crisis of prayer. In this most important and difficult area of worship we offer some helpful reflections which come from the liturgical theology and life of the undivided Church.

To a certain extent, the archaic language of worship hinders contemporary people from active participation. On the other hand, it is true that a considerable effort is needed in order to go "within" oneself for personal meditation. Full participation in worship implies an *askesis*, a discipline, an honest eagerness to catch the hidden message. It is the same with understanding the Bible. Any translation of the language of worship, however necessary it might be in order to make our worshiping relevant, is not sufficient in and of itself. What is required in addition is a mobilization of our own spiritual and intellectual powers in order to bring about a perceptive communion with God, who wants to speak with us.

St. John Chrysostom explains the reason why God wishes to transmit his ineffable truths through visible channels:

> For Christ hath given nothing visible, but in things sensible, the meaning of which is to be determined by the mind. So in baptism, the gift is bestowed by a sensible thing, that is, by water; but that which is done is perceived by the mind — the birth, I mean, and the renewal. For if thou hadst been incorporeal, he would have delivered thee the incorporeal gifts bare; but because the soul hath been locked up in a body, He delivers thee the things that the mind perceives, in things sensible.

How many now say, I would wish to see his form, the marks, his clothes, his shoes. Lo! thou seest him, Thou touchest him, thou eatest him. And thou indeed desirest to see his clothes, but he giveth himself to thee not to see only, but also to touch and eat and receive within thee" (*Homily* 82,4 on *St. Matthew;* PG 58.743).

The West suffers from a reluctance, mixed with a kind of prejudice, in observing the liturgical feasts. This crisis happens in the midst of a historical moment when man becomes more self-confident, rationalized, individualized, and technicized. For this precise reason, man now more than ever before needs these feasts in order to warm his frozen feelings and to find once again his profound identity. This liturgical decline took place as as result of secularism and the anarchic liturgical reform. It is true that the civil or secular calendar, with the inclusion of all the designated prescriptions of civil feasts and holidays, originally, emanates from the Christian feasts themselves, i.e., Easter, Christmas, Epiphany, Pentecost, etc. Citizens have retained the exterior form and the accompanying non-working days, but instead of using the available free days for something spiritual, uplifting, and essential, they just do nothing, preferring to remain idle, with the exception of taking automobile trips from one countryside to another. Consequently, during such feasts, the family and the parish in general are scattered. This massive exodus then constitutes a new and alarming phenomenon from a religious point of view. Christians in this way are less and less nurtured liturgically, resulting in a spiritual anemia. The local Church then is amputated from the major symbol for its vitality. Its ecclesiastical visibility and its faith in the risen Lord are dangerously weakened. Even on Christmas night, when families are supposed to be gathered together in worship, the TV and other secular preoccupations or amusements become tempting diversions and thus serve to work against the observation of the purely religious feast.

One asks the question whether or not it is time that the local community rediscover the very meaning of celebrated feasts, whose absence is so strongly felt by many of the faithful, in order that they may live the mysteries of Christ in symbols and in sacraments? Many related liturgical traditions, such as processions, vigils, worship over the tombs or relics of martyrs, etc., are slowly losing their interest and in time may even be abandoned.

What above all else unites Christians is the same faith, the *symphonia* transmitted by the early Church, and subsequently concretely manifested in the Eucharist. This is the very mystery of unanimity, of unity, and of the true *koinonia*. In the Eucharist the faithful unite their entire being with that of Christ, after being purified from envy, selfish piety and sectarianism through a cathartic *metanoia*. Worship is the very moment to proclaim "with one voice and one heart" the blessed Triune God, to pronounce, in common with other fellow-Christians, the *amen*, to act out liturgically our sanctification. In such a context, St. John Chrysostom, with his mystical lyricism, presents Christ as inviting us to become one with Him: "I came down in order to meet you and to make you mine. I want to attract you. Eat me! Drink me therefore . . . I wish that we, the two, make nothing else than one." (*Homily* 16,4 *On 1st Tim;* PG 62.586).

The worshiper is surrounded by texts and liturgical forms conveying salutary messages and reminding him constantly of certain basic truths as soteriology, eschatology, and doxology. The faithful are not left to themselves to express their feelings to God without any guidance. Their prayers are shaped and sustained by the prayers of the whole community. The individual is called to join, to adapt, to conform himself as a spiritual being with the spirit and the requirements of the *ekklesia*, which incorporates in liturgical life the perfect type of prayer, the eucharistic prayer.

Let us look at the setting of these worshipers. The theology of the new creation, the *kaine ktisis*, during the Liturgy, is exposed before them. The common material world, the world of decay, instead, is put as secondary in a marginal place. The "darkened or unclean image" of man, which resulted from the fall (Rom 8.22) is contrasted by the Church to the image of man renewed by Christ's redemption, and by his overabundant grace (Rom 5.20). Hymns, icons, prayers, and liturgical forms were creations of a particular morphological conception which seeks to remove the worshiper from the transience of this world and impose upon him the idea of the reborn creation, of the eternal kingdom. This idea of the "new" man prevails everywhere. All texts again and again focus and aim at "fashioning," *morphosis*, namely, that Christians are entering a new world redeemed and Christified. These texts educate, lift up the mind, and put it into a celestial reality. The hymns of Advent or Lent seek to instruct and to lead Christians directly to the thought that God dwells in the fullness of his divinity among them. According to Theodore the Studite, "if we say that Christ is the power of God and the wisdom of God, by the same manner his representation must be said to be the power and the wisdom of God" (*Antirrheticus* 2,16; PG 99.361). The Seventh

Ecumenical Council insisted on the reality of the hypostatic union: "May the memory be eternal of those who say that the flesh of Christ was overexalted by its union and is found beyond the highest honor, being equally divine by utter union, and remaining immutably and invariably with the Divine Logos who received it" (*Letter on Sunday of Orthodoxy*). Theodore the Studite goes on: "The unmixable were mingled; in the uninscribable, was found the inscribed" (PG 99.409).

The most revealing experience which one can have concerning Orthodoxy is a visit to a church. There the visitor is reminded of the Old Testament's verse: "This is the gate of the Lord. The righteous shall enter into it." There one feels the *communio sanctorum*, worshiping with all the members of the mystical body: patriarchs, prophets, saints, apostles, martyrs, confessors, and ascetics. Christ as Pantokrator and a plethora of the early saints appear on icons and it is as if our prayers *hic et nunc* are answered by an echo of the whole angelic choir: "Holy, Holy, Holy." But only those who have ears to hear might hear it. The passage of time as *chronos* does not obscure its size and duration, or its strength, of the ever-recurring scenes of devotion at its Holy Eucharist, and even we can compare our present difficulties and tribulations with early sufferings and martyrdoms within its sacred confines.

The uplift one experiences during worship is so strong and so influences our whole being that our very nature is inundated by the divine, to such an extent that it is no more we who live, but God who lives in us. This may be called "enthusiasm," the same enthusiasm which the first-century Christians experienced who, through John's epistle, shared with us what they had heard and seen and handled of the Word of life. Enthusiasm still seems the appropriate expression as people explain how the Logos came alive for them in the here and now. It is a pity that in its modern usage the word "enthusiasm," has become so suspect, even though it has distant but Christian origins. The word literally means "possessed by the Spirit of God within." During the divine Eucharist, we sometimes feel that the Spirit takes possession of a large part of the congregation — not all of it, but of a sufficient cross-section. It creates a new generation of "enthusiasts" for whom life, after this mystical gathering, will never be quite the same again.

Sharing this vision and experience with those who have not as yet seen or felt it will be difficult. We have to make known to others the extraordinary operation of the Spirit, which happens when we breathe in deeply the fresh air of our communion with one another.

"Unity," after all, is becoming a common slogan. We need to make a particular effort to distinguish this word from other notions of togetherness, fellowship, or human association. "Unity" was always‾ clearly understood in church history. It is visible, concretely manifested, and highlighted in the eucharistic fellowship. Those who proclaim one faith, one Lord, one baptism — they become the one Body of Christ, experiencing the word of redemption and participating in the bread and wine, these two things which bind the community together.

What then has happened to the cosmos, to the orderliness of God's creation, as a consequence of man's rebellion and fall? Where does this orderliness remain in a fallen world? What is the nature of this orderliness? In what sense has Christ by his sacrifice restored this orderliness? In what sense is this restoration complete, and in what sense is the restoration on-going? What are the main lineaments of the restored order? What are its permanent, and what are its dynamic elements?

All these questions can best be answered in the context of a eucharistic theology of the creation and the Incarnation. And this kind of eucharistic theology related to society can be acceptable to Orthodox, to Catholics, and to Protestants alike.

But a certain stream of theology is too man-centered to deal with the Eucharist in its fullness.The Eucharist is not simply a matter of Christ's feeding us; Christ's offering of his Church to God constitutes the primary meaning of the Eucharist. The bread and the wine are not simply elements of food. The words of St. Augustine are relevant in this context:

> The whole redeemed community, the congregation and fellowship of the saints, is the universal sacrifice offered to God through the great High Priest who offered himself in his suffering for us, that we might be the Body of so great a Head — that is the sacrifice of Christians: the many made into one body in Christ. It is made manifest to her (the Church) that in that which she offers she is offered herself . . . If you are the body of Christ and His members, it is the sacrament of yourselves (*mysterium vestrum*) that is set upon the Lord's table, the sacrament of yourselves that you receive. Be what you receive and receive what you are." (*De civitate dei* 10,6, see also 19, 23; 22, 10, *Sermo* 48, 2).

And again: "Be what you receive and receive what you are" (*Sermo*

272). That is how St. Augustine puts it. Clever, but still a bit inadequate: the tendency to individualism is still there. Perhaps we need the corrective passage of Cyril of Alexandria, who says:

> With one body, and that his own, he (Christ) blesses through mystic communion those who believe him, and makes them one body with himself and with each other . . . If we all partake of one body, we are all made one body . . . The same with the Spirit. All of us by receiving one and the same Spirit are in a way fused with one another and with God. For even though we are many individuals, yet Christ causes his Father's and his own spirit to dwell in each one of us. But the Spirit himself is one and indivisible, and it is he who collects into a unity spirits that are distinct from each other — since they exist as individuals — and makes them all appear as one in himself. For, as the power of that sacred flesh makes those in whom it is one body, so, I venture, the indivisible Spirit of God by indwelling in all brings all to union in the Spirit" (*Commentary on the Gospel of John* 11, PG 74:553-61).

Enough has been said to show the inseparability of a eucharistic theology and the proper understanding of unity. The deeper dimensions of God's purpose for man cannot be discovered outside of a eucharistic theology. Fundamental principles concerning unity can only be recovered from a eucharistic understanding of the body of Christ.

It is true that the Orthodox place greater stress on the eschatological aspect of faith rather than the temporal, earthly situation. They are less inclined to see churches marching through the world side by side, and they highlight the kingdom of God which is within us, which is to come and which is starting from this very moment in time just now before us. The vision of glory is, in fact, revealed in the sacredness of church buildings. Entering a Byzantine church we feel a change of atmosphere. We are not penetrating into the ark, or the tabernacle of the desert, but into God's palace. We find no lofty naves, so common in Western chapels, over which steeples soar like masts pointing towards heaven and reminding us of the transitory character of Christ's Church, or the ark of Peter sailing across the seas of this world; on the contrary, we find a solid building, looking no further than itself, whose square or basilica design surmounted by a single cupola or multiple domes, expresses by such a geometrical representation the union of heaven and earth, and thus is a symbolic image of the whole universe. Again and again we find this architectural form exactly the same, whether in the sixth century "Great Church" of Constantinople or in the smaller ones with Byzantine crosses of the fourteenth century. The form is not arbitrary; it fulfills a theological purpose.

In what proved to be the classic manual of religious iconography for Byzantine art, the *mystike theoria* of Germanos, Patriarch of Constantinople, we find this description of the church as a building: "The church is the earthly heaven wherein the heavenly God lives and moves" (PG 98.384).

In these days when the climate for organic church unity appears so chilly, it seems more important than ever before to know and to experience one another's worship and depths of spiritual life. At this time, prayer and thought for the future are needed, more profound references to the prompting of the Holy Spirit. Today we all might with profit learn more about the ancient Orthodox Church. It is possible to understand more clearly what is meant by the early church, because Orthodoxy in so many ways is the early church. You will detect the true worth of the unchanging and of changelessness. You may indeed find yourself experiencing a dimension nearer to paradise than you ever thought possible in this heavily-laden, modern, permissive society with its confusing and incoherent liturgical changes. A church with its gracious apse, its iconostasis and its beautifully carved ceiling beams, has about it a quality that makes the passage of time almost meaningless, and gives a sense of reaching out to eternity which is born of so many centuries of prayer and liturgy.

For the Orthodox believer, the worshiping place is associated with the generations of the faithful, the context of the *communio sanctorum* — of prophets, patriarchs, martyrs, and confessors — of meditating upon Christ almost as long as Christianity has been in existence. Only when you have experienced this to the fullest degree can you turn your attention to the congregation, which is a mirror of the celestial, worshiping assembly of angels and saints. Depictions of Moses appear in two scenes above the apse: in one he kneels before the burning bush and in the second he holds the tablets of the Law. But the main scene is that of the transfiguration — Jesus flanked by Moses and Elijah. One is also conscious of the overwhelming magnificence of the quiet landscape. The spiritual *koinonia* which is expressed in Church decoration has done as much as anything else to shape the spiritual growth of the parish, a tangible demonstration of the ephemeral life of man against the timelessness of the primordial magnificence.

This conception seems to be entirely in conformity with patristic thought concerning a "paradise upon earth." The Church is considered, first of all, as a society and this suggests to an Orthodox the glorious community of the elect. Furthermore, this heavenly community is anticipated in the liturgical community, and thus the worshiper sees it and experiences it as represented in the act of worship called *leitourgia* or the Holy Eucharist. Whereas, for a Westerner the eucharistic sacrifice is envisaged above all as an actualization of Calvary and a means of communicating sacramentally with the Christ immolated, the Orthodox sees in the Eucharist the service of divine *oikonomia* and the *philanthropia* of the great King, both as an anticipation of, and a participation in, the celestial liturgy. It is a hommage paid to the victorious Lamb rather than a commemoration — *anamnesis* — of his sacrifice. Is it not just this connection with the celestial liturgy that we feel in one of the most solemn moments of the Orthodox Eucharist — during the Great Entrance — when the assembled faithful seem themselves to be an incarnation of the glorious vision of the Apocalypse?

We do not just attend — we participate in the sacred mystery. We associate ourselves with the choirs of the court of heaven, sharing in a certain way the life of eternity.

Here, in this profound mysticism, flooded by the splendors of another world, is that antiquity which the first Christians experienced united for the eucharistic synaxis, living the mystery of the Church in the expectation of an imminent Parousia, and singing the beautiful prayer which the Didache attests: "Let grace come and this world pass away" (*Didache,* 6). Paschal joy even fills the funeral service, while the Latin liturgy of the dead abounds in accents concerning the "*Die irae*" and the "*Libera me*," with its sombre perspectives of the last judgment, creating an atmosphere of dread and sorrow. The Church is a liturgical community, exercising to the full its special mission of sanctifying both man, the universe and the entire cosmos. In short, the Eucharist aims at embracing the whole of mankind, dead and alive, present, past, and future — the *eschaton* — redeeming and bringing into the kingdom all things and all created beings.

It is not accidental that in the last four years Orthodox theologians lay a strong emphasis in Orthodox ecclesiology on the *eucharistic* understanding of the Church. The main reasons are: 1) The modern strong trend to change the Church into a mere socio-political institution, or into an ally of the established government. (Therefore, many Orthodox theologians today, laymen as well as clergymen, constantly urge the churches to persevere trustingly in their appointed role as "bondservants to God," for only by doing so can they maintain their freedom over against *ideologies* and *political systems* which the Church cannot under any circumstances or for any considerations of expediency enter into coalition with or even identify herself with, but of which she must always remain the prophetic "crisis.") 2) The modern misunderstanding of the nature and mission of the Church, which was originally understood and experienced as Christian *diakonia*, witness and promotion of God's Kingdom on earth, and as a contribution to the creation of a fellowship of solidarity, in the sense of a metamorphosis of "natural" orders and the outlook of a society of individuals formed into a *koinonia of persons*.

The Liturgy is not an escape from life, but a continuous transformation of life according to the prototype of Jesus Christ, through the power of the Spirit. Each of the faithful is called upon to continue a personal "liturgy" on the secret altar of his own heart, to realize a living proclamation of the good news "for the whole world." Without this continuation the Liturgy remains incomplete. Since the eucharist has even incorporated us in him who came to serve the world and to be sacrificed for it, we have to express in concrete *diakonia*, in community life, our new being in Christ, the servant of all.

The sacrifice of the eucharist must be extended in personal sacrifices for the people in need, the brothers for whom Christ died. Since the Liturgy is the participation in the great event of liberation from demonic powers, then the continuation of Liturgy in life means a continuous liberation from the powers of evil that are working inside us, a continual reorientation and openness to insights and efforts aimed at liberating human persons from all demonic structures of injustice, exploitation, agony, loneliness, and at creating real communion of persons in love.

30. Reality and Anticipation

Nothing is monotonous and static, even detached or isolated, in the Divine Liturgy. Everything is interdependent, interrelated, alive and moving harmoniously in perfect unity towards its fullness. Everything takes on a meaning. Everything is concentrated into a whole entity. New aspects are revealed and everything becomes known in developing the various parts of worship which are communicated to the congregation. Their nature and the reason for their existence in "rational worship," in the liturgy of the Logos (Word), "through whom everything was made," is revealed. And while we talk about everything, we see everything as if it were happening right now, at this very moment. Everything comes near to us, becoming relevant and familiar; nothing is unfamiliar to our deepest problems, to our culture, because the Liturgy is transcultural. Fundamentally, the subject matter is one; but this oneness is inclusive, containing a whole world, synthetic and complementary. It is the blessed kingdom of the Father, of the Son, and of the Holy Spirit, which by revealing itself, welcomes and sanctifies creation. It is the uncreated grace of the Holy Trinity which rejuvenates the whole creation.

The Liturgy begins with the solemn proclamation in the form of a doxology to the most holy triune kingdom. Afterwards we ask only: "That the grace may come, that the world may pass," according to an ancient text (*The Teaching of the Apostles*). The faithful offer themselves in it, entirely and forever.

Thus, the Liturgy becomes the theological place where the diversity of the creation meets. Beyond its ardor, the totality is irrecognizable, frozen, and isolated.

The unity of faith of the participants appears in the way that the totality is vivified, transformed, and rendered incorruptible, immortal by the uncreated grace of the Trinity. In this way the original unity of the present structure and of the eschatological entelechy of all appears as the cause and the end of everything.

"All things rely upon you and the unique one. All things together are expecting you. And you are the fullness and the end of all," says Gregory the Theologian (*Carmen* 1, *Poemata Theologica* 29, PG 37.508).

The genuine liturgical experience affirms that: "We saw the real light (reflected from the whole transformed world), we received the

186

heavenly spirit.''

The natural world in which man lives, however fallen and cor-
rupted, as a divine-human reality, is the liturgical world. Neither
history in the form of time, nor creation in the form of space, nor
logic of fallen man, nor art of wavering person constitutes it. In the
Liturgy everything is altered, uplifted, eternalized, and immortaliz-
ed, having undergone a profound metamorphosis. Everything is tested
and restored by the cross and the Resurrection.

Indeed, the task of the eucharistic service is to Christify the worshiping community. Each one thus becomes a chosen instrument of
the Spirit; ''you did not choose me, but I chose you and appointed
you that you should go and bear fruit and that your fruit should abide''
(John 15.16). Being chosen by God seems odd and frightening: odd
because it smacks of favoritism, frightening because it presents a God
who intervenes in a less than understandable way for us. The ''divine
likeness'' is destined to be accessible to all and to be our own
possession.

One of the ancient spirituals said, even if only one human being
were on earth, Christ would come down and be crucified for that man's
own salvation alone. How extraordinary is this immense love that God
has for man, which results in man's immeasurable value, beyond any
human calculation. That God accepts his own sacrifice for the sake
of man shows what dignity he attributes to our humanity. Thus in
our social relations, each person must see the other in a similar way.
We judge unjustly when we look on others and see only sad and dark
aspects and nothing positive or bright. No matter to what degree one
is a sinner, fallen and prodigal, one does not cease to be ''God's child.''
We have to see ourselves and others too, in the light of this principle, and behave with honor and reverence at all times. To this end
we are helped by the way the Eucharist treats the subject of God
and the human relationship.

The whole world of the Church, the new creation, is a divine-human
reality. The created world is united immutably, unalterably, and
distinctively with uncreated grace; it is neither abolished nor destroyed,
but it is transformed and rendered imperishable. This is the weighty
insight of Maximos the Confessor:

All the reasonable creation can be seen in a mystical way through
the sensible means, figured symbolically in different forms. And
they can be perceived only by those who can see them. The whole

sensible world is found in the insensible one, and each existence can be seen in the ones which are reasonable through a special knowledge (*Mystagogia* 2, PG 91.669c).

When the seer of the Apocalypse writes: "I, John, your brother, . . . was in the Spirit on the Lord's day, and I saw a new heaven and a new earth" (Rev 1.10), it seems as if he were telling us: I, your brother, John, celebrated the Eucharist.

Liturgy brings us in front of the open window of the revelation, of the incorruptibility. It enables us to breathe pure air which revives and refreshes our innermost depths. In the Divine Liturgy this event takes place and we experience it. Everything becomes new through the grace and the communion of the Holy Spirit. It is not the sun that lights up the earth, nor the imagination which opens the sky — "Heaven and earth shall pass away" (Mt 24.35) — but it is the very presence of God which renews, renders imperishable, and unites the earth and the heavens. "And the city had no need of the sun . . ." (Rev 21.23). The liturgical reality cannot be illuminated by a lighting which will pass away, "what is evident (is perceived by our senses) and what is visible, is not the supreme good."

The invisible presence of (God) the Lord enlightens and reveals the totality of existence. The shining light will not perish. It is inextinguishable. What we perceive is perishable, subject to the law of decline and disparity. It is not, therefore, the really good, because it is not permanent. "That they might have life" (Jn 10.10).

The liturgy of the altar creates, regulates, and constitutes every part of our existence. What is admirable is that the liturgical spirit is incarnated in our life. The liturgy of the sacrifice of Christ, which the priest offers on the altar, constitutes the center of our life and of our self-consciousness. It animates and forms our life. It holds together the person of every individual as well as our liturgical community. It composes and contains everything in us and around us. It incarnates and it brings near us and in us, consciously and obviously, what is invisible and uncreated. It transforms and sanctifies what is visible and insignificant. We experience the unconfused succession of the uncreated and of the created; of life and death, of motion and immobility, of the mystery and of logic, of miracle and of law, of freedom and of nature.

What is invisible is seen in a visible way. What is unutterable is expressed. What is inaccessible, far and beyond, dwells in us. We are a minor thing (a non existent thing), which contains something unlimited and unattainable. The more that we advance voluntarily towards the lessening and the disappearance of pettiness, the more the inaccessible glory shines, creates the essence, and draws out into the light from non-being innumerable new creations and pleasures.

At the end one does not know if the invisible things are more perceptible than the created things, or if the created ones are more sacred than the invisible ones. Everything exists and is valuable because the Holy Spirit enlightens it (illuminates it).

Our whole life has meaning only when it is illuminated by the light of the love and grace of the Trinity. It preserves its freedom when it has surrendered itself to the redeeming action of the Trinity. It is not decomposed into the sunless space of the insignificant when it is expanded by the Savior's straining on the cross whose sacrifice the mystery of the altar reveals. Life consoles us when it is tormented by the spirit of freedom, which blows in whatever direction it wishes. We exist as we are, constantly expanded by eternal life, once we have surrendered the arms of our cowardice (that is, of our own desire) and have allowed our destiny, as well as "our whole life and hope," to be entirely dependent on the will of the incarnate God.

The Eucharist baptizes, with the fire of the Holy Spirit, man, nature, and time. Out of this Baptism come as tangible blessed fruits, the saints, paradise, and eternity. All these things are tried in the incandescence of the prolonged Pentecost of everyday life, and they are deeply refreshed. The only thing that concerns us is: that the Spirit may do whatever he wants. That his wish may be fulfilled. This is what constitutes the eternal paradise for man.

31. From Earth to Heaven

The liturgy may at first glance give the impression of being merely a commemoration, an exclusive *anamnesis*, belonging to the past. But the wonders of God which it commemorates are linked to the mystery of the Resurrection of Christ, which is already accomplished in him, and which is being accomplished in his Church. Moreover, in the liturgy we are constantly experiencing the different stages of Christ's life on earth and the climax of all, the mystery of Easter, with all that it encompasses and all that it announces.

Far from disassociating us from the actual world, the liturgy embraces all the daily realities in human life and the material world, as well as the people who are not yet gathered into the Church. The liturgy thus undertakes a magnificent task as it reaches out towards all men. But this outward reach also explains why the liturgy may give the impression of being provisional and imperfect. However, it is not merely introductory. The liturgy is already, here and now, the presence of the heavenly world and the communication with it, because our Lord is the High Priest in heaven and on earth, because the Church in heaven and the Church on earth form a single fellowship of prayer.

When the Christian participates in the Eucharist, he does not feel alone — that terrible feeling of being abandoned, of being isolated, and imprisoned inside oneself. He is fully aware of his communion with his creator, the Lord of the universe. Moreover, he trusts the Pantocrator completely, he is filled with hope, he does not fall into depression, and he is not torn by melancholy. The Eucharist thus becomes a power in daily life and supports the combatant in his struggle against depression and against those who attack his security. Indeed the Lord's Supper is life itself and it is food, but above all else it is a close communion with Christ as the second person of the blessed Trinity.

St. Averkios, Bishop of Hieropolis in Phrygia, (died c. 300) is famous for the inscription which he set up over his future tomb:

As a citizen of a distinguished city I have set up this monument during my lifetime. My name is Averkios; I am a disciple of a holy shepherd who leads his flock over hill and dale, and whose eyes see everything. It is he who taught me the true scriptures, it is he who sent me to Rome to contemplate the queen

190

with golden garments and golden shoes. There I saw a people which bears a shining seal. I also saw the plain of Syria and Nisibis beyond the Euphrates; and everywhere I met brethren. The faith led me everywhere; everywhere it provided me with fresh fish, large and pure, caught by a pure virgin. Faith gave this to her friends unceasingly, together with delicious wine and bread. This I have engraved, I, Averkios, at the age of seventy-two in the year 300, the sixth month. Peace be to those who pass by and who remember me!

While he mentions his travels to Rome and Nisibis, he makes allusive use of early Christian symbolism and above all, a testimony to the contemporary dynamism everywhere of the Eucharist. For this pious bishop, the body and the blood of Christ constituted the central focal point of his very being. He could not pass a day without receiving the celestial food. It is in this sacramental context that he uses so many metaphors to describe the nutritive nature of the Eucharist.

The response of God's people to this revelation must be a total one: obedience and self-giving in terms of the given conditions of life. Inasmuch as the offering to God made by the Church of its own life prefigures the offering made to the Creator of the whole created world (which includes human existence and culture), in order to accomplish his eternal design, the Church commits itself to work in order to integrate man's cultural life within this total offering in the form of service and worship rendered to God. This role of the Church implies an obligation. It is the Church's duty to express its faith and its life in terms which the "world" can understand, so that the Gospel and the Christian life do not seem foreign, but a part of human life in a given cultural situation. Indigenization is, therefore, a universal obligation that is incumbent upon the Church. This principle was already professed in the Church of the martyrs, when it permitted certain brothers to observe the Mosaic law (Justin, *Dialogue* 47,2; Eusebios, *Eccl. Hist.* 5,24, 13-16).

The forms of worship must be related to people's lives. It is not sufficient to adapt the liturgy to a certain culture, because the indigenization of the Christian faith is based not on the indigenous culture but on the "style of life" of Christians today. This indigenization must be carried out in response to the searching questions which present themselves when the Church makes the laborious experience of participating in secular life. Inasmuch as a technological civilization is spreading all over the world today, the forms of worship must be adapted to that culture as it is manifested in certain geographical regions.

Worship has lost much of its meaning for many of our contemporaries, even for many members of the Church. For man today, more or less "secularized," the very word "worship" has lost its meaning and no longer arouses any response. In the steadfast soul where worship still means something, it mainly arouses the recollection of archaic church customs which have gradually become largely unadaptable to modern life. A careful examination of worship and of man today must not be confined to the evolution which has influenced man from the time of Bacon to the age of technology. The structure and quality of human sensibility have changed during the centuries. The Church must, therefore, take the necessary measures in the sphere of worship, showing its centrality in the life of the faithful, while focusing on the fundamental impact of the Eucharist as the very source of all sacraments.

Human contact with God, especially the *koinonia* with the Holy Spirit, has lost its edge through long familiarity. Besides, one suspects that "fellowship" has fallen in the social scale of words. Yet words are our servants not our masters, so if we retain the word *koinonia,* let us be clear about the world of difference between the cheaper forms of modern usage and that which indicates so inadequately the depth of the riches of Christian experience during the Eucharist. The central fact of Pentecost was that an apparently fortuitous assembly of Galilean peasants suddenly became aware that they stood in the presence of the Holy. They were under an overwhelming conviction that an unseen and living presence, *parousia,* was among them and that in his life they possessed life. It was an experience shared in common, transmitted in ever-widening circles, and clearly of a unifying quality.

Tertullian, an early doctor of the Church, after observing from his own experience and the experience of his friends how they found spiritual fulfillment in the Church upon abandoning pagan superstitions, exclaimed: "O human soul, you are Christian by your very nature." Indeed, man is a continuous seeker of the permanent and of the absolute; he is created for that purpose, and is perceptive and ready to accept it. Man is a worshiping being. Our very nature craves for union with God, and out of this inner need the worship of God is born. Symeon the New Theologian considers as heretics those who think that such communion is impossible, beyond man's nature:

A heresy is to deviate from one of the established dogmas concerning our true faith. To say that they who love God are not sound, neither are the baptized sons of God and gods granted the privilege of receiving the Holy Spirit nor of possessing the Spirit in vision, in knowledge, and in experience — such contenders who deny these things subvert the entire dispensation of God and of our Savior Jesus Christ. . . . This is the worst heresy among all the heretics!

But I call heretics also those who say that in our own day and in our midst there is none who is able to observe the precepts of the Gospel and to become as were the holy Fathers. To begin with, the most reliable and practical consideration of all is the fact that faith is demonstrated by means of works in becoming illuminated and in receiving the Holy Spirit and through the Holy Spirit beholding the Son together with the Father.

Those who contend that this is impossible are guilty of not simply one particular heresy, but of all heresies, and if one can say, exceeding and surpassing them all in ungodliness and excessiveness of blasphemy. . . . Those who state such things close heaven, which Christ opened to us; they obstruct the ascent to him which he himself initiated. Standing at the gates of heaven, bending down, seen by believers, and declaring through the Gospel, he invites: "Come unto me, all ye who labor and are heavily burdened and I will give you rest," while *antitheti* God-opposing ones, or rather the antichrists, cry out, "This is impossible! Impossible!" (*Catechesis* 4,25).

Such an experience could not but be thought of except in terms of something new. The reflective mind of subsequent generations has discovered in the experience of Pentecost a fulfillment and a vindication of the life of Jesus. The clue may be found in his reinterpretation of the holy. In sharp contradiction to current ideas which regarded the holy as something so separate and aloof as to be beyond any common experience or possession, Christ taught both by inference and by example, rather than by words, that the holy is a gift to be shared, and that the Sabbath could be enjoyed by man. The Holy, as a common heritage, and the profane and secular are to be transfigured by the holy. This change was revolutionary. This change constituted an attack on all commonly accepted values of the times and the blasphemy which ultimately led to Golgotha and the cross. Thus, the self-emptying and self-giving of the divinity to man as seen both in the humility of the Incarnation, as in the tranquil yet powerful witness of his life, and in the mystery of the Passion were followed by yet another self-giving of the holy in the power (*dynamis*) of the spirit of Pentecost.

Is this theme remote or detached from reality? Surely not; Can anything but a recapturing of the meaning of the *koinonia* of the Spirit close the broken ranks of the Church and replace the impotence with which a divided humanity faces so many miseries? In our effort to understand God as much as is humanly possible, we need to keep before us a basic fact, namely, that God reveals himself to us in order to save us. He offers himself to us and calls us to receive him. This offer is God's *philanthropia*, his love of mankind. The records of the four Gospels are nothing other than the early Church's experience of this joyful redemption, which the Evangelists empirically wanted to witness and interpret for others. This desire explains why the Eucharist was not celebrated before the catechumens and those who were in the process of initiation or who were receiving instruction. It was celebrated for the intimate friends of Christ, who had already studied the Gospels, who had come to recognize him as their Lord, God, and Savior, thus identifying themselves fully with him, even at the cost of sacrificing their own lives if necessary for their confession of faith in Christ.

Thus, the Eucharist is the triumphal celebration of those to whom St. John refers as "born again." Orthodox worship is the sublimest expression and most joyous song of the children of God, so well expressed in 1 John 1.5. Attending and/or participating in Eucharistic service means sharing in holiness and partaking in what is really "holy," for God alone is holy (Lev 11.44). Such a God can be glorified by an assembly of saints. The multitude who have joined this eucharistic gathering were born within the Church "of water and of the Spirit" (Jn 3.5) and were cleansed of their sins. They constitute the mind which alone can drive away every worldly care, and thus participate in beholding the glory and love of God in heaven. In liturgical life, God is the cause of man's salvation. On the other hand, man becomes fully resolved to serve God and his fellow-men. Through this service, God provides a heavenly content to man's whole life, so that he might become a partaker of God's kingdom. The eucharistic grace is both on earth and at the same time in heaven. It is both earthly according to its external and visible aspects and heavenly according to its spiritual content. The ultimate goal of every sacrament is to arrest the destructive process of one who is drifting away from the family of the redeemed and then to revitalize the flow of vital forces of the "living water," of the grace-bestowing life into man's life. All the prayers which are offered by the Church militant and by the Church triumphant seek to protect and to strengthen the faithful. Thus, God bestows sacred content to human life by drawing near man through the sacraments. As a result of this nearness, earthly life participates in the process of the divine economy of salvation, and life becomes imbued with holiness. The Eucharist becomes in a sense the ladder of Jacob by which man's reason ascends and descends from earthly to heavenly realities and from the celestial to the temporal. Along this ladder the mind moves back and forth between heaven and earth.

Every contact with eucharistic worship helps man to enter into communion with God and to remain truly alive, truly pure and even purifying others. In this sense worship is indispensable as the path of ascent to holiness. Being sanctified, we then return to the struggles of daily life with new strength and vigor in order to continue the good fight.

Westerners often refer to Eastern worship and the Eastern way of thinking as totally devoid of rational thought, identifying it instead with abstract and vague religiosity. While we maintain an ignorance on the spiritual issues of our faith, it cannot be held that this ignorance is complete. Symbols and analogies convey to us in the form of images what our spirit cannot otherwise attain. Cyril of Jerusalem, instructing the catechumens, states that after he exposed his catechetical homilies, yet another kind of language for the communicating of the supreme truths of our faith also existed, namely, the mysteries. For him the " mysteries," that is liturgical offices, with all their rituals and symbols constitute another way of teaching, of educating, and of uplifting listeners to other-worldly realities. An apocalyptic imagery goes beyond man's ability to know. It stands for something that we do know and even completes what we do not know. When Plato warns us that we must be content with a "myth," he is very far from suggesting that any myth will do, or that one myth is as good as another. Plato held the strongest opinions possible about the misleading tendency of the old myths. In fact, he chose his own myth with the greatest of care. If we tell a myth, he would say, it must be a "likely myth," a myth that suggests the right meaning and contains the right moral values (*Timaeus*, 29). Since human nature, fallen and finite, cannot attain to the whole truth that God offers to reveal, he is caught up in awe, ecstasy, and divine love. God must be sought and loved for his own sake. St. Augustine says: "All human perversity or vices consist in wishing to enjoy what we ought to use, and to use what we ought to enjoy" (*Quaestiones*, 30). At the heart of the Christian life lies this paradox, that only by coming to care more about God than about either our own character or our own destiny can our character be transformed. The transference of attention from the self to God is the secret of noble souls aflame and burning with the fire of divine *eros*, of self-conquest, and of hope.

32. A Crisis in Man's Understanding of Nature

Humanity needs a different set of priorities in order to better administer the world and its natural resources. In this respect, what patristic spirituality defines as *askesis* can serve as a useful guide. *Askesis* means to limit one's needs, to impose restrictions, to put earthly appetites under control. In terms of the human commodities necesssary to his existence, man must impose imperative guiding principles and a certain discipline. Such a discipline cannot be attained only by means of laws and/or by some universal declaration by the international community. How many wonderful laws remain only on paper and are not respected by the citizenry? Each person must take seriously the effects of his lifestyle upon his environment as well as on the human or natural milieu. My attitude to the material, the arrangement of the economy, or the philosophy of a factory owner, taking into account the existing relationship between the foreseen gains and the eventual repercussions upon the natural wealth, of irresponsible publicity and a disregard that often even small deviations become, on a wider scale, an important public matter — all of these are important. They are important because even small things constitute a serious threat to the natural balance and the survival of vital raw materials. Statistics on the resources of nature show that these are continuously diminishing and declining.

A selfish approach to such matters, the counting on schemes exclusively for profit and commercial success by the powerful industrialists, who put a priority on their own comfort and an unnecessary accumulation of goods. The excessively consuming societies in which we live now, by all estimations, cannot be viable for long. They will inevitably die if they continue to follow the same mentality and ignore the immense risks for our common future. The modification, therefore, of our habits and ways of living becomes urgent. Our actual order of priorities is based on miscalculated, short-term aims and goals. We become difficult to restrain or control when we want to increase the production and expansion of industries at any price. Sometime soon, before it is too late, man must impose a self-discipline upon his insatiable appetite for wanting more, spending more, and wasting more. In order to achieve this vision, man needs to think in terms of a global view and not of a narrow outlook which only serves his own personal greediness and bows before the idol of the self.

The whole question concerning the use or misuse of material resources is not purely an economic issue. It is related to the finality of human life. What is the purpose of man's life? His goal and his exclusive interest cannot be restricted merely to profits or to investments serving endless avidity, "bulimia," but all these interests should serve a higher plan, a different view of our existence, because the life hereafter very much depends upon how we conduct ourselves with the resources and gifts entrusted to us by God during this lifetime. Going beyond the pressing compulsions of the self and the flesh ceases then to be merely a utopia and becomes a victorious reality because we are not left alone in this immense universe. We no longer only serve the earth, but we place earthly needs on a higher perspective. We are under God's care. There is, in each one's life and in the general history of mankind, a direct intervention of God's love and power. The God of Christianity is a God who is the Father of all, full of *philanthropia.* We then are not only God's creatures but also God's people. We have also received from such a God a specific mandate, innate within us, to become like him, to become his image. Consequently, it is in such a continuously controlled process of correctly administering the natural resources of the earth that we realize our important mission as God's children, which consists in transforming the world in conformity with its sublime dignity, since it was redeemed by the Incarnation of Christ. This redemption of all earthly worries will result in hindering the spread of anarchy, will keep natural wealth from becoming a tyranny or a source of conflicts, tensions, and slavery for human beings because of God's continuous mandate to us. This control must be exercised in response to God's explicit mandate to royal service, that we administer goods on his behalf. This implies that man's liberty is conditioned. Man must give an account of his assigned management to his Creator, as is recorded in Genesis 1.28. In assuming such an attitude, he can show, in concrete ways, how great is the degree of his participation in God's plan, which is sharing and thus reaffirming the "community aspect" of the universal family.

A rigorous diagnosis of our technological civilization reveals the damage previously made by scientists and economists by their paroxysmal praise of production and consummation as the two factors which guarantee the dream of prosperity and economic growth. Our society has to be liberated from all such pernicious ideals, attitudes, and similar theories about progress which were expressed during the last century. What really is progress? Instead of moving onwards and upwards, we are, in fact, relying exclusively on economic growth as a sole criterion. As a result we are now standing before a terrible degradation of human relations which threatens to devastate even our educational system and to produce generations suffering from hypertrophied rationalism, overladened brains, but empty hearts. Our generation, moreover, no longer believes in our culture. It is with sad feelings that we witness a certain systematic accusation which enumerates all our misconceptions and which for decades influenced our way of life. Reason was excessively deified, and all its worshipers were proposing a glorious future. But in the midst of this hysteria and enthusiasm about industrialization, man forgot that the human spirit is merely an instrument and nothing more. It is not a sovereign conscience controlling the mystery of human life and destiny, or even of God and his transcendence. Reason readily knows its limitations, that it does not know everything. Subsequently, a space always remains for the unexpected possibility, for what is "probable." The real value, the real pleasure comes only when human existence is open, looking beyond its own needs, when it is related to, and in attendance upon, the other. Reason, also, must be redefined. It accomplishes its role when it desires properly and honestly, when it keeps well within its defined place. Within such dimensions, a balanced life is constructed. Success must never be sought at the expense of other vital requirements and, above all, at the expense of our own real selves.

A relationship also exists between overstated reason and subjectivism. Up to a certain point, subjectivism is legitimate, but not when it is taken to excess. Excess of subjectivism which dogmatically affirms opinions, or the inverse excess of pseudo-objectivity, can only be confronted by people who are engaged together on behalf of the real welfare of the world. The human spirit seeks a liberation from its self-imprisonment and from its oppressive chains, as it did in the days of Epicurus. This philosopher expected nothing from the gods. For him, the world had nothing to do with metaphysical research. This universe in his view was a mechanical dance of atoms, regulated by *tyche* — mythical fortune. But such views lead to despair, paralyzing any creative effort on the part of man. They create a fatalistic approach expressed by a contempt and indifference for the universe, and furthermore, even lead to the abolition of any reference to God, or of any religious quest, as well as to the disappearance of links with otherworldly realities.

Human greed and an irrational attitude to the blessings of the earth do not know any limits today. Man proceeds from one abuse to another, always wanting more, while offending the biophysical balance, always exploiting more, at the expense of man's own interest, both material and as well as spiritual. When in Genesis the Creator asked our forefathers "to cultivate" the earth, he gave them at the same time all the necessary criteria to distinguish between the limits of what is legitimate and useful and that point when everything becomes illogical, destructive, and abusive. In recent years, because of pollution, alarming voices from all corners indicate that the industrialized countries live beyond reasonable limits. This charge must be applied not only to particular cases, but must also be applied in more general, global terms. Isolated countries do not alone bear the heavy responsibility for such violations and transgressions; all humanity seems to be living a lifestyle that is beyond what is sound and reasonable. How then, one may ask, is this possible? Statistics do not reveal any noteworthy commercial deficit, but announce prosperity and higher output of goods. We must examine this extremely vital problem from a totally different angle altogether.

Man's abuses actually are alarming since they are made at the expense of his own personal future. In other words, man borrows or takes a loan in order to build his future, but in reality he is consuming the capital and the effective yield of that capital at the same time. Specialists on this topic speak about vital human resources which are being wasted or misused. Humanity, in other words, has become self-destructive and suicidal. The case of petroleum, for example, is significant. Petroleum's very cheap cost over a long period played a role. As a result, petroleum was used instead of other energy resources thought to be more rare and even more costly. The extensive use of raw materials derived from oil, in addition, obscured the problem, and, because natural fibers were not grown, there was an increasing limit to cultivable land. Synthetic fibers replaced the natural fibers. Such a comfortable pillow, upon which our society was lazily sleeping, was overthrown by the two recent terrible international oil crises. Only then did humanity begin to become conscious of the progressive shortage of certain resources and began to readjust itself to new realities. Today, we are able to estimate the world oil resources with greater precision. Experts now conclude that in approximately one hundred years all oil reserves will allow only for minimum production and perhaps may even have disappeared.

Such awareness, which may at times reach even to apocalyptical visions of disorder and its concomitant panic, has obviously had a blessed effect. All efforts and plans toward conserving energy and reclaiming it for reuse, however, do not offer the real solution to the grave issue before us. Although this awakening has already had a salutary result, it is not enough. It is only marginal in comparison with the importance of the whole problem which is the proper existence and future of humanity itself. The acute problem of the lack of cultivable land reveals the importance of this problem, since at first glance, land constitutes such an enormous source of potential wealth, about which nobody must worry. Nevertheless, realities have shown that it is time to question frankly all our accepted criteria and to see the dangerous world-wide situation.

In reality, the cultivable earth is a species in the process of gradual extinction. The actual methods used in cultivation, of the Third World and industrialized nations as well, require more space and more extended areas. At the same time, all kinds of abuses are indirectly producing an alarming erosion of the soil, making many parts of the earth completely unusable for cultivation. How strange it is that nobody speaks of this particular crisis which, unlike the oil crisis, already exists now and is slowly but invisibly persisting on its destructive course. Is it necessary to await the destruction of enormous territories of good soil or the appearance of dramatic droughts and famines in order for humanity to become conscious of the imminent danger? Forests are also progressively disappearing since they are attacked by foolish human activities and pollution, victimizing meadows, fields, and woods. And what is true of the earth is equally true of the sea, which is affected by continuous pollution and by unbalanced fishing procedures which take excessive quantities of fish. Statistics clearly reveal the results of such policies — the fishing catch is decreasing every year while some species are becoming very rare or are totally disappearing.

Many scientists fear that any loss of the great genetic diversity which characterizes a "natural" world might put the survival of the world itself in danger, since the human and the natural world are totally interdependent. Are we capable of facing all these accumulated dangers with less superficiality and more generosity by adopting less destructive ways and more constructive strategies? (See: Edward Way,

State of the World 1984 (New York, 1984).

How long will human beings treat these natural resources as an enemy by being bad neighbors to nature in its cosmic dimension, and not as a friend? Every time man ill-treats the earth, it takes its vengeance, not because of any fault in it, but because the earth is continuously provoked and insulted by its inhabitants.

A relationship was established from the very beginning so that humanity might take advantage of the earth as much as possible, but always bearing in mind certain conditions and limitations. Thus, patristics state that man is the *oikonomos,* the steward and administrator who is able to develop a clever "economic cybernetics," by the use and not the misuse of his natural resources. But man in his paroxysm of greed persisted in unacceptable, anarchic, disorderly exploitation, and today we see the disastrous results of such disrespect of the laws of nature.

Most of the proposed alternatives regarding the vital problem of maintaining the environment in as healthy a state as possible ignore reality. A risky proposal without discernment or sufficient research becomes in the long run dangerous for the whole community. In other words, the "better" way is often the enemy of the good. For example, many of those who desire the abolition of automobiles are victims of pure demagogy. At present, there is no alternative to private cars as a means of circulation and transportation.

The historically sharp separation of intellectual disciplines inevitably led to the fragmentation of man's very being or psyche. Indirectly, this separation contributed to the production of certain types of closed individualists whose capacities of perception became limited by an over-specialization. Often a specialist is in reality scattered in incoherent worlds. Let us look a little deeper as to how this problem came to pass.

Knowledge originally aimed at the acquisition of universal and general information. As time passed, this method became defective; its lack of unity gave way to a multiplicity of approaches on scientific matters. It became even more impossible to know everything within one specialized field. Paradoxically, the more one takes up a field, the more unknown elements eventually emerge. Sometimes, higher university study leads to an accumulation of more ignorance rather than of more knowledge, thus confirming that Socratic paradox: "All that I know is that I know nothing." In this way limited science was inaugurated and consequently the limitation of real wisdom.

Now western philosophy, deviating from classical roots, began to be separated from nature and consequently from a living wisdom. One of the sad effects of the Renaissance was the confusion between individuality and personhood. The human person should be seen in its relationship — its openness, its social life — and not as the egoistic self-centered unit of individualism. Such a risky departure started with the invention of the concept of "being," which was separated from objects, and accentuated not simply the will but the undisciplined, egoistic will. Descartes' statement: "I think, consequently I exist," resulted in a hypertrophy of the self, limiting it to thinking, but at a great expense to its ontological, infinite, and unlimited realty. Thus, Western philosophy became a theatre of light and shadow, where object and subject fight each other. From such a philosophy about an exclusive, independent, and exaggerated being, separated from his action, there emerged in time many other issues. In the East, on the contrary, truth was associated with human life, in deeds lived and experienced. Truth transformed into mere thought was impossible, because of the living reality. But science in the West became detached from living wisdom.

Thus, as an inevitable result, we have the primacy of "infinite evil," so important to Hegel. By by-passing transcendence, the West tried to find the infinite not in an interior life, but in matter, in strength, in speed, in material success, and in a spectacular outcome. But even when all these things are gained, we realize how little meaning they have given to our life. We see the futility of such motivations in many sporting events, where people with cars are forever seeking the speedier, the super, the more, a competition without meaning, without the cultivation of a noble spirit as in classical athleticism. For a passionate driver, what counts is the supreme pleasure of driving at a maximum speed even if he goes nowhere. This divorce between science and wisdom has resulted in an accumulation of explosive, original ideas, but since it was not guided by any moral principle whatever, it inevitably lost its consistency and consequently only served vanity and ill-conceived liberty, which is an evil thing. But nobody can put a halt to such a widely accepted notion of progress. Man, in this way, has lost sight of the possibilities of inner progress and inner expansion. In such a paroxysm, of course, he blindly perpetuates an economic machine whose progress has become synonymous with self-destruction. Our view of things, although it may seem to be rather pessimistic, nevertheless, bears within it an optimistic ethical lesson, namely, the need and the imperative necessity of reconciling science with wisdom. This is the urgent task of future pedagogues and a necessary orientation for teaching at our universities.

The intellectual systems in ancient Greece were rather synthetic and unitarian. Teaching was based upon an encyclopedic formation, that is, a circular perfection of a wholistic knowledge, containing many elements. For the Greeks and the Latins, the development of the intelligence in general presupposed the accomplishment of a long intellectual voyage. The *orbis doctrinae* was marked by successive initiations necessary for the knowledge of one's self. In the Middle Ages, the West still managed to preserve the universality of knowledge in institutions which sought to provide authentic instruction of those generations. A course of studies or "liberal arts" was instituted in order to seek and to find the unity of man and of the cosmos. It was during the Renaissance that a revolutionary fragmentation broke down the ideal circle of the *orbis doctrinae*. Frustrated humanity, marching along in confusion and in darkness, ignores the sense of real solidarity or any need of a transcending help and wisdom as a complement. Specialization thus produced an epistemological cancerization. The many various schools of humanism, each teaching its own system of "how to know," hardly helps man to find his deeper needs and his exceptional place in the immensity of this universe. This "distortion of the mental space" destroys any possibility for a universal or encyclopedic knowledge, and consequently fullness or completeness is not attained.

Scientific inquiry and wisdom became dissociated by means of the rise of specialization which became a dividing tool rather than a uniting agent. This division caused a general alienation which terrifies and alarms the human mind, because man no longer knows himself and he behaves foolishly against his own interests. But the human man is the goal as well as the source of knowledge, and the development of a certain sub-activity remains our last hope of unifying all knowledge by providing a fulcrum. Real knowledge, in fact, is based not only upon the mind but also has reference to, and is structured in, the conscience. Excessive attention to specialization itself could lead to a grave blindness, if the means for the unification of the diversity of knowledge was not sought at the same time. There is an urgent need to reunite all the disciplines in question for the benefit of our sick civilization. Only in this manner can man escape a new slavery which may come from science. This unification also implies a reformation of any distortions in an all too human-centered anthropology and the necessity of showing that any technological progress and discovery is being made precisely for the sake of man's welfare and not as an end unto itself. In addition, we need an interdisciplinary concept which may also open man to his neighbor and which might reveal their common similarities rather than their dissimilarities. Far from us is any underestimation of learning and progress. What we mean to say is that the quest for more knowledge in modern times is really situated within a passionate, disorderly, onesided, intellectual situation. Limitless specialization, idealized by the passionate worshipers of a certain form of anthropocentrism, has brought about an epistemological fragmentation. Scientists, expending all their efforts to know more and more in fields which are less and less spacious, will finally end up knowing far too much about nothing. Starting from an unbalanced attitude affects the human personality in its entirety. Such a scientific alienation, no doubt, remains one of the causes of the malady in our contemporary civilization. At the beginning, knowledge (from the Latin *scio*, to know) was the search for a science of totality, embracing the fullness of human life. Such knowledge, sanctioned by tradition, gave access to the secret reality of the soul and to the wisdom of life. The Socratic "revolution," in opening the way for an intelligent and comprehensive knowledge-learning, led to a salutary evolution of the idea of the conscience in its connection with the object and laid the basis for a proper kind of rationalization.

History is written between two diametrically opposed concepts. The one wants to see God alone as entirely responsible and the sole factor for determining the continuum of human affairs. The other, reaching the other extreme, seeks man alone as the only factor responsible for the shaping of the affairs of this life, refusing to recognize any interference from God. We may call these two opposite streams providentialism and activism.

Providentialism teaches that all events in life, good or bad, are God's entire responsibility. God is bound to his creation. He alone, therefore, must show his almighty power by taking care of all; otherwise, what kind of God is he and should he reaffirm his lordship over the universe? Such a divine "providence" in the minds of a few people, in order to justify its divinity, has to show its might in terms of continuous miracles, and consequently has to do things that our limited competence could not accomplish. We need, of course, to pray for the poor and hungry, but as human beings, it is not up to us to go beyond in order to change structures, injustices, and to invent the means for helping and manifesting our solidarity. But such a prayer life, separated from any human action, runs the risk of distorting our image of God and of diminishing man to a childish, impotent level.

But God in no way wants to replace man's liberty and capacity when he can do all things that are assigned to him, but he only wants to inspire, to sustain, and to help him in order that he might do his duties well.

God's role and attitude are very discreet, even in moments when he seems so terribly silent. But it would be blasphemous to imagine our being in this cosmos as simply a passive marionette, played from behind a dark screen by God, while we ourselves are unable to do anything by our own will. Total resignation and submission, like a slave blindly executing God's orders without showing the least degree of sharing, would be unworthy of a Christian god as well as unworthy of man or woman.

The activist approach proposes that man alone can carry the future of the world on his shoulders. Being empty of any esoteric life and deprived of any moments of contemplation, man comes to the stage of living the stress or fever of "doing," "overdoing," "now," all being urgent, quick, efficient, productive, regardless of whether they serve a higher purpose or not. For such a human type, the formulation of projects and plans is foremost, because they are accountable and measurable by man's brain and so will certainly lead to successful completion. But then, he does not dominate his action. He is turned to the left and then to the right by the winds of upheaval and is not clear of events. He often shows moments of triumphalism, trying to persuade himself that all is going well, as if they were foreseen. Such an activist runs the risk of reducing the good news of Christ to his own limited measure and horizon of interest, confining God to his own proper projects, to his social class, and even daring to identify God as an accomplice to his dubious passions or weaknesses. He also risks the danger of sacralizing his ideology as truly human, absolutizing what is only human or even letting himself to be chained or unconsciously led by it, overestimating it, and reaching such degradation as to become a simple tool.

Neither the providentialists nor the activists have ever realized the honor and the grandeur of the collaboration between God and man. We can never increase God's dignity by decreasing man's dignity. They never elevate man by lowering God. Only man, being both free and responsible, reflects the devine image bestowed upon him and actualizes the action of God. In such a case, prayer constitutes one of the greatest activities of man. Prayer stands at the crossroads of this extraordinary collaboration between Creator and creature. If God takes the initiative in this adventure, he nevertheless can do nothing without the consent of man. Prayer, therefore, above all else allows God to do his divine duties, while man, as a truly human being, is enabled also to do his. Prayer is not simply a theoretical acknowledgment of God's majesty, that he is one in three. It acknowledges and accepts God's action within the individual and often through him even for the benefit of others and of the world. The most privileged place in which God desires to realize his plans, to create, to be revealed, and to work is man's conscience, his innermost being.

Prayer is to be loved by God, to allow him to express his love to the supplicant and to shape him according to the measure of his love, so that he can create in him what he wants him to become. In the silence and tears of his prayer, man does not flee from his responsibilities. He can reconvert and re-orient his daily deeds in the dynamism of love and Christian hope. Indeed, at the heart of human history two agents work together: God and man. How can a Christian remain vigilant in the midst of this chaos of contradictory forces, adversities and the turmoil of life, if he does not possess an inner life? Who, then, is the main actor in his life: God or man? Both, of course, together. For this reason, God creates within us renewed appeals, calling each one for new commitment and re-orientation of his life.

The Orthodox are often accused by Westerners of following an ethereal approach to life and of not taking seriously the importance of the economic order and the administration of everything which is connected with money. On the contrary, the American clergy are said to be more pragmatic and to penetrate better into the economic world of what is called "business" and "marketing," thus influencing the earthly city and the wider economic life. Orthodox clergy have, in fact, never produced any economists in the strict sense of specialists who could produce a moral deontological code of "affairs." Max Weber in 1905 wrote a book entitled *Protestant Ethics and the Spirit of Capitalism*. In this work, the whole spirit of a reformed economist tried to express his feelings, fully aware of an individual's conscience concerning economic matters in the presence of the Lord. Taking into account the gifts which have been a divine blessing and recognizing a responsible stewardship, reformed scholars more than others favored development and the spirit of success, of prosperity, and of initiative in a capitalistic business. Puritan morals offer a firm attitude concerning the multiplication and earning of money. Surely idealizing wealth and affluence merits further investigation of its real underlying motivations. One must remember that those community-traders, bank owners of the Middle Ages, were mostly Protestants. It is a fact that Anglo-Saxons have no hesitation dealing with the most complex questions concerning earning.

To produce a parallel ethics or "spirituality" dealing with money-earning, exploiting capital, and other material resources is distant from our understanding. This "spirituality," namely, that manual work has a redeeming effect on the soul and all that concerns the inner world, seems rather to be related to a Jansenist rigorism which contributed to the formulation of a conscience of labor rather than of success and profit. Profits are placed on a secondary level. If one could assess the value of labor from a Christian point of view, he would state that the conscience of work and doing this work well and honestly must have priority and indeed predominate. In this way whole generations of administrators and honest dealers were formed. A systematic guide for the morality of affairs will not have a difficult birth in the Orthodox Church. It is equally true that in our day with unemployment and monetary uncertainty, a clear position becomes impossible on such controversial questions as higher industrial output, investment, productivity, neo-liberalism, planification, etc. What should count above all else is that every task be well done, rather than attaching any excessive importance to the resulting profits and/or successes.

Modern life is developing at such a rapid pace and in such a way that man is constantly forced to seek more and more comfort, more irresponsible jobs, and less labor, manual or intellectual. All lips seem to repeat the slogan: easy earning without doing anything which involves hardship, pain, or effort. Some of the poor seek wealth at any price. They are eager to become rich, the sooner the better, just by relying on unreliable lotto, sweepstakes, and on gambling. Such dubious games as card-playing, prognostics on horses, betting on football players, animal races, etc., are therefore flourishing. All these get rich quick schemes should be seen as the deformed view of life of a consuming and permissive society. We avoid, even loathe, the slightest degree of difficulty. Even in maternity hospitals, childbirth is made as painless as possible.

Consequently, "this is a great problem" is used only to describe a normal, important obstacle. Today people designate as "problems" things which are elementary and small — the smallest of things. They dramatize them, exaggerating their gravity adding: "This is a great problem." Such an excessively sensitive mentality reveals a forgetfulness, an amnesia, that our life on earth is full of hardships and cannot be conceived carelessly or without worry. Such a life simply does not exist and has never existed. Life as such is always associated with one or another kind of suffering or warfare and with endurance and work. We are dreamers if we think we can live in the real existential sense of the word without doing anything, preferring to remain idle, fatalistically allowing all things to come to us by themselves, ready-made, without our moving even the tips of our fingers. Indolence and idleness cannot be reconciled with living organisms and with human beings. As such, man has to work continuously against his own distorted nature, overcoming difficulties, disturbing sufferings, and even managing to transform them into productive channels for his spirituality. And more so, he cannot rely on what others do for him, even the benefits of the welfare state or organizations and protecting laws. He has to contribute to the general good, becoming creative as much as possible, not remaining a simple consumer or spectator, but being instead an effective contributor. We forget that obstacles exist for our own interest, namely, to awaken within ourselves inactive inner resources, to stimulate sleepy forces, to push us toward a more constructive and creative life. Without adversaries and difficulties life loses its meaning, its purpose, and we are all the more attached to a futile, ephemeral existence, cut off from the ultimate goal.

To a great extent, the solution and successful approach to the human tragedy depends upon man's own capacity. Sometimes he insists upon facing this tragedy by himself. But in the case where he systematically ignores that he is a created, temporal being — fallen, distorted, and therefore depending upon an outside "thou" — then the problems will accumulate even more and become even more tragic, because he is a referential being, compelled to seek some reference for everything that he is doing and looking for concerning his innermost aspirations and visions. Any self-reliant attitude which refuses transcendent help, God's intervention, not only leads to a kind of *hybris*, an unattractive self-confident arrogance, but will actually undermine man's own security. We always risk overestimating our "scientific conquest," progress and potential force, to the point that we may even misinterpret the Psalmist's words, and, seeing our own proper splendor, be led to a blinded autonomy: "You have beset me behind and before, and laid your hand upon me" (Ps 139. 5).

There is no doubt that powers of enormous potentiality have been bestowed on man. Angels are "below him in honor," and he is somehow godlike. But the delicate and decisive point is whether he wants to go it alone, by means of his own powers. Certainly, he is created in the "image of God" and is created for an ever-increasing advancement. But he is not an accomplished god — he is a god in a process of becoming. This implies that he is called to become another God but only together with the Creator God, and never without him. The cause of spiritual growth and of sanctification is found not in man but in God. He is unable to do even the least of things as long as he distances himself from his Creator. For this reason, the Bible often reminds him that God is always "near" to him, "available," "ready to help," Emmanuel, the Pantokrator, co-runner, etc. Without this theological prerequisite, man makes himself the measure of all things, the center of the universe, falling into all kinds of extreme, egoistic, self-centered philosophies, cultures, and systems. He absolutizes things which are only relative, futile, deceitful, and temporal. Obscured thus by his own pride, he is made dizzy, and consequently he is unable to catch the mystery of life.

The more he ignores God, the more he is bound to his own passions, attached to himself, and yet leaving his own self forgotten in an illusionary state of pseudo-progress. Thus, the alienation is consumed, he remains a stranger to himself, dispersed and scattered in the attractive pleasures which are in him and around him. Finally, he remains empty and alone, plunged in a tragic vacuum, both spiritual and social. It is a pity that he even intentionally ignores his own fallen nature, inseparably surrounded by sufferings and adversities. As a result he sees so many false, unreal hopes dying in his inner world, while he refuses to live his real humanity.

The churches are questioning themselves concerning the changes and mutations going on within themselves. Particular groups are organizing themselves such as the laity, clergy, etc., and initiating new experiments in community living. Some people suggest that parish institutions and apostolic movements are no longer adequate to the current needs of Christians. It would be naive to believe that new church forms will suddenly spring up miraculously from accidental and often very brief encounters.

But parishes sometimes lack the flexibility and the dynamic breadth of outlook: they want to control everything just as if they by themselves represented the whole Church of today and tomorrow. A better solution could be that instead of being suspicious of every new community experiment, those responsible for the parishes should, rather, encourage such initiatives. These little communities of

Christians who know each other well and are conscious of gathering together around Christ's eucharistic table could stimulate the larger parish or apostolic community on the condition that the latter not reject them.

This cooperation demands a serious effort within the domain of theological education. A temporal-spiritual distinction is insufficient. To get out of this dilemma, the terms of the problem must be modified. Today we stand in need of a form of thinking that is unifying, capable of envisaging the whole of man's future in the light of the Word of God, and of a new Christian synthesis, which would guarantee the inclusion of the contribution of modern culture. This synthesis must also be implemented with a view to action which presupposes a Christian analysis of human experience. What is man, and what is that society which must be aided by different efforts in the fields of teaching, liturgical sanctification, education for life in the community, and social commitment? What can be the specific contribution of Christians to this new civilization and the innumerable absurdities that one has to deal with so frequently?

To meet this situation and its demands, Christian mission should have no other aim than to set the good news before men in search of hope, to encourage, and to arrange contacts. We must offer this service in this world which makes us strangers to each other. To gather together around Christ those who are seeking him, whether they have already found Him or not: this task is not optional but a major one for all practicing or militant Christians, who are always inclined to give value to secondary matters. Should not the prime responsibility of the ministers of the Gospel be to keep these little communities alive through the Word, the liturgy, prayer, and fraternal sharing?

It would be an over-simplication to believe that a totally new Church is in the process of coming to birth and that the existing parishes and movements are about to be replaced by far fewer communities, whose vocation would be to bear witness rather than to organize or act. The reality is more complex. These little communities, the current forms of Christians coming together, can reanimate yesterday's institutions and structures — which are often very heavy and cumbersome and which often lead to weariness and confusion. To that end the bringing together of Christians, on the basis of the Gospel, must become the principal aim of the Church. Given these conditions, ecumenism will be concerned not only with relations between the churches, but also with relations between the larger and smaller communities. The institutions, on all levels, will have as their aim the fostering of communion. The risk, and it is a real one, is that one might end up with the pulverizing of the Church, but this risk could be avoided if, beginnning now, we were able to pick out and favor those community experiments which are capable of reforming and forming the Church from within.

Christianity aims at the normal functioning of all that constitutes the human being, thus reconstituting the order or *taxis* which we lost because of Adam's fall. Nothing in itself is satanic. On the contrary, natural human instincts are the raw material of both virtue and vice; they may be "a savor of life unto life or of death unto death" (2 Cor 2.16). Because man is not only an animal but also a spiritual being, the merely instinctive gratification of his natural impulses cannot, as with the animals, be the fulfillment of his nature. He must transform the disharmony and asymmetry which come from the striving of the flesh against the spirit and the spirit against the flesh. This should be done neither by the suppression of the flesh nor by the quenching of the spirit, for a victory of the one which involves the crushing of the other can only issue in a maimed sort of life. True victory is the unification of a full human nature under the freely accepted way of its highest faculties.

Man so often chooses what can only hurt him, because the strength of his appetites, his impulses, instincts, and passions and his nature in a very imperfect society impair his vision and determine those choices in which the apparently desirable usurps the place of the true good. Christ regarded sinners like sheep gone astray, as lost or blind; this understanding is often the most true precisely when the sinner thinks he knows full well what he is doing. If the light within is darkness, how great is the darkness?

Without the consciousness of a *telos*, an ideal for human life, a sufficient motive for the self-regulation or sublimation of natural inclinations is hard to find; without the inspiration of a divine activity the sense of higher obligation is feeble and fitful. The realization of the presence of God is the surest means toward the transvaluation of life's values which, by promoting harmony in human nature, opens the door to its true joys. "When a man . . . has attained to a genuine religious faith and convinced himself that he stands in the presence of God, he is sure he has stood there from the beginning." He is unable to conceive his initial turning to God other than as a response to the divine action upon his soul.

33. Transcending Structures

We were mistaken in the past, and perhaps are mistaken in the present too, in relying on the adjective Christian in Christian society, Christian civilization, Christian school. We were thinking, perhaps, in terms of a security, a defensive line against secular forces. Once somebody entered into such a setting, he was thinking not so much of his own initiative, but that of others — of the existing structure — and this would do the rest for his spiritual growth. It is now time, however, to rediscover the real way to our salvation. It is not to be found in the number of values, commandments, ideas or established rules reflected in a given society. Christian life, above all, is to be found in the mystery of Christ's incarnation. It is on this basis that the daily life and behavior of a baptized person is developed, grown, shaped. Such a life is not always spectacular, visible, or tangible, like a human work. Like Christ, it, too, is something humble, invisible, calm, quiet — and for a secular mind it is sometimes painful to discover this hidden thing. Such a life does not make any noise or publicity. A special effort is required to see it, and once you discover it, then you need to proceed toward it with admiration in order to communicate with it.

Such an authentic life, at first sight, does not attract, because it is not ornamented with attractive or impressive jewelry. Its very essence is that of the simplicity and poverty of the shepherds at the manger of the baby Christ. A pure soul has other distinctive elements which often escape the profane eye. A special way of reaching it is imposed, and Gregory the Theologian helps us to understand this mystery: "All those who want to penetrate this mystery are driven by a special motivation, and having entered into the very interior place, they are worthy to see that beauty and then are illuminated by the light of celestial knowledge" (*Theolog. Oratio* 5). We are mistaken if we identify a Christian with the exterior appearance, or his religious observances, thus thinking that we can so represent the Gospel. The identification has to do with genuine simplicity and sincerity rather than any self-reliance. Often we think that we are self-sufficient and what is needed is a small bit of Christianity as well. This is a kind of Pharisaism which contaminates many religious circles. We seem to be like the Pharisee of the well-known parable — feeling filled, complete, full of ritual piety. Real faith has little place when

Christianity becomes a scholastic system, with rules and external observances — leaving the inner world empty, without holy visions, flame of the heart or the fire of truth.

An approach to Christ is made with sincerity, but accompanied also with a quest for more and more, with an open heart, which the Gospel designates as trust, attachment that is deep and continuous. It is not enough to pretend that "I am Christian living in a Christian milieu," and therefore justify the fact that we are not "complete" Christians. We become Christians continuously until the last moment of our life. I am en route — *in via* — on an ascending route. Whoever has closed his dealings with Christ, thinking that nothing more is left for his advancement, will remain on the periphery of illusion, and not in communion with Christ. Gregory of Nyssa helps us to understand the way to meet Christ and to remain forever with him:

> The discovery of God is a continuous following after him, a seeking of him forever. There is a difference between this movement towards searching God and finding God . . . And seeing God really is this, namely, never to feel a satiety of our holy desire. Yet, we must always look forward, as much as possible, more and more being burned by this ardent desire (*72 Comment. on Ecclesiast. Homily* 7).

This patristic reminder is timely, because we are surrounded today by so many depressing factors in our society. These factors often become oppressive idols, driving us by their fascination against our will to ends which do not correspond with our aspirations. Consequently, if one does not possess strong roots of personality he, like the wind, is led here and there by the many pressures of an affluent society. A type of unstable man results who is not really what he seems to be. Many people speak of liberty, but are far from capturing its reality. Man becomes impersonal, anonymous, unknown. He ceases to pose questions, since everything is done by the State. Finally, he finds that he has to do what others do. A Christian resists such a danger of subjugation, and this resistance differentiates him from others who accept such enslavement. A Christian freely chooses his own way of life. In this lies the real sense of liberty, in refusing compromise with evil. The life of faith cannot be counted by economists; it is out of reach of ethnologists, with their statistics and laboratory observations. Here we see the greatest miracle in history — the miracle of the people of God, the miracle of all the saints.

Absolute self-surrender to an established totalitarian regime and socially-accepted moral code or institution, excluding the elementary liberty of choice and of personal cooperation of men and women, will sooner or later show its weakness, namely, its lack of viability. Its strength will remain doubtful and uncertain. To be sure, a minimum of popular consensus, in the wider sense of the term, is necessary for the proper functioning of a moral principle as the foundation of a healthy society. But above all, moral principles do not depend on people. They must be based upon a full contribution of each one concerned, so that they do not stand in a vacuum, as a sort of misleading exterior cover, while the interior is desperately empty, hiding all kinds of anomalies and deviations. In order to make this point clearer, we can take as an example the current, well-established belief about the value of marriage and its institutionalized respect in most of the world's societies. Much of its credibility was perhaps due to its sanctity as clearly stated in the scriptures, to the praise of the institution as offered by the churches, and to the traditional patterns of more or less Christian societies. Civil legislation also sustained its legal authority and its prestige, severely punishing all violations, i.e., adultery and all other kinds of unfaithfulness, with severe consequences, as, for example obliging the guilty partner to suffer all the material and all the moral consequences. While civil legislation in the most official way confronted the deplorable consequences of matrimonial decline, little was done to remind couples concerning a right sexual behavior. Little was done to cultivate the creative process of improving the lives of the two partners, in keeping them truly united in mutual respect for their vows as consecrated bodies and souls, and in the upbringing of their children in purity and chastity. Marriage implies mutual enjoyment and support, responsible parenthood and the common life of two beings, but as such, it inevitably brings tensions and unforeseen conflicts. Couples need to be prepared and strengthened so that both parties will be able to face life's difficulties and challenges and to maintain unity, sanctifying themselves and each other and being sanctified by the grace of God.

Due to the absence of a common commitment and a conscious engagement, we are facing a precarious situation concerning marriage as the foundation of the family's sacred bond. We need to look at the present situation and its causes with courage and honesty. Not only in what are called industrialized societies, but even in rural ones, the number of officially registered marriages is declining. Marriage is becoming an obsolete and outmoded practice. Divorces are rapidly outnumbering contracted unions, and the number of natural children is growing in an alarming rate. The first explanation for such an alarming phenomenon seems to be the dissolution of the old patterns and of the social constraints which are still characteristic of some modern societies. Today some believe that it is not absolutely necessary to be married in the Church or before a civil authority in order for two people to live together as a couple. Very rare after all are those parents who are upset and who revolt because their children from an early age insist on going away from their parents' home, arguing for their right for self-expression and for living by themselves with another partner. If marriage was until recently the only way for women to acquire a status and to reaffirm their womanhood, this is no longer the case.

Another aspect concerning the social advantages of marriage arises from the accepted, highly esteemed value of a valid and legal marriage, involving the sacred right of a person to dispose his own self. We arrive now at the enjoyment of an absolute self-determination and an uncontrolled liberty. In such a context, marriage seems to offer little interest. The existing system of taxation, instead of encouraging legal marriages, heavily penalizes such a marriage, imposing a disproportional tax on the income of couples when the two partners are both working, but this is not the case when they live together unmarried. Another explanation, more directly effecting the general weakening of marriage and its meaning, is the increase in the concept of privatization in our societies, by which many young people begin to contest the state, the law, and any other authority's right to interfere in their personal and private life. The whole affair is a private one, and in the name of such a sentiment marriage is being contested today. Triumphalist and absolutist love has become a new idolatry. It is the all and the everything. Upon this *eros* or sensual love, and only on this basis, the relationship of a couple has to be based and to be realized. In the name of such a chemically pure love, young people reject the classical idea of marriage, considering it as anachronistic and useless, like a prison, and harmful to the development of their own self and the expansion of their natural liberty. Because of such an overemphasis and overestimation of an idealized physical love, we have regrettably so many quick divorces.

Thus, we observe a catastrophic crisis in the matrimonial relationship. But one may ask whether this is something transitory or accidental? Does it inaugurate an abrupt end of marriage as an institution? The answer may be formulated as follows: from the moment an institution loses its pressing and sustaining power, then it unfortunately becomes an optional matter, as are so many other matters in everyday life. Consequently, it undergoes a certain devaluation or underestimation and encourages an unbalanced freedom or even license. It also leads to a weakening, a lethargy, and a complacent attitude. It is time once again to redefine and to reinterpret, on a more solid basis, what marriage really means, that it is more than just a simple biological co-existence of two human beings. We need to move towards providing a more dynamic and creative explanation of the importance of marriage in terms of the spiritual growth of persons and of their offspring. Until recently, marriage was seen as a static principle and the whole concept of marriage was taught without adequate information and pastoral help being made available. No adequate reference was made to the sanctification process within the marriage bond. It was considered sufficient that the two were married, thus concluding that they were safe and this was enough of a guarantee for them to be happy and to accomplish their task. It is time to help people to find a more profound, real sense to their matrimonial state and to explain that their choice is binding for the cultivation of a better quality of life, something which involves their whole personality.

Marriage remains, it is true, a personal as well as a social contract, an intimate everlasting alliance, a project never achieved, always being restarted, which reposes just as much in the will of each partner as in their love for each other. Only then can marriage become, step by step, a profession, a commitment, and an experimental *praxis* of the faith of both parties. It becomes an effort for mutual correction, for the uplifting of one's character higher and higher, never, however, with a blind toleration of and compromise about the faults of each other. Such toleration, on the contrary, destroys the harmony between the partners, endangers the real spirit and harmony of marriage and its harmony and pollutes the health and the spiritual beauty of both. Married people must struggle not only against their own personal faults but equally against the exterior polluted air of the times. All this struggle may perhaps seem foolish to some people, in view of this era of alienation from moral standards and of general permissiveness, wherein people prefer what can be easily done, the instant, the ephemeral, and the futile rather than a laborious spiritual fight together and the engagement of the couple for life. But in reality, man cannot live alone and only for himself, not only because he can never really be self-sufficient, but also because human beings cannot live by reason alone, and guided exclusively by rational criteria. There are instances where what is called "foolishness" is absolutely required in life, when one lives fully dedicated to the other, when one cares, when one is ready to suffer for the other. Only then has togetherness a real and everlasting meaning.

The above reflections show that to stand superficially upon traditionally accepted norms or institutions while at the same time not trying to engage in a dialogue between persons is unreliable.

God, desiring our advancement to the highest point of sanctification, established marriage not as a simple *symbiosis* of two beings, who procreate and help each other in moments of need. Such elements, of course, are included. But they are only parts of the whole. The wider goal of marriage is that each partner, animated by real love, try with patience, deep affection, and an unselfish attitude, to improve and to influence the other partner to the common end — perfection in Christ. This goal involves a long term process, to be sure, but one that is noble and necessary. A passive attitude, fatalistically accepting one's own faults, is not enough. In time such an attitude can even become dangerous. Because as time goes on these acquire deeper and deeper roots and finally whole characters become petrified, incorrigible, and desperately intolerable. At the same time, promoting the "romantic" relationship is also dubious, since this relationship remains on a very low level, namely, the physical and/or sensual level. Real unity cannot be achieved at once. It is a process that needs to be achieved in stages. Both partners must move from the level of an earthly relationship to a real "communion" of their innermost selves, to a real *koinonia*. Real love must not be understood only in physical terms, because this seems to exalt the most destructive enemy of happiness, namely, selfishness, resulting in the domination of one person by the other and unavoidable rivalry between them. Lack of respect, as well, will sooner or later wound the sensitivity of the other partner.

Love or *agape* means living for the other but equally correcting the other. Such a longing for a creative love, for a correcting love, often tends to appear too late, the autumn of one's life. Looking back on their past, the partners then begin to appreciate better the necessity of one's correcting concern for the other, or they may admit the bitter results if their life has passed without the least amount of effort expended to improve the quality of their life. But in such a case, from a Christian perspective, life has already lost its real content and meaning a long time ago. Everyone admits that it is then too late. Many would wish to be reborn or to return to the early days with new insights for mutual correction. The task remains, however, for Christian couples to continually make this unity between themselves visible in the divided world in which they find themselves.

34. Law and Justice in Ancient Greece

Ancient philosophers always tended to be sceptical about the effectiveness of laws and of otherwise excellent rules and regulations which were promulgated even by the best of politicians, if at the same time, the very character of their human behavior was not in compliance with these laws. What was needed then was above all a deep sense of duty which is the harmonious cooperation between excellent legislation and the spiritual growth of citizens, so that inner justice meets the social setting and thus sustains the external justice. The term "justice" is used here in the wider sense, implying a correct way of living and at the same time protection by the state, so that public evils and social disorders might be reprimanded. Thus, Anacharsis, a Scythian philosopher and poet in pursuit of knowledge, came to Athens about 594 B.C. and became acquainted with the current Greek intellectual ideas of that time. Solon, the Athenian legislator and statesman, had such confidence in human ordinances and laws that he exacted from the people a solemn oath that they would observe his laws for a certain period of time, and then absented himself from Athens for a period of ten years. While everyone marveled at the famous laws formulated by Solon, Anacharsis, with reasonable doubt, pronounced the following words which, to this date, remain a good lesson for all to keep in mind: "The law resembles the spider's web. It certainly can capture small flies and insects, but it is unable to capture the great ones. Such are those in power, the rich and wealthy, who by bribes and other means succeed in escaping the existing laws."

Solon, while guiding his illustrious guest around the city of Athens, arrived at the agora. With a degree of pride, Solon showed him the wooden rollers and triangular tablets on which his laws were inscribed, and he was highly impressed by his Asiatic visitor's ironic remark showing the insignificant impact that legislation has without deeply rooted morals and an honest respect of one's civil obligations and duties. Plutarch (*Solon* 5,2) records this story while expressing his approval of the relative nature of external laws.

Such mistrust of institutional systems and established laws must not be interpreted as a contempt or underestimation of their real value. Instead the intention is to expose the absolutization and excessive authority that is attributed to them which ignores what is hidden in human nature. Man stands, thinks, and reacts regardless of any given structure and beyond laws. He, as a free being, if he wills, can violate law, finding ways to escape the consequences. At the same time he can do more good than even the minimum which the law requires or asks. A certain lawful structure can be useful as a deterrent to evil-doers, but only in certain limited cases and for a certain category of people. The best elaborated legal system, as daily experience and reality show us, do not prevent criminality, violence, immorality, etc. Along with law something else is needed, something that can reach far deeper into the human heart, that sacred and impenetrable area. Not that laws and structures must be abolished, but the consent, the understanding, and the cooperation of the people are also needed, on the basis of which legislation is enacted. Most social disorders do not result from lack of good systems, laws, or elaborated structures. Quite the opposite is true. Never before in history were societies protected so well by excellent laws and by-laws as in our days, guaranteeing human rights, liberty, and peace, condemning injustice, every form of exploitation, and the ill-treatment of defenseless persons, the weak, and the poor. And yet, in spite of such euphoria of local and international laws, unemployment, inadmissible poverty, the decline of moral standards, broken families, deliquency, conflict of generations, and deficient educational systems continue to exist. To all these anomalies must be added the scandalous misbehavior of those who are responsible for administering public affairs and controlling the respect and the proper application of the existing laws. Who and how will supervise these law-keepers, those supervisors of the common welfare who themselves scorn and disrespect that order by breaking those same laws that they themselves legislate? It is right, therefore, to make an honest diagnosis regarding the limits of the influence of such rigid laws and structures on human behavior, which, while maintaining a minimum degree of order, are unable to permeate the will and heart of man.

In human society throughout the course of history, accumulated traditions and habits related to established human life are crystallized into concrete systems and structures. However good or bad they may be, they certainly exercise a considerable influence upon human behavior. In some societies, citizens cannot escape their influence, and consequently, to a certain extent, they are formed after such models. What must then be a Christian's attitude toward such socio-political structural pathogenics? Is there any chance for man to develop his potential and manifest his faith above and beyond such restrictive structures? Is their omnipotent dominion inescapable and, therefore, is it necessary for one to submit totally, having very little commitment and being largely restricted by exterior factors?

The question, perhaps in a different form, was asked by the early Christians of Corinth. Those who had married pagans were frustrated, not knowing whether they had to abandon their partner because he or she was hindering the realization of life in Christ in its fullness. Another question was raised concerning the legal acceptance or rejection of that pitiful class called slaves. Is it allowed for them to revolt against their masters, defending their God-given rights, refusing any cruel dominion over themselves as free beings created by God? Both issues carried, at the same time, individual and social implications. Paul answered the following: "A Christian transcends any structure established by a given society. He can live above any situation imposed upon him or his faith because he enjoys the gift of self-determination, because his existence transcends human conditions. It is something based within his very heart and nature, thus is invisible, and relates to his being in a continuous communion with Christ." In 1 Cor 7, St. Paul enumerated all the categories of persons involved in this situation: women married with unbelieving husbands; slaves; circumcised and uncircumcised. "Let every man abide in the same calling wherein he was called," was his basic and crucial advice.

Paul argued that, by using such situations they were given exceptional chances to witness to their faith and finally to bring those with whom they were living to Christ. Particularly, the unbelieving husband may be sanctified by the persistent example of his Christian wife. A servant must not care so much about his state, because, in the eyes of the Lord, he is free. Circumcision is nothing, and uncircumcision is nothing, but what counts is the keeping of the commandments of God. John Chrysostom drew valuable lessons from these Pauline answers, pointing out that external conditions in a given society cannot alter the identity of a man or a woman, which is rooted in the innermost part of his heart, and in the essential distinctiveness of his being. We may live in such a setting and yet feel quite above, free, untouched. In mixed marriages, opportunities are given for the unbelieving person, by appropriate evangelistic action, to become Christian and accept the truth. Coming into matrimonial relation one member of the couple being pagan, does not necessarily make the other one unclean, because, after all, everything depends upon secret feelings and the inner will. A great gain, therefore, may come about from such an attitude: "Do not revolt, stay where you are, but admonishing, advising and persuading. There can be no better teacher in such a case than a faithful woman."

Even more interesting is the case of slaves. For John Chrysostom, there are no such things, ontologically speaking, as "slave" or "free." Both are equal in Christ. Slave and master are both Christ's creatures, reborn children, because Christ has freed the slave from sin and has abolished all by taking account of the external, humiliating condition. Consequently, a slave in reality is no longer a slave. He is free, because he is liberated from the evils polluting his soul, from iniquities, and all other kinds of evil. He was redeemed by a great ransom and a high price. Within this logic, the slave is in reality no more a slave, while a free man, considered free by worldly criteria, may easily become a slave. The first man, compelled by the existing law to serve men, is in reality obeying God's will. On the other hand, the apparent free man becomes a slave when he yields to attractive, human vices, when he desires by all possible means money or power, or when he seeks earthly pleasure. Such a man, in reality, becomes the worst kind of slave, although socially he is free. Remember Joseph as a slave, and yet not serving men. Thus, although being a slave, in fact he was freer than all the others, who humanly were seen as free, "τῶν ἐλευθέρων ἐλευθερότερος."

On the other hand, the wife of his master, considered free, in reality was overcome by lust and unclean desires and became a slave of all: and what a paradox! She was a matron condescending to but also flattering and begging her servant. In spite of all that, she did not succeed in persuading an obedient servant to do what she wanted him to do since he did not want to do it. The state of slavery did not at all prevent Joseph from remaining pure and chaste. There may be oppressive rules about slavery, but if a slave keeps his own inner freedom and integrity, then he proves to be above all restrictive conditions, and is really free. This is why Paul recommends: "Be not the servants of men" (v. 23).

Joseph was truly free and, by his attitude, he showed it everywhere and in everything. Nothing, absolutely nothing, can dominate such a man — neither bondage, nor slavery, nor the most tempting woman's desires — to be a "stranger in a foreign land," as is seen in the case of Joseph. He showed himself a free being. This is the mark of authentic liberty, to be able to shine, as he did, even in the state of the worst slavery.

This is indeed Christianity, making men free even in slavery. It is as though one has an invulnerable body which does not suffer or become wounded even when receiving arrows; so a really free man shows himself as such only when he does not allow himself to suffer, and when he refuses to be dominated even though subjected to masters. It explains why Paul recommended that slaves remain in their status. In addition, Greeks would discredit slaves who were unable to show themselves as real Christians merely because of a certain social condition. Furthermore, the Greeks would begin to accuse us of having a weakness in our faith, if we were unable to accept such a class within our ranks. On the contrary, if we would admit such a class they would admire our faith, since nothing hinders the practice of piety even among slaves. None of all these things — death, flogging, imprisonment, fire, tyrannical situations, sickness, poverty, wild animals, or so many other tribulations — could hurt or damage the faithful. These evils might enable them to become greater. It is not social slavery which really endangers, but another type, the natural slavery produced by sin. Take heed you do not become a slave of this kind, and rejoice when you overcome it. Nobody can harm you if you keep your behavior from being subdued. But if you allow yourself to become a slave of sin, however free you may be, there is no use for your liberty (*Hom. 19, 3-5 On 1 Cor.*; PG 61.156-58).

Thus, we can see that love towards Christ provides wings, so that the soul enters into another space of life, beyond the repressive structures made by men. In addition, it shows that however right a structure may be, however scientifically perfect or anthropologically correct, if it does not take care of the very human beings within it, it is useless. Plato already noticed this when he distinguished between a pure science and virtue or righteousness (*Menexenos* 13).

Christ never underestimates the charismata of his image, namely, men. He believes in his creative force, especially at critical moments when human beings are surrounded by negative forces or structures. Man, therefore, is enabled to effectively transform this earth. Instead of becoming a dead field where real life is replaced by a distorted existence, a real expression of God's family is possible. Man is able to face destructive structures and to build up a new world. Man remains the hope and the glory of God, as Irenaios states.

The ancient pagan world, filled with unusual religious and cultural conceptions, never accepted the Gospel's revolutionary views about human dignity and elementary rights. But one can see a slow but remarkably manifest regeneration, namely, the gradual infuence of Christianity upon that society. Antoninus, the pious Roman emperor, was the first to punish by legislation the exploitation and even the sale of a child, when the parent is rich. Until the destruction of ancient Rome by the barbarians, the Church did not hesitate to promote the renewal of social ethics through the personal commitment and ethics of its neophytes. The twelfth canon of the Council of Elvira in Spain (300) prescribed severe discipline "for parents delivering their children to debauchery." The Constantinian legislation, published in 315, decrees: "That a general law promptly be decreed in all towns of Italy, preventing parents from killing their newborn children ... We have learned that citizens of the provinces, suffering from shortages of necessary provisions, dare to put on sale their own proper children. We declare, nevertheless, that those who have not enough personal resources will be helped by our competent offices."

Little by little one discovers the effective impact of the Gospel on society in general. Thus, we see that Gregory the Theologian, at a critical moment of his career, seeking the peace of the Church above his personal comfort, decided to resign before the whole population in tears, a sign of how Christianity had already penetrated into a nation's structure and become the people's religion. Of course, here and there sporadical traces of inhuman treatment were still found, indicating that the pagan world had not yet died completely. Thus, Basil of Caesarea in a moving sermon defended unprotected children so dear to the congregation. He painted a sad picture of a poor miserable citizen, in a most tragic situation, who, chased by the tax collector and seeking a solution, the funds to pay his debt, finds that the only solution to his problem remains for such an unhappy father to sell his own children.

> He possesses no gold. His house is for sale. But his house is only a miserable hut, really poor. There remains nothing else other than to sell his children in order to cover his debt. He decides for it, but then again he hesitates, and finally he yields ... But which one of the children should he sell to the trader? To sell only one? Or to sell two? What a terrible conflict between starvation and paternal feelings? Again, how will the other children see it, considering such a sale as an offensive betrayal of their

dignity? To sell all of them at once? But then how could he dare to live henceforth, after such an inadmissible betrayal, in this house which he himself in this manner made empty? How would he dare to sit at the table, to eat, knowing quite well that the abundance that now was created had cost him so dearly? (*Homily in illud. Lucae* 12,18, ch. 4; PG 31268-69)

When the barbarians from the North invaded the Empire and became masters of conquered European countries, the Church continued to extend her influence regarding infanticide, still existing customs and to cultivate a respect for the child and the sacredness of the family. In the fourth century, newly established monasteries become sheltering asylums for the increasing number of orphans. Schools were opened. Slowly society becomes even more organized, and so more social concern and protection were offered. Churches offered hostels. Love's history, born in the days of Caesar Augustus in Bethlehem with its climax on the cross on Calvary, was manifested in *philanthropia* through the concrete *diakonia* of the Church, faithful to the teaching and the example of Jesus.

35. Personal Evil — Structural Evil

Sociologists of all ideological tendencies agree upon one thing: amelioration of our society demands first and foremost a change in society and an improvement of the human condition, not so much progress in morality. Thus, for many of them, criminality is a purely sociological problem, touching upon the individual, and is, in fact, an effect of the actual organization of the sick society. When society will have evolved, the death penalty will be abolished and every citizen will respect his fellow citizen. In the present structure, we are all pressed upon and influenced by superior forces, mostly economic, which produce aggressiveness. For instance, an unemployed person may be led to criminal conduct since he despairs concerning the prevailing injustice caused by the dominant class. Society is responsible. Society puts obstacles in the way, thus provoking indignation, bitterness, and revolt. And so, guilt must be placed upon the present form of society.

Changing a given society means the rejection of the evil which the leading classes worship and sustain. Social unrest and problems cannot be produced but appear only from a collective sin — from the sin of classes abusing their privileged positions and their possession of power. All forms of hypocrisy, therefore, must be fought since they feed inadmissible systems which exploit the weak, the under-privileged, and the oppressed. The poor and powerless must get freedom at any price. The unique and ultimate liberty inherent in all of us compels us to become authentic human beings engaged in a fight against a given world. But in what case does the free choice of human actions exist, or is it only the negative attitude of revolt? We are responsible for fighting against the established, even institutionalized, disorder. Negative uprisings and movements can be creative and constructive in a certain sense. To deny this fact would mean that we might end up with something worse than what we expected. Overcoming the limits which the world imposes on him, man conquers the world and himself as well at the same time.

From such conquest could come a new creative humanity, an invention which no rule could define or limit. From the moment man becomes a fighter and accepts the contingencies of a cause, he reveals himself to be an absolute autonomous being. His will becomes his *raison d'etre*. There is no other, more noble vision to follow nor other ultimate goal besides this one. Man becomes the highest goal. He is the author of his own destiny. Here we encounter the well-known theories of Jean Jacques Rousseau, for whom the general will becomes, implicitly, the main principle — replacing the will of God. This substitution is more explicit in another French philosopher, Diderot. For certain thinkers, the golden age can be found in a mythical past. For others the ideal lies in the future. Real freedom is invented every day, by finding new ways, new forms of freedom, inventing a new different world in which man is going to grow and develop his potentiality, thus organizing the ideal future society. Such views also echo the existentialists' position. In different philosophies, the goal is to contest any power above and beyond man, any taboos, religious or moral, which may influence man. Some philosophies tend to individualize absolute freedom, becoming a form of anthropocentrism, while others seek to collectivize the same freedom, yet both eventually arrive at the same conclusion. The dialectic takes many shapes in *forma mentis*, even in the theological sphere, covered with excuses.

The inevitable result of such a tactic is a variety of contentions against alienating structures rather than ways to attack the inner cause by an interior warfare. According to such established theses, the more a society is sinful, the less a person seems ultimately or even directly responsible. Social fighting takes priority, excluding any interior fight, moral or spiritual, where the very cause of the social problem lies.

Structures, which must be refuted in modern society are to establish peace, to prevent the danger of nuclear war, to rectify violations of human rights, to limit the influence of multinationals, etc. But such commitments to general problems risk overlooking any serious consideration, particularly for the personal and spiritual progress of the person as such. All the fervor and zeal is not directed toward discovering the primary source of human misery. And yet, this attitude is one of the main factors dividing and poisoning man and the world.

However, evil is not so much engendered in the form of psychological or social realities. Evil, above anything else, is man's free choice to abandon God and to refuse his lordship. Whoever tries to explain evil, by the pretext of not being responsible, and attributes all existing anomalies to the structure of human society, simply underestimates man's value and falsifies his own capacities, gifts, and privileges. From such deviations come many human disorders. Losing the sense of personal sin also alienates a man from the truth. Consequently, Christians maintain that social anomalies in the form of concrete structures are the effect of personal sins, which, in turn, produce more sins and multiply in different similar evils. It is quite easy to manipulate the whole issue of a man and human structures by proposing various alternatives.

In one of his expositions on human behavior, Dorotheos of Gaza in Palestine, a famous ascetic father (580), dealt with how to walk with vigilance, without wasting our precious time during our earthly life in the paths which God has established. Among other arguments, he addressed the burning question of what is evil? Fully aware that in human society unjust structures and wrong situations will always exist, he, nevertheless, does not see them as self-existing imperative powers ending and determining human beings or forcing themselves upon human aspirations and existence. Such structures for him, on the contrary, are neither almighty nor absolute. Consequently, it would be wrong to place exclusive blame on them, attacking their existence as if they were the main generating causes, while overlooking their primary cause, which is hidden behind them, namely, man himself. All human vicissitudes and calamities proceed from man's inner disorder, from man's destructive inclinations, which finally reach their concrete form in projects which affect the entire planet, resulting in wrong traditions and rules. Man above all else must renew himself if he wants to reconstruct a more healthy life and its socio-political structures. According to Dorotheos:

> Evil itself is non-existent; it is a non-entity. It has neither substance nor hypostasis. Woe if it were like that! Behold, what really happens. The moment our soul departs from the royal way of virtue, it imparts a lot of destructive passions which thus work out the evil. In this process, the soul is punished by the evil itself, since it loses for itself the indispensable restful situation which it enjoyed when it was living with virtue. Let us look at what happens in another case, that of wood. Wood does not, of course, at the very beginning contain any worms. But in time, it becomes rotten and from this state comes the worm. And in the course of its development, the worm itself then eats all the wood. A similar

thing happens with copper. It itself engenders the stain, which in turn eats the copper . . .

Likewise, the soul commits evil to its own detriment, without the evil previously possessing any substance and hypostasis. But gradually, the soul finds itself punished by the same evil that it has engendered. Gregory the Theologian was right in saying that "the fire is born from the wood, while in turn, it burns all the wood," thus following the example of evil which in turn destroys the evildoer. Evil is produced by the wicked person, but at the same time it eventually destroys the wicked person himself (*Oratio* 23,1; PG 351152).

Dorotheos further applies this principle of causality to the analogy concerning suffering and physical illness. The lack of attention to the states of the body endangers the entire physical state of the body and finally results in a total loss of good health. But beforehand sickness in fact did not exist at all, and after the body is healed, sickness can nowhere be found. In the same way, evil disfigures and distorts the whole being, becoming a sickness of the soul, because the soul, when it is polluted, loses the natural state of its health which is none other than virtue (*Instruction* 10, 106).

Such an important emphasis on man's total responsibility — as over against the assertions made about impersonal, external abstract forms and factors causing the disorder and misery of human society — is held by many church fathers. Thus, Basil of Caesarea, focusing on the source of miseries, stated:

It is not people from outside who teach us to hate and disdain sickness. We by ourselves automatically from within detest all which might produce pain. And a hostile attitude towards evil is inherent in our very own souls, so that every evil seems to be a sickness for the soul. On the contrary, virtue becomes for us the very health of the soul. Very rightly, certain people have given a definition that physical health is the well-being of energies in accordance with nature. A similar statement can be made about the well-being of the soul, if we want to speak comparatively and precisely (*Homilia* 9, 4 in *Hexaemeron*; PG 29. 196).

Nevertheless, a deplorable social and economic climate can result from the misbehavior and the selfish attitude of individuals. Whatever may be said about particular responsibilities, society as a whole suffers. Like an epidemic it propagates and contaminates and thus permanently creates pollution. We find ourselves before realities which enclose within themselves disruptions and unrest of all kinds, from which innocent people may suffer. Even in the ancient world, evil's consequences were pointed out, as were their wider effects, direct or indirect, which cause passions, enmities, and divisions (*Hermes Trismeg.* 1 *Sermo* 7).

Even if it is legitimate to underscore the "temporal" nature of life, Christians, nevertheless, cannot ignore the tragic visible disorders of this life, remaining coolly indifferent and leaving the responsibility to others. The Church does not confine its mission to preaching only a disincarnated ethereal love in an academic way. She must also put into effect, in every situation, principles to transform society for the better. St. John Chrysostom, by establishing humanitarian institutions in Antioch, sought to widen and further enhance the social services of the Church. In his days, there were three thousand unprotected girls in Antioch, as well as widows, to whom he offered food and every possible assistance on a daily basis. In addition, special care was extended to those in prisons, the sick, foreigners, and disabled persons lying in the streets (*In Math. hom.* 66,3; PG 58,360).

According to his biographer Palladios, St. John Chrysostom built hospitals in Constantinople which were directed by two presbyters, with a full staff of medical doctors, cooks, and nurses selected from the monastic ranks. Specialized help was designated for foreigners coming from Asia and the Middle East, flooding the imperial city to seek shelter and employment (*De Vita S.J.Chrys.*; PG 47,20).

A well-structured philanthropic *diakonia* was also developed by St. Basil. Historians record considerable activity in the whole region of Caesarea. If we take into account the complete absence of social security in those days, this social assistance represents a fantastic and concrete social achievement. Series of buildings hosted all kinds of social activities. In a letter addressed to the Governor of Cappadocia, the Archbishop enumerated the enormous difficulty he was encountering in running such an immense charitable enterprise. All kinds of foreigners found generous hospitality. The handicapped found lodging and medical care. Even more than that, because of the specialization of the staff, a permanent school instructed future nurses and health personnel (*Epistola* 104; PG 32,488).

Later on, Saint Basil's friend, St. Gregory the Theologian, invited his listeners to go outside the town of Caesarea in order to admire the size of the buildings constructed from private contributions. To a town, he added, no other could be compared. Neither Thebes in Boeotia with its seven gates, nor Thebes in Egypt, nor the Babylonian walls, nor the Mausoleum of Halikarnassos, nor the pyramids, nor the bronze colossus of Rhodes, nor the beauty and fabulous size of all the ancient temples could be compared with them (*Oratio* 43, 62-63; PG 36, 577-80).

Remarkable leprosy dispensaries were made available for a class of miserable persons who were the most neglected and the outcast of society. In those days lepers were ill-treated, expelled from inhabited areas, and relocated outside the city limits like circulating "dead before death." To all these Basil manifested a particular affection, often embracing them like brothers.

In the dwellings he constructed, even the most incurable cases found a warm welcome. We are in fact presented with a systematic program of social concern. For the fathers, the Church should always be present, near the sufferers. Their problems should also become the Church's problems.

Convinced, in face of such a scandalous and inhuman attitude of the upper classes, that the abusive employment of wealth and power are roots of many subsequent social evils, the fathers undertook an extremely difficult pastoral task by recalling their heavy responsibilities before God and men. But they maintained that the people first must be formed and reborn, and then things would follow for the better. Thus Basil warned: "Be mindful, O man, who it was that gave you all these goods. Remember who you are, what wealth you administer, from whom you have received all these, and why you were chosen as a steward rather than another. You, indeed, became a servant of God who is merciful, a steward of other servants who are equal to yourself. Therefore, do not think only of your own stomach" (*Hom. in illud Lucae* 2; PG 31.264).

Gregory the Theologian recommended, in the same spirit, "Friends and brothers, become not unworthy administrators of all that was given to us, in order not to receive your condemnation. Every time you give alms, you give nothing from your own, since all comes from God. Even if you offer a big donation, and another bigger one, it will always remain insufficient" (*Oratio* 14, 22-23; PG 35, 885).

John Chrysostom also developed an argument that everything we possess, in reality, does not belong to us. We are trustees, responsible users of goods and money: "All that we have as our own, comes from Christ. When we claim that this or that is mine or yours, this is only a light, superficial expression, but it does not, in fact, correspond to reality. What indeed is appointed for you is their use, and even this remains uncertain" (*Hom.* 10,3 *in Epist.1 ad Cor.*; PG 61,85).

Fully conscious that we, as reasonable creatures, are invested with extraordinary gifts, Basil rebuked any selfish attitude in dealing with earthly goods. Nothing must be used exclusively for our own sakes only. Others also deserve our generosity and a Christian spirit of sharing — brotherly sharing — because by its nature all wealth is for the common benefit. Commenting upon the parable of the foolish rich man who in prosperity thinks "I shall demolish my stores," Basil mimics his words, full of egoistic feeling: "To whom do I cause an injustice if I keep the goods that are in fact mine? But are they really yours? From where have you borrowed them and brought them into this life? But such is the logic of self-centered wealthy thinkers. Because, by chance, they have managed to possess common things, they pretend that they are exclusively their own. But if each one kept for himself only just what was necessary for him, distributing the rest to those in need, there would not exist either rich or poor. Those who take away clothes from a dressed man are called robbers. But how you could call somebody who, while able to dress a naked body, does not do it? The bread you possess belongs to the hungry. The vestments you store up belong to those naked. The shoes to those without them, which remaining in your hands, are rotten. And the money hidden belongs also to those in need" (*Hom. in illud. Lucae* 3; PG 31,276-77).

This sharp protest against the rich constitutes in reality an outcry of disapproval and a plea for the poor. At the same time, it is a passionate effort to persuade the rich to change their attitude, and instead of exploiting and earning illegally, to be helpful to their fellow man. The language used may be full of pathos and emotion, rather than a philosophical approach to a burning, eternal issue. It would be useless to try to find a system of sociology or economic philosphy in these reflections. Neither can simple almsgiving be accepted as the best solution for the healing of society's wounds. Occasional signs of human solidarity admittedly may relieve temporary sufferings, but generally speaking, it leaves the problems unsolved and in a stagnant state. Selfgiving cannot bring about any large-scale economic justice, and contributes little to bridge the gap between rich and poor. For the fathers, however, love in all its dimensions and implications still remains most important. Christian love, when applied, animates and inspires new relationships, new attitudes, and a new regard concerning one's responsibilities about management and administration of wealth, of capital. After all, history teaches us that many radical changes took place through the initiatives of godfearing people. New laws were promulgated, thanks to individuals who had been renewed by the evangelical spirit of charity and mutual solidarity. Humanity owes an immense debt to such men of God. They showed, in their daily lives, a love toward God and to their fellowmen as well as to society in general, suffering with the sufferers and often emptying themselves of their own comfort in order to bring assistance and relief to others.

Each Ecumenical WCC Assembly provides us with opportunities for and gives us the right to make an honest evaluation. Things that have been sufficiently or properly assessed, or have been underestimated, invite the member churches to give them further consideration. With a heavy program, and a busy schedule, many issues at such gatherings remain either untouched or may still await more profound study. In addition, each post-assembly period provides for a gradual reception of the decisions. This is the "conciliar" process which was practiced after the convocation of the Ecumenical Councils in history. Member churches are asked to examine various aspects of the recommendations and after a thorough study to formulate reactions, constructive comments and appropriate proposals. This present text claims to be one such proposal, reflecting the Orthodox perspective.

The chosen assembly theme was recognized by all as of immense value. It sought to stimulate, to guide, and to inspire all discussions beginning with the keynote speakers to the various committees and different sections. The meeting at Vancouver very wisely issued a paper concerning future study projects, programs, and guidelines — where we can find a common challenge, namely, that there is a long crossing ahead. In most of the churches, a certain number of things cannot be done together, because each one lives in a particular situation. But there do exist a number of issues where a common effort is urgently needed and where we can complement each other. There are no sicknesses but only the sick. No violence or oppression, but only violent people — unjust, racist, and militaristic oppressors. Sometimes we run the risk of absolutizing the exterior structures, forgetting that all such phenomena are products of human deficiency and sinfulness. Another danger is trying to capture God and making a theology to justify exclusively one's own case. We must take theology far more seriously.

If the Assembly's theme had really permeated the debates in all the clusters and the sections, it would have produced a common challenge for all, namely, by what means can we relate the modern life of our congregations to Jesus Christ? The benefit and service we as churches could render to a frustrated world would be beyond imagination. The emptiness and the confusion of a society totally immersed in worldly happiness awaits our reaction, it awaits the constant reminder that life is not truly life without God or against God.

The issues which surround the main theme of every ecumenical assembly need more theological consideration. Some delegates may stress the socio-political implications of the theme as priorities, but we need to relate also how humanity can be restored to its dignity as a brotherhood and how the family of man can have harmonious relations with God. Such a step would naturally lead to the harmonizing of human relationships, making them more just and correct. We know that the amelioration of human conditions —improving salaries, material happiness, etc. — however legitimate do not necessarily lead to a full reconciliation with God. Anthropology, if not treated in the light of redemption, runs the risk of bringing about a greater polarization with its vague slogans of continuously seeking rights and privileges which may never be satisifed. After all, this dissatisfaction emanates from man's concern and quest to attain earthly gifts and pleasures, and clearly demonstrates that solutions must be sought elsewhere, that in the human being there exists a thirst for another nature which is not purely human and temporal. Rightly, then, the post-Vancouver follow-up work includes the oportunity for deep theological consideration. All departments of the WCC should wrestle with the call for a more creative and coherent theological action, and these various approaches should be co-ordinated by a theological advisory group.

36. Surrounded by Sinful Structures

No social structure or law ever appeared in human history all by itself as a product of human intelligence or bad intentions. They have become permanent institutions in the course of time, thus being changed for the better or worse, according to existing moral attitudes or given situations. It would be unfair, therefore, to see such structures as determining in an absolute manner the life and destiny of individuals or of societies. They do exercise an immense influence upon man's behavior, but they are not the only determining factors. As human beings, endowed with free will, we can allow a structure or system to have a limited impact, which we can accept or reject. How many Christians, in the early days of Christianity, lived under deplorable pagan traditions, laws, structures, and inhuman customs, and yet did not allow themselves to be fully dominated by them, but felt themselves to be independent and free individuals. To a certain extent, of course, as citizens they had to take into account certain realities and to obey these laws without allowing them to offend their personal convictions. They attributed to worldly traditions their due respect but never permitted them to pass the limit, always keeping in mind that, above everything, reverence and obedience are due to the Lord of heaven and earth. The epistle to Diognetos designated a certain privileged place of Christians within a pagan surrounding.

Our reflection leads us to another thought. Certainly the milieu — the given socio-political structure — cannot leave Christians entirely indifferent to the evils around them. While admitting a proportional degree of authority to such a structure, nevertheless, a man or a woman still remains above all else free to yield or to resist. It would be superficial to deny the force of a given structure accepted by the majority. Living, for instance, in an atheist, or secularized, permissive society, or even in the midst of an Islamic state, many factors, sooner or later, challenge Christians with problems and dilemmas which are often sharp and painful. After all, being human, we cannot dissociate our daily life and attitudes from that of the existing and surrounding milieu. This phenomenon explains the importance attributed in recent years to "structuralism." Although the problem raised above is actual and pressing and we are often reminded of its influence and importance, it deserves a more penetrating study.

This study should be undertaken from the perspective of its influence upon human behavior, whether man is superior to or only the fatal slave of the established structures.

In the Christian life, legal prescriptions or canonical ordinances, especially the disciplinary canons formulated by the Ecumenical Councils, are subordinated to their spirit. Life cannot be imprisoned in rules. The spirit inspires and dictates. Even the ancient law of Judaism ought to be taken according to its spirit and not its letter. At this point, we enter into a central truth touching upon Christian ethics, the danger of falling into formalism and legalism. Andrew of Crete (circa 660-740), a famous hymnographer, in his great Canon used during the great Lent, compared the Mosaic law with the era of grace:

> The law was vivified by grace and placed at its service in harmonious composition and fertility. Each one of these two elements has retained its characteristic, without alteration or confusion. But always, the law which previously constituted a heavy burden and a tyranny now becomes, through God's intervention, a light burden and a source of liberty (*Discours* 1; PG 97,806).

This spirit which is offered to the faithful, and written in our innermost selves as God's law, is understood not to have been ordained exclusively from the outside but, above all, has been implanted as well within us. This divine grace offers us space for free action according to one's own discernment, guided by the voice and the inspiration of the spirit. Thus, holiness, while receiving stimulus from outside, takes its initiative from an inner communion with God, thus keeping its autonomy above any structure surrounding man's earthly existence.

Christians consider it a priority to promote men and women as persons in the sense that they are created by God for a higher task than a simple existence. Every social change, therefore, must contribute to the accomplishment of the inner life. Such growth will have as its model Jesus Christ incarnate, who assumed our nature in order to remain the *typos* and the everlasting example for us all. Humanity is aware that it lives in the era of many changes. An epoch is dying and a new age is dawning. Many challenges, therefore, touch humanity in the process of growth in the midst of so many ambiguities in this new technological culture. At the same time, we know that most of the existing structures have become dehumanizing and degenerating. An overwhelming example is the contrast between production and hunger. In spite of food production increase, official statistics tell us that fifteen thousand persons are dying every day either from famine or from malnutrition. The world's population will increase fifty times by the year 2000. This increase will be felt mostly in the poor countries of the Third World. The stockpiling of nuclear arms, sufficient to obliterate every town on our earth seven times over continues. And yet the arms race continues causing an economic hemorrhage — forcing the poorer nations to enter into enormous debts for vital needs: food, health, education, employment. Such alarming issues illustrate the deficiencies of the existing structures and the absence of systems favoring the normal expansion of human life and peaceful existence. How, then, can such inhuman structures be changed? Can we as churches work out a new order on an international scale, based upon dignity and human values? Is it possible nowadays to shape a new society based upon justice and equal rights?

All these reflections invite us toward a more dynamic presence of the Church in every field where human problems are discussed and where humanity is in danger. And when we use the term "Church," we mean the assembly of the faithful. It is up to such living, radiating, witnessing, active Christians to influence the sociopolitical setting and to transform it for the better. St. Augustine expressed his disappointment to his flock when he discovered that many, called by the name of Christ, in reality were not actively manifesting their faith. They were not what they pretended to be "in daily life, in their behavior, in hope, and in charity" (*in vita, in moribus, in spe, in caritate, In Epist. Johannis tract. 4, 4; PL 35,2007*).

Due to the existing structures, not corresponding to our generation's aspiration, many dissatisfied young people have either become uneasy and now struggle for a new society, or they live completely indifferent, refusing to make any positive contribution. Thus, instead of having a participatory society, we have many people living on the periphery. They openly declare that what was inherited from the past is only a caricature of a society which is built upon outdated principles, transmitting adult values in a paternalistic way. Many people think that they are thrown into a society which does not offer any security — either economic or moral — and they openly cry: No future! They live in a frustrating universe. Under such circumstances, parents and clergy are surprised that they cannot understand the younger generation's language. Credibility is lost, and a possibility for dialogue does not exist, either because commitment is seen to be useless or the parental language is seen as archaic.

As individuals seek another person as a partner in a dialogue, so human society in general is searching for a supreme partner in dialogue, namely, God. This is the sociological aspect of common prayer — dialogue with this supreme interlocutor. At the same time, man tries to improve what already exists. But once he arrives at his goal, he realizes that perfection remains something that is beyond his reach. And he asks: order or chaos and why one or the other? Man is seeking the ultimate meaning to the human condition. In bygone years every human action was sacred, in the sense that it was connected to the mystery of creation. Even discourses bore religious references, referring sometimes even to the Logos. But nowadays, language and science have become autonomous. Religion is losing most of its temporal influence upon social affairs. Faith is not totally excluded or banished, but it is withdrawn. What still remains is the vacuum and the hunger for the mystery and the sacred in daily life. We hunger for the influencing of the existing human reality with spirituality, with this "plus" or "more," because we often lack the finality of goal, and we sense that progress and technology are not ends in and of themselves.

By refuting religion, atheists try desperately to match Marxist "axioms" with counter-truths equally categorical, but also equally unsatisfactory. Is it too much, therefore, to say that up to now man has never been able to live without faith or divinities? True, they may often fall from their thrones, but the thrones have never remained empty. The only difference is that alternative or substitute gods and beliefs are placed there. Today's society — de-Christianized and desacralized — has produced its own secular priesthood in the verbalizing classes. A desire for social change, in which the community is transformed to fit preconceived notions of political good, bestows on many spirits an important role, in which they interpret reality on its way to the utopian vision. These people are hot for certainties but somewhat wantonly cool about the consequences.

Society, like the individual, is above all the idea which its members form of themselves. This idea is not simply the product of merchants but is based on many other things as well — words, structures, images, and mysteries — all of which combine and confound attempts of codification by unitarians in search of the master code. Virtues and values, in their real essence, are not "things" and never exist as such by themselves in an autonomous way. They become incarnate, visible, living realities inasmuch as they reflect an eternal reality in our daily behavior. Thus, when I say "love is good," or "justice is good," I mean that love realized in a personal life is good, that justice as manifested in a man's life is good. I do not mean that the mere abstract quality, love or justice, is also good. The mere quality "love," conceived abstractly and without any reference to its realization in an individual's personal life, is not good. Good cannot be predicated in the abstract. It belongs only to the concrete, to persons. Similarly, when we speak of virtue, health, etc., as having *value*, it is never virtue, health, justice "in the abstract" to which we refer, but always to the actual virtuous conduct, the true thinking, or the healthy bodily functioning of persons conceived as existing, either in fact or *ex hypothesi*. Candid utterances, the comprehension of truth or the vigorous performance of the physical functions of life by existing things — in fact, by persons — are the real objects to which we ascribe a certain value; we are not giving value to the logical "concepts" — virtue or health. The "truth," "goodness" to which we ascribe worth are in all cases "hypostasized" — incarnate, personified, and concretized in individuals of which they are the constitutive *forms*, and our ascription of worth is only significant in relation to this embodiment of the "universal" in the individual.

One more aspect should be mentioned here, namely, the relative nature of exterior structures. A law, however strict and perfect, exists only to prevent violations and departures from the established order. It acts rather as a deterrent — preventing outbreaks and upheavals — but it actually helps very little in the promotion of virtue and spirituality, since it is a negative rather than a positive force. In general, people are afraid of the law and they limit their activities at a certain point, just so far so that the law is not transgressed. Laws and given structures cannot go much further than this. But what about the human heart — the explosive nature of so many passions, desires, atrocities, aggressiveness, and inclination to sin? Who will treat this enormous inner world, where nobody else can penetrate except God? Keeping in mind that tangible evils proceed from the heart and evil thoughts, the Church turns to the very pathogenic source of it all in order to work out its ministry of correction, healing, and recovery — enabling the recovered penitent to become a new creation, doing good in all its dimensions.

In Christian life there is no logic. One cannot rely on good deeds and, following their number and high amount, demand salvation. A solid spiritual edifice is based not on the number of virtues, but rather on pure intention, on the heart's innocence. Even if one virtue is absent, all the rest are voind, as Chrysostom shows us:

> Christ discourses seldom concerning doctrines, for the subject does not need labor, but often or rather everywhere, of life for the war about this is continual, so also is the labor. And why do I speak of the whole code? "For even a part of it overlooked brings upon one great evils; as, for instance, almsgiving overlooked casts into hell those that have come short in it; and yet this is not the whole of virtue, but a part thereof. But nevertheless both the virgins were punished for not having this, and the rich man was for this cause tormented, and they who have not fed the hungry, are for this condemned with the devil. Again, not to revile is a very small part of it, nevertheless, this, too, casts out those that have not attained it. For he that says to his brother, you fool, shall be in danger of hell fire" (Mt 5.22).

Even continence itself is a part of virtue but, without it no one shall see the Lord. For "Follow peace," it is said, "and holiness" (I Thes 4.3), "without which no man shall see the Lord" (Heb 12.14). "And humility, too, in like manner is a part of virtue; but, nevertheless, though anyone should fulfill other good works, but have not attained to this, he is unclean with God. And this is manifest from the Pharisee, who, though abounding with numberless good works, by this pride lost all" (John Chrysostom *Homily* 64 on *Matthew*, 4).

The necessary effort to overcome both the internal and the external obstacles to a godly life implies a series of steps to be taken daily. Let us not be intimidated by the terminology: effort, feat, ascetic steps. The Christian athlete of today must expend a tremendous effort in order to overcome the worldly structures, the sinful nature which impedes our real happiness and deprives us of eternal life. How does one begin the struggle against an inhuman setting and a secular milieu? By finding the power which destroys and renders evil powerless. One should reach the very source of the *dynamis* — the power source — because the attractive power of evil is always rendering our feeble efforts useless, and without God's help we are powerless to change our fallen nature. God is near us and immediately comes to our aid. The *Kyrie eleison* of an Orthodox conveys to what extent our life is linked with God the omnipresent Pantokrator, as well as our dependence on God's love and protection. This cry "Lord, help me" pierces space from earth to heaven and helps grace to descend into the heart and a ray of light to illumine the darkness.

This movement into another sphere is an accomplishment, a real effort to free ourselves from the conditions of corruptibility. This effort results in another blessing, the dormant good, which is hidden in us, is potentially called forth and made manifest. The personal conquest of evil becomes the asset of the whole community. It is the bedrock of global rebirth and it reduces evil on earth, which in turn increases the impact of virtue in society. Every time evangelical principles advance God is brought into the whole society, reducing the influence of moral misery. By showing spiritual values, by living according to his dignity, man also enriches others. Each person has his own mission on earth with which he serves the whole world. The more we are engaged in our struggle against evil, the more we become strong, meek, generous, self-giving, merciful, and steady. We experience a true renewal, the formation of a new humanity. This is transfiguration. This is the new heaven for which we all yearn. Man has been endowed with the great power of transforming the dubious structures of a given society into a new redeemed community. We can on this earth engage ourselves with another reality, thus creating and transforming our own nature and that of other persons. Each person is thus a miracle-worker since he has performed a miracle by vanquishing evil.

Between good intention and its realization there lies the unknown, the unforeseen. How many good projects by contemporary theologians, fighting for a better world, for a more just society, with emphasis on a kind of Christian Messianism, suddenly collapsed. They miscalculated the nature of Christian hope and its limitations, forgetting man's fall, the existence of evil in the world, that we all are sinners. All the means employed do not always have the expected response and the result which was hoped for.

When comparing the potential offered by a faithful person and the expected corresponding outcome, one must not forget the unforeseen factors, the strong opposition of wicked persons; such factors may intervene and overthrow the logical estimation of the outcome.

As an example, a certain amount of food in normal situations produces a measurable amount of energy. And yet, what in theory is correctly calculated, in practice might give an unexpected conclusion, because to produce energy, in terms of healthy blood, and to activate the consumer, a series of preconditions must be fulfilled. How will the energy be produced if the consuming body is unable to absorb, to digest and properly transform the food? Or again, how will energy be proved if the consuming body is defective or if the blood does not collaborate? How often is first class food offered to patients in our hospitals, but in vain, without any positive result. Lack of energy is due to the improper functioning of the body, and the amount of vitamins or calories ingested cannot be transformed to blood, as healthy bodies do.

John Chrysostom's statement remain true: "It requires only one single person, filled with divine zeal, in order to totally change a whole city." However, how often even such remarkable persons, consumed by desire for the transformation of a society or fighting for a better living and witnessing Church, wearily see at the end that their efforts and labor have become void, fruitless, and even deceptive? How often is everything prepared for the renewal of an institution, of structures and even more, accompanied with a general mobilization of all forces, and yet produces such disappointing meagre results?

This mystery is due to the resistance of evil forces or enemies of our faith, who do all they can in order to hinder the reign of truth, of God's will on earth "as it is in heaven." This failure may also result from an inconsistent attitude, one day engaged in a passionate desire for the defense of good and after a few days compromising with the spirit of this world. In general, the most noble of people and the best intentions can be contested or refused simply because human nature is not what idealists suppose it to be, when they dream of a return to the paradisiac state. Justice, happiness, and godly life are all relative on earth, in spite of all constructive efforts. The Church's mission, after two millenia, did not attain its objective in quantity or in quality. Christian society does not behave as truly Christian and the non-Christian world, vast and more numerous, has not yet been entirely evangelized.

In this respect, Jesus remains the example. With the best of intentions to offer ideal conditions for a new redeemed humanity, his mission was rejected and finally he himself, though innocent, was condemned to death. In the history of mankind, we find many instances of people who lived for others and not for themselves and who did not succeed in restoring humanity. A great gap exists between excellent plans and the realities of life. We must not idealize laws and principles. Society cannot throw away its familiar demons while relying only on the good intention of a newly organized system. These demons are pathological individualism, absence of the sense of civic responsibility, the endemic violence of a society, and the hidden intentions of powerful and high ranking individuals. A group cannot wipe away, as with a sponge or with the magic touch of new structures, the accumulated evils and continuously emerging problems or the profound misery resulting from human sins.

Life, therefore, cannot be judged with arithmetic precision according to a human measure. We do not always reap in our human struggle what we sow. The harvest does not correspond to the sowing. A mysterious law, it seems, does not allow us often to see the realizations of our visions and of our efforts. There is the fall, the omnipresent sin with its consequence, and only in the afterlife shall we find a full reward — the absolute satisfaction of all our efforts. Sin, in spite of Christ's redemptive work, limits our joy and happiness on earth. Above all we must free ourselves from evil. We must admit that being sinful and possessed by passions is not our real essence. Sin is not part of ourselves but something which, intruding in our lives, contaminates us and brings us anguish. Then we will want to rid ourselves of this strange element which is so alien to us. By doing evil we do not reveal ourselves in our true aspect. Evil is not our natural state — it is a mirage, which does not exist as an hypostasis. Virtue and God alone are real and hypostatic. A mirage when taken as reality is a darkness which brings us unhappiness and prevents us from enjoying that moment of joy and light given to us each day. Evil, further, robs man and prevents him from revealing himself in the fullness of his spiritual powers. If we do not recognize this, then we ourselves willingly create our own hell.

Often we do not try to free ourselves from what is not ours and which also brings us unhappiness as well. A substitution of something false for something real is always taking place within us. We set forth evil for good. Our actual steps, stemming from the unreal, bring corruption, dissatisfaction, suffering. We walk as if in a dream, immersed in the darkness of our illusions. Our being was created for eternity, but we are not concerned about it at all.

Plato regarded goodness as something which saves the whole of society, while evil distorts it. Iniquity and selfishness harm the body, and on a wider scale, leads to degradation (*Republic* 609b). We must not blame God for social miseries, because man by his own fault disturbs the harmony and wellbeing (Iamblichos, *On Pythagoras* 32). A close relationship exists between an individual transgression and the whole community. A single act does not stay within a limited sphere. It influences others also and even the innocent suffer — a theme which remains a mystery. Basil of Caesarea dedicated an entire theological treatise to this topic in which he proves at length that God is not at all responsible for any evil (PG 31.329-53).

One particular disorder affects a wider circle, thus touching the state, the law, and established institutions. Once the root of a tree is rotten, inevitably the rest of the branches are touched by this corruption. Basil, commenting on a Pauline verse, ''for the reward of sin is death; but what God freely gives is eternal life in Jesus Christ our Lord'' (Rom 6.23), remarks with profound insight:

> The more primitive man was estranged from life, the more he was reaching toward death. This is because life is God, while privation of life is death. Adam, by departing from God's presence, fabricated for himself death, as it is said (Ps. 72.27). Consequently, God was not the author of death, but we ourselves by our free will created such a sinful situation that we made ourselves mortal (*Hom. Quod Deus non est auctor* 7; PG 31.345A).

The disastrous results of evil can be seen in heavy inhuman taxation, in bureaucracy, favoritism, bribery, and all kinds of corruption and demagogy at the expense of the poorer classes. John Chrysostom in a shocking statement remarked that in the great city of Antioch one percent of the population was entirely poor, ''having nothing at all'' (*Hom.* 64,3 *in Matth*; PG 58.630).

While the fathers were criticizing the egoism of the rich, at the same time they attacked as inadmissible the general social disorder. Their hearts were burning with love towards man, but also for the whole country. For this reason they made an effort to solve general problems, attacking inequality, scandalous misery, and the misconception which led to different laws for men and women. All the fathers declared that God created human beings equal. Differences and inequalities result from human injustices and not from God's will. Gregory the Theologian, commenting on the text of Prov 22.2: ''Rich and poor have this in common: the Lord is the maker of them all,'' stated that the Lord never created the one rich and the other poor. The division does not originate in God's premeditated action. All are creatures of God, however much the exterior conditions seem to be unequal (*Oratio* 14,34; PG 35.905).

With regard to women's dignity and equal rights, sometimes known as feminism, the fathers disapproved of social discrimination of either sex. Gregory the Theologian, condemning certain unjust treatment, did not hesitate to oppose even the unjust legislation of the emperors. Why, he asked, can the law punish the adulterous woman and not the adulterous man? I shall never accept such onesided legislation. And I know the real cause of this discriminatory attitude, namely, men that exclusively were the legislators and consequently the whole legislation goes against weak women. It was partial, serving only men's interest and favoring the masculine sex, discriminating in a scandalous way against women. But God, on the contrary, did not treat us in such a way, rather he said: "Honor equally your father and mother" (Ex 20.12). "Do you not see here the quality of the rule of God? One and the same is the creator of man and woman; therefore, it follows that one and the same law must be applied to both. No legislation is equal. One and the same is the Creator of both man and woman. Both are earthly. There is one icon, one law, one death, and one resurrection for both. We are all made equally from man and woman. One is the debt that is due by children to their parents" (*Oratio* 37,6; PG 36.289).

Laws and structures are thus relative, ephemeral. To a great extent they are influenced by this or that human attitude which develops in history. Man has enormous possibilities for forming a good socioeconomic climate or, on the contrary, for endangering the social setting by his greed and arrogance. Systems and structures certainly influence but do not absolutely determine our final individual decisions. Yet, it would be too theoretical or utopian to show ignorance of these structures by insisting exclusively upon determining human values and by disregarding the milieu in which they exist. Sometimes external factors can be so depressing and humiliating that they make life a non-life, an anti-life.

37. Changing but Not Being Changed

Very often people who suffer from human injustices speak about changing this or that. Certainly, a lot of ill-situated things need radical change. Change is an imperative need in all human life. Wherever there are living beings, changes are inevitable from time to time. But with regard to the question of change, the real problem is not to change something that is structural or external but rather to change somebody, namely, the members of a given society in whose minds, wills, and hearts are social evils. Christians hold that inasmuch as human beings in their inner world need redemption, a change in their innermost lives, so, too, is there needed a change of structures where values are supposed to reside. Structures, surely, are not *innocent*. They are badly constructed and in need of therapy. They are the carriers of certain abstract ideals, embodiments of errors or truths held by a given society. But to ignore the therapy of society as a priority for living people, who by their thinking determine and produce the subsequent structures and rules, is to sacrifice personality upon the altar of the impersonal, and to prefer abstract nouns to living beings. Abstract universals are indeed involved in all our ascriptions of value, but that to which the value is ascribed should not be the universal itself but the individual in which it is embodied.

A characteristic of every age is to decry and disapprove the decline of morals and of general human standards. But the decline of "structure" and its subversion by some should be a particular warning to Christians, because it will diminish and ultimately destroy our ability to perceive the existence of any standards at all. These standards are declining because without structures they will no longer be capable of a just expression or a fair evaluation.

We should not belittle the subversive effect of using technique to sustain vague and meaningless terminology whose interpretation can be changed under different circumstances adapted to sometimes altogether different goals. In doing so, the users divorce words from their accepted meaning by repeating demonstrably untrue statements. There is no need to lie openly when truth, well doctored, gilded and shrewdly distributed, will serve the same purpose. A society built only on such hypothetical structures is corroded when deprived of the meaning of words, and thus loses its critical faculty and the alternative

247

concepts necessary to support true criticism. But it is in the roots
of a pluralistic society that the roots of individual freedom and morality
can be found. These are nourished by the gentle rain of a million
words and ideas. If there is no rain, then there are no roots, no words,
no freedom. We know that some materialistic systems adapt and promote any misuse of language and structure as long as they contribute
to the ultimate ideological goal. We know that any systematic criticism
becomes impossible when demonstrable falsehoods are persistently
considered as admissible — in order to serve a political purpose or
end. We know that a conspiracy exists to corrupt, subvert, and
ultimately destroy all "religious language" because atheistic ideology
does not recognize it. More difficult to discern is a certain widespread,
indigenous debasement of our language and terminology which cannot be attributed to any clearly-defined conspiracy or ideological
assault. Language and terminology should act as custodians of values
rather than as instruments of their corruption.

Nowadays we use vague, abstract concepts such as stabilization,
interdependence, and so forth, but these words are often susceptible
to various incompatible interpretations. These methods, in reality,
intend, through a conscious manipulation of facts and minds, to
substantiate wholly invalid predictions about the future. They have
a tendency to depersonalize and to politicize the environment which
in turn affects persons. An example of this is the family question.
The family, a living organism of infinite value, is often treated abstractly as a mere index for social determinists. Such a tendency should
not be considered to be an iconoclastic conspiracy. It more likely
springs from a reaction among intellectuals who, though seduced by
the magnetic power of Marxist certainty and dogmatism, are
themselves searching for a freer way of expressing their identity and
affirming their personhood in a civil or state setting.

A diagnosis is easy when it looks only upon the exterior side of
a bodily or spiritual disorder. Often this exterior facade hides much
deeper causes beneath it. Most economists and sociologists,
overestimating society's weak, unjust and sinful structures, fall into
such a trap. Their morphology and phenomenology are inadequate
and terribly misleading. Each time they attack a certain way of life
instead of penetrating deeper. And the ills and deviation within man's
own person, mind, or deliberate decisions and false approaches tend
rather to criticize laws, political systems and social structures. Then
people will be corrected, discipline will be established and men and
women will feel happy, behaving in a more correct way. Marxism is

is one of the defenders of such a line, followed by dozens of similar ideologies of socialist inspiration. Perhaps the truth is somewhere in the middle, and the wrong must be fought from two sides. Human hearts need to be healed by education and evangelical training, on the one hand, and on the other, the necessary infrastructure for public order — disciplinary measures, sound rules, and inspired legislation — need to be estasblished. Human beings need to live in a sound, properly structured milieu. In such an environment, the practice of spiritual values will be facilitated and the faith will be safeguarded. Suicide, depression, unemployment, and crime may in fact result from money manipulations as well as from the natural resources boom which is sweeping many parts of the world. No society can be complacent about the poverty induced by compulsive exploitation and its damaging affect upon many families. In such cases, the Church must raise its voice in order to urge governments to tighten their laws, to regulate salaries, to prevent excessive profitmaking, to give inducements for participation, and to stop the exploitation of victims in the crazy cult of money.

The radical socialistic approach fails to show how to alleviate the problem and who are the responsible persons. Getting tough with oppressors sounds good but misses at least half the point. What their selfish policy has accomplished up to now has been to make the other half worse. Their poor results show to what degree they have been particularly myopic about our distorted human nature, about institutionalized egoism, avidity, and corruption. Reality cannot be masked. We cannot make justice work with only regulations and administrative controls, by launching fervent appeals, whatever the merits of the civil servants who do. Thus, in spite of all, social sins still survive and easily escape the laws and the law-keepers. Governments fix the main lines of an equitable strategy, but from then, the inner values of entrepreneurs and the creators of enterprises are decisive. Herein lies the drama of the human condition — the absolutization of organizational rules and of human structures. An excessive confidence placed upon superficial exterior changes, forgetting that redemption is more than a modification of simple organizational structures, in the end shows its weakness in a most flagrant manner.

38. On the Surface and Beneath

Christians are obliged to put into practice that which they believe and profess. Liturgical order and ceremonial rites are of little use if the person, the worshiper, does not engage in the most profound part of his own being, the songs, hymns, the ordained prayers, and the whole message of the eucharistic service. The divine liturgy is a "happening," an *opus Dei*, an event which implies the active participation of the assembly. As such, people need to put their feelings into a certain frame of reference, i.e., to worship in uniformity, but at the same time to accept by means of their active participation, what this liturgical content demands and indicates. Both formalism and ritualism are deviations because they rely exclusively on the exterior forms without involving the whole being of the person in the mystery of the worship service. Since our common calling is to become saints, we must mobilize all our being during a religious service. If not, attending services may degenerate into a parody, falsifying the whole concept of worship and Christian prayer itself. Symbolic actions and signs are there to lead us to the underlying facts. A virtue which is not actually embodied during prayer becomes superficial, fragile, and sooner or later will collapse. Like those foolish virgins who were unable to enter and meet the Bridegroom because they kept their lamps in their hands without sufficient fuel, so, too, in the same way, empty virtues, without being lived, consolidated and renewed, cannot lead us to that door where Christ is waiting for us.

Most of the changes and the reforms demanded in our liturgies may become, in fact, futile, since whether they are shortened or lengthened, they do not produce the desired effect. This failure may be the result of an error in the anthropological field. The word, actually, precedes the individual. The truth and the word also precede the structure. We feel or we think before we speak or sing. The anti-formalist movement, which has been in existence since the sixteenth-century Reformation, may distort the praying assembly by the number of its rules, which are at the mercy of changes made without first considering the implications of such changes. Man lives and resides within all these forms with a full liberty and commitment and does not remain indifferent and on the periphery. Exterior forms only serve as an introduction or an initiation. Every liturgy essentially implies a "work" accomplished, a personal action fulfilled, thus justifying the real meaning of the term *leitourgia,* namely, an *ergon,* a work performed on behalf of another. All the liturgical gestures, the rubrics, directives, etc., are only auxiliary elements which correspond to man's double nature of body and soul. All of these must be articulated within the living presence of God, in an inner meeting or communion with Christ. We do not "read" the Gospel pericopes as we would any other secular texts. The early Church did not start its worship from zero, but based it on the existing Jewish rituals and rites of the temple. But all things were seen and elevated in Christ's death and resurrection.

Rites may be changed when necessary. But such innovations should not become change for the sake of change, because we risk making the liturgy more like a consumer product and liable thus, to continuous change. We need to understand the very nature of Christian worship: actualization and contemporization of all that the liturgy reveals as being essential — what is not invented by the human mind, but is given to us directly by Christ. Every prayer, is at the same time an intervention from God. He intervenes but not always in the expected way. Thus, God intervened in the world in Christ — not from on high, but lowly; not as an irresistible power, but as a vulnerable persuasion; not as a detached visitor, but from within the world process itself. The incarnation of Christ is unique and it provides a paradigm of God's intervention within his creation at other points, too. God is not a puppeteer pulling the strings, or the master of a gaming table pushing chips across the board of the world. He intervenes in the world through persons — through people who are open and responsive to his promptings.

To be in Christ may be a purely individual act, but it also involves one's incorporation into the Body of Christ. This incorporation means one's integration into a community that is so close that, if one member suffers, the whole body suffers. If we are incorporated into the Body of Christ, we are involved in doing Christ's work. But words have to proceed from our way of life. What we are speaks louder than what we say. No structure or human condition can prevent such an affair. What we are depends upon how we apply our faith to the problems of life, regardless of any social or ideological conditions. "A new signboard over an old shop," Arabs say when they want to stress the purely formal, superficial nature of changes. It appears often that some Christians want changes to be confined to the replacement of a signboard. These are changes without a change.

Let us live not only according to the flesh, but a little also for God. The taste and enjoyment of food pleases only a small part of the body, the mouth; but after the food has rotted in the belly, it has its end in the draught. Compassion and beneficence on the other hand are things which are dear to God, and make man partaker of the divinity in whom they make their dwelling, implanting upon him the seal of the good so that he may imitate it, and that they may exist as an image of the first and uncontaminated being that surpasses all understanding (St.Gregory of Nyssa, *De Pauperibus Amandis*; PG 46.464-65).

39. A Thirst for More Spirituality

The role of the Holy Spirit seems to us to answer an imperative need of that modern consciousness which will have nothing to do with any alienation. Just so long as the word of God only impinges on man from the outside, only stems from some external authority, whether it be the Bible or the liturgical life of the Church, modern man feels led to reject it. If, on the contrary, this external outer word is but the revelation, the unveiling, the service of the inner word, that of the Spirit, he will understand that it is not only useful but essential. The discovery of the role of the Holy Spirit actively at work in the hearts of men permits us to understand in a living fashion that dependent relationship to God, a dependence which is faith and, far from giving rise to any alienation, constitutes his freedom. The Holy Spirit progressively reveals to man that it is a question of his willingness for him to receive all gifts from God in the form of freedom in Jesus Christ. Only the experience of the *love* with which God loves man and by which he enables him to love, and this enabling is the specific task of the Holy Spirit helps man to discover that his longing for liberty and autonomy, far from being presumptuous, full of pride, or a desire for power, is instead faithfulness to the gift God gave to him when he made him a man, a man able to share in the divine sonship of Jesus Christ, the Son equal to the Father and one in essence with the Father by the gift of the Father. Christianity has revealed to us that man has been created as a creator, a co-builder of the kingdom of God, a collaborator with God's plan on earth. This attitude, never firmly set once and forever, grows and ceaselessly deepens in us, as a result of the discreet and ever faithful action of the Holy Spirit within us, in accordance with our humble and ever more willing submission to the Holy Spirit of love, who is given to us by the Father in the Son.

Inner life, contemplation, personal intimacy with God, all of which characterize the spiritual tradition of the Christian East and which are none other than involvement in all things with the Holy Spirit, have always received recognition in the Christian West. But, at the same time, these words which imply a mystical relationship "inner life," "contemplation," "personal intimacy with God," which are summed up fairly well in the expression "life of prayer," give rise today

253

to a mistrust which is to a certain degree both instictive and reflected upon. One sees the danger, the temptation, the illusion of turning in upon oneself, of disguised egocentricity, of a fear of action, of an individualistic self-satisfaction, of self-withdrawal, in short of an escape from the human reality. This is due, it seems to me, to an opposition or even a competition between contemplation and commitment to the earthly city, between the love of God and the love of men, between the life of prayer and engagement in the realities of life — an opposition which culminates today in the exclusive predominance either of what is called verticalism or of horizontalism. In such a context, the claims of the Gospel are confusing; God appears to be man's rival, or man the rival of God.

The spiritual tradition of the East must help us to overcome this divergence between the two essential aspects of any authentic Christian life so that they may converge together.

True inner life is not a turning in upon oneself, but a constant return to the source. The disciple of Jesus, submissive to the Spirit, knows that the source of action is in him, but not of him. By this humble concern to remain dependent in faith on him who, in the words of St. Augustine, "is more inward to a man than his own self," the Christian discovers today's imperative of fraternal charity and service to mankind. He only relates to those whom he serves because he constantly hears within him the call of the Spirit of love, the call of love; but he really depends on this Spirit of love only to the extent that he allows himself, willingly, to be sent forth to others in order to serve them.

Spiritual experience, in which contemplation and action, the spirit of prayer and apostolic action, make but one whole, is a perpetual Pentecost, wherein faith in God and fraternal charity are discovered to be indissolubly one and an inexhaustible spring of liberty, hope, and joy. Is this not what Jesus reveals to us when He says: "It is not they who say to me 'Lord, Lord' who enter into the kingdom of heaven, but they who do the will of my Father which is in heaven"? Now the will of God, as Jesus has also said, is that we should love one another as he himself has loved us. Is this what St. Paul discovered on the road to Damascus, when he asked of the risen Christ, who was revealing himself to him: "Lord, what do you want me to do?" The Christian seeks the source, the inspiration, and the animating power of his acts even of the least, the most material, the most technical acts in God, who loves him and teaches him how to love. Prayer for him never consists of asking that God act as a man in his place, but that he permit him, by bestowing his Spirit, to discover ever more fully his own responsibility as a man and what he must, in freedom, decide to do.

Many Christians have the persistent fallacy that "theology" and "spirituality" can not only be distinguished but even isolated from each other. The teacher must always remind his flock that the very use of the word "God" is to make a most profound and fundamental theological statement. Knowledge of God which is wholly cerebral is an abstraction and is a spiritual awareness which *per se* leads to pietism. If a Christian is to be true to his calling as a "peacemaker," he must recognize in the worldwide apathy and spiritual decline the stirring of that higher spirit within mankind. Not that we must be engaged in any socio-political movements. While the biblical command is quite clear on the personal level, we must remember that often a number of the saints, whom we revere and with whom in Christ we share a mystical fellowship, have taken concrete steps at given moments to purify a polluted society or to defend a threatened family life. A Christian may have to fight in some circumstances for the survival of Christian values and spiritual life.

The second step would be for those theologians presently engaged in the ecumenical field to update their theological methods, deliberately ignoring certain easy solutions which can only be damaging in the long run.

First and foremost of these "easy solutions" is the emphasis upon eschatology, in opposition to a presumed "this-worldliness" in non-Orthodox modern theology. This emphasis serves, of course, to highlight Orthodoxy against the background of non-Orthodoxy, but it can be utterly misleading, as it can lead to an irreducible interpretation of Matthew, 25: 31-46. This situation is not only bad ecumenism: it is bad Christianity. A far more fruitful and harmonious, doctrinal exposition would start, quite simply, with the Lord's Prayer, laying stress upon the petition, "Thy kingdom come, thy will be done, on earth as it is in heaven." Here Orthodoxy could draw on many factors related directly to its centuries-long experience: the liturgical tradition, the *askesis,* the cenobitic tradition and — with greater or lesser success — the "theocratic" tradition. This last point holds particular relevance for today, since it answers the question of the legitimate relation between Christianity and ideology, the latter being distinguished from the former by the admission of political and sociological factors not bound by Christian ethics, but purporting to be over and above Christian ethics. The problem can thus be seen as less of a theological than an ethical one.

Orthodox Christians have a unique witness to make at this point, since Orthodoxy from the time of the Ecumenical Councils has survived, and even flourished, under a wider range of social and political systems and ideologies than any other Christian denomination. Its crises have been of an ethical nature (the morality of a rapprochement with Rome, for example, when material advantages were at stake. Even in the *'filoque'* controversy, the problem for certain Greeks, was not so much theological — the Roman explanation of "spiration" was generally considered satisfactory — as ethical — the ethics of adding even one word to the Creeds when additions were expressly forbidden by the Second Ecumenical Council) rather than of a truly theological nature. Today, as in the sunset years of Byzantium, true Christian ethics are again undervalued, being replaced by a popular "permissive" theology, which can only lead, in turn, to a Montanist revival. Neither is it a true solution, in accordance with the advances of modern society which calls for an enlightened religious equilibrium. Thus, for example, it is less the theological aspect of ordaining women to the priesthood than the ethical dangers of a competing feminine priesthood that requires examination.

The Christian family — as a microcosm of the kingdom — with all its inherent problems of family planning, sexual behavior, divorce, etc., should be accorded far greater importance on the ecumenical scene, since deviations from its ideal norms have been shown, by recent psychological and psychoanalytical research, to have been the causes of deviations in social (and political) behavior. Orthodox research on this subject, in relation both to past and present historical events, could be extremely helpful in determining future WCC international policy, weaning it away from one-sided, socio-political activities and options to an impartial general reminder of the ethical and moral responsibilities of Christians. This policy would include the replacement of partisan theorizing by plain common sense, in accordance with the (higher) laws of human nature.

To bring the wheel full circle, only when Christian morality has proven itself in society, can the supernatural claims of Jesus to be the savior, in the form of "God made man," have any meaning for the man in the street. Even in looking in the history of the Christian east, we must remember that theology — the patristic theology of the so-called "Golden-Age" — was an offspring of Athenian philosophy, and that it drew its strength from the superiority of Christian over pagan morality, even over Jewish morality. Idolatry was seen to be fundamentally the worship of bestiality. "By their fruits shall ye know them," is the Gospel reminder. Our Lord himself healed many people before asking: "Who do you say I am?" Also, Jesus prayed to his Father, on the night of his betrayal, that the disciples might be united as the Father and Son are united, "that the world might believe that thou hast sent me." In other words, a grasp of the moral requirements for salvation is the prerequisite to an understanding of eschatology. Jesus himself made it clear that he was castigating the Scribes and Pharisees of his day, not for keeping the Mosaic Law, but for keeping it hypocritically and for hedging it about with so many prescriptions that those who could not comply fell into the sin of despair, and neither group could distinguish the true meaning of the law any more.

The Christian is a contemplative in a double sense (both in his action and by his action), thus uplifted in otherworldly realities and joys: in faith he contemplates the demands of love, the imperative of God, the source of his action; in concrete social action, with which he loves his fellow men, — by his action attuned to the action of God in him and in the world — he also contemplates the laborious but sure progress of the creative design of God.

Today's society needs this message in order to fulfill its human, let alone its Christian, potential. The fate of all ideologies, even the most promising revolutionary ideologies, is to become pharisaical, tyrannical, the very opposite of liberating. In reaction, Christian theology can also become pharisaical, inward-looking, concerned solely with rites and with witch-hunting among its members. Modern Orthodoxy, especially that of the Diaspora and "exiles," has not escaped this pitfall, alas, but the young are anxious to escape from this hothouse atmosphere and to bring the essential flavor of Orthodoxy to the rest of society, no matter what its worldly allegiances may be. Ways and means need to be found, whereby this can be done without hurting and causing any misunderstanding. Probably the time has not yet fully come, but it could well be at hand, especially if the pan-Orthodox movement truly shows itself to be that of the one, holy, catholic, and apostolic Church of Christ, and not a motley assembly of local Orthodox churches, each seeking its own advantage. Once the churches of the East have achieved this, other churches may be moved to adopt the same conciliar system — which can only be advantageous to the ecumenical movement as a whole. For the Anglican communion, it could be a means of uniting and building up Anglican theology, while in the Roman Catholic Church it could provide a way out of its dilemma of decentralization versus the re-mythologizing of the papacy, or independence and conciliarity of each local church versus reunion under the papacy in a new guise.

Present-day society, no matter in which country, under whichever regime, is itself rent by this dilemma of state versus individual rights. If future wars are to be avoided, economic malpractice (such as distinction of food surpluses) stopped, and limited global reserves preserved for future generations, some solution must be found. It is not utopian to assert what the churches are theoretically capable of achieving in practice, what political and economic caucuses can also achieve, provided they accept and abide by the same basic moral rules.

In short, Orthodoxy should, by its leverage in the ecumenical movement at large, persuade the Christian churches to campaign for *moral hygiene* as an essential part of human hygiene, beginning, like other forms of hygiene, at the nursery and kindergarten stage. The way things are at present, no other form of evangelism could be as effective as this. Through experiencing the little resurrection already in *this* life, within their hearts and among their contacts, ordinary people come to recognize Christ. Then — and only then — can Christian theology take on meaning for them, since the nature of sin and sinlessness will have been revealed to them. It could take place just as with the Roman centurion who, unperturbed by the squabbles over the remainder of Jesus' worldly goods, stood before the cross when Jesus died and was able to say — seeing *how* he died — "Truly this man was the son of God."

Christ's teaching, like a white light, has been broken into many colored fragments by the prisms of men. But truth is not something we change through our own reasoning and reasonable theology. Knowledge of God is a gift given by God himself, and the quest for the truth of God is an ageless phenomenon.

40. Applied or Incarnate Theology

Christian faith is not a simple matter either of a knowledge of certain religious articles or of intellectual concepts. Consequently, it does not become the possession of a believer nor does it grow by simple observation and scrupulous intellectual study. Faith and truth, as confidence in God's word, mean self-surrender to God, inner communion with God as a person, and therefore are related to love, since God is love. By loving him we belong to him, we conform our life to him, we become identified with him. Thus, we offer whatever we can possibly offer him and only then do we begin to know him and to feel his presence. Then faith increases spiritually in length and in depth and theologically in all dimensions. The whole of our being is filled with his divine power which can resuscitate every dead life. From that moment, no doubts poison our minds. We possess a rational peace of mind, and even more, we feel that our entire being is enveloped with an unutterable serenity and blessing which is a source of incorruptibility. Because we are unable to express this kind of joy, the only way to manifest these inner feelings is through a continuous praise, a doxology, an uninterrupted *Te Deum*. Thus, we can say a true theologian has reached his main objective, to know God and to feel his presence and almighty wonders. Without such an experience, our relation to theology and God is inadequate, poor, and defective.

God can be known by a *koinonia* of our innermost selves with the ineffable God, by faith, not rational but ontological and existential, which involves the whole human being. We see then in our deepest and innermost being amazing similarities with our Creator. We see that we are more than flesh and bones, that we are indeed entirely his image, *imago Dei*. In other words, we believe because we accept a certain number of concepts and also because we feel his presence and we find him within ourselves. God is not like an outsider, an "object" being touched and rationally observed, since all human receptive criteria remain inadequate and poor. In fact, in the Christian experience of living one's daily life in communion with the will of God, there are most noble and sweet feelings which can hardly be conveyed by words, but which permeate the whole being and its whole setting. But we hold it as an icon which is caught and seen in the framework of love and sacrifice, following the principle of John 4.12:

"Are you greater than our father Jacob, who gave us the well, and drank thereof himself, and his children, and his cattle?"

One of the most famous ascetic fathers, Isaac the Syrian said: "When we shall reach this love, then we have reached God. That means that our way is accomplished and we have passed to that island beyond this world, where is found the Father, the Son, and the Holy Spirit" (*Sermon* 72).

Thus he described the relationship between life and faith. Life is shaped according to the degree of communion with God, implying total faith and confidence. The saints are called to follow Christ himself. The Christ-like life is a life of obedience to his sufferings and a renunciation of the desires of the flesh. The ascetic vision is a daily following of the incarnate and risen Christ. Christ is also the focus of patristic theology: God deals with sinful man according to man's faith in Christ.

Thus, love and faith in the Orthodox perspective are acknowledged as two interrelated realities, distinctive and yet complementary. We cannot refer to one without mentioning or knowing the other, too. Herein lies the dilemma and the tragedy of contemporary non-liturgical liberal theology. Doctrine and religious instruction must be sustained, completed and confirmed by spiritual *praxis*. Every theologian is a martyr. He is a true martyr of the Christian faith, always confessing what he has already experienced or proclaiming his faith in love for Christ and for his mystical body, that is, the community, the *ekklesia*. In this way noble souls coming out of ancient pagan society, as Justin the philospher, Clement of Alexandria, Athenagoras, Augustine, etc., were able to recognize the distinctive character and the superiority of Christianity as opposed to other gnostic or philosophical religious trends of their times. In Christ they found the true faith because it was grounded in love, in personal surrender, and founded upon ultimate union with God.

This love, far from being sentimental, is linked with binding engagements and requirements known in general as *askesis*. Without the ascetic element — the continuous renunciation, struggle, sufferings, self-denial, refusal, resistance, keeping faith's demands without compromising with the world — faith loses its renewing element and dynamic revolutionary character becoming just another ordinary and conventional ethical system. Such was the dynamic asceticism that the early Church lived, as many early writers witness. In this particular ascetic life, the Church's tremendous attractiveness and the secret of its expansion were to be found. If today the too distant and academically colored theology faces critical moments and is in crisis, it is precisely because it has lost its spirituality. This loss explains why many theologies turn into a religious vacuum, causing man to seek after pseudo-ascetic movements from the East. Historical errors and compromising attitudes of a worldly theology have thrown a cover over the authentic face of the Christian faith. Our duty, therefore, consists in uncovering it by removing the accumulated dust and whatever else has been added.

The ascetic life is extensively emphasized by patristics because the basic principle of the Gospel remains forever that man's earthly life is just a pilgrimage, and, therefore, only transitory and preparatory. His permanent dwelling is in heaven, not in a topological sense of course. To possess "eyes for seeing" and "mind" is the result of an inner fight, an abnegation of sensuality, and an ascension. To follow Christ requires an abandonment of one's iniquities, a refusal of futility, and the overthrow of earthly priorities. It means to carry one's cross throughout this life. In this context it is very significant that believers from the earliest times have chosen the cross as the most eloquent symbol of their Christian identity: as the model of self-emptying, self-surrender, unselfishness, evacuation of the old man with all evil and sinful passions.

The Gospel's message, therefore, is betrayed by all those who try to intellectualize it, or even worse, to secularize or to evaporate its high standards by adapting it to man's measure, as opposed to adapting man to the requirements of the faith instead. Such theologians — abundant in the West — try to misinterpret the authentic meaning by introducing strange views, as if the Gospel were known and understood without pain or hardship; as if it were an earthly Messianism, full of enjoyment and permissiveness. Joy and optimism are doubtless its elements, provided that this joy remain a permanent, constant joy in Christ. Gladness must be nourished and consolidated in the struggle against evil. The cost of Christian joy and optimism is heavy and is borne by all the faithful on account of the triumph of Christ's resurrection, his victory over the powers of evil, sin, and death. But if one wants to share in this triumph, one must first pass, as did Christ, the way of the cross and suffering. To hear the risen Christ's joyful greeting "Rejoice," spoken to the women bringing myrrh and to his disciples, one has first to be crucified with Christ and to share in his passion. Any external, mechanical union with the risen Christ during church festivities is no help to us unless we, too, in our personal experience participate in and pass through all the

saving and redeeming stages as he and all his followers did. Only
under such presuppositions and considerations can we begin to touch
upon the very important task of a true Christian theology. Only in
this way can we avoid falling into traps or extremes or arriving at
a kind of utopian or unrealistic, or other worldly approach. The main
task of theologians and devout laity remains to reformulate and to
assist in this earthly life, in order that we might be formed for participation in eternal life, having first lived the Gospel in all its dimensions here and now and in all spheres of human existence, regardless
of the sociological or ideological conditions in which we may find
ourselves.

If we could define approximately what is meant by the common
use of the term "theology," we could say that it is the science *par*
excellence of God. By such a definition, one places emphasis on the
word "theology" and, contemplating its status, restricts oneself only to the methodological requirements, the role of human culture,
etc. But one may also put the emphasis on the word "God" and thus
pay more attention to the possibilities and content of the modern
understanding of reflections on God. It is, therefore, natural that
psychological and sociological conditionings of the idea of God are
unavoidable in such research.

One of the weaknesses of the present state of theology in the West
is that the confrontation of emerging earthly realities with theological
thought becomes disproportional; hence, the polarization and high
intellectual level of such a theology. While it may appear to be an
attempt to get free from the pressure of academic influence, in the
last analysis it remains less creative. The consciousness of local engagement of theology with temporal issues should not hamper the feeling
of *sentire cum ecclesia universal.* This leads to a spiritual openness
to the thought of other parts of divided Christendom without any
inferiority complex or any other prejudice.

In prior decades the struggle was against pietism. Today the situation compels yet another struggle against the exaggerated rationalization of faith. The development of philosophy is a predominant factor here especially, the birth of existentialism, which inspires
theological thought to encompass the whole man in his relationship
to God and to put the problem on a subjective rather than objective
level. Theology should be, from its very nature, closely linked with
the whole life of the Church in a given social setting. An authentic
theology does not develop in a vacuum. It grows out of the concrete
problems and needs with which the faithful must cope and which

they must overcome and which quite often make people more deeply aware of those issues. Questions should arise, constantly disturbing and challenging the minds of theologians.

The lack of any sufficient consideration of Orthodox theology by Westerners deprives the West of a basic link with the very roots of the early Church and condemns it to a certain isolation. Patristic and Byzantine writings are little known to the majority of Western theologians. It is hardly possible to speak today of a true "catholic" or "ecumenical" theology if the latter does not take into consideration the thought of the Church which, in the first centuries, was shaping a tradition which remains common to the whole of Christianity. These traditions, because of the schism and the reformation, have ceased to shape the theological consciousness of the West and have not been able to receive until now a due expression in the life and theology of the West. To rediscover a living bond with the early patristic era is one of the requirements of a true theologian. After the frequent contacts and improvements of inter-confessional relations, we have every chance to contribute to the implementation of this task.

Curiously enough, although many national churches of the West, in Poland, Czechoslovakia, Italy, etc., were greatly influenced at that time by Eastern Christianity, they were suddenly cut off since the great schism.

It has been said again and again, on the occasion of a quest for spirituality that the Orthodox faith, while formulated by the Ecumenical Synods, is lived out in daily life and incorporated in its worship. We can find this relationship in the liturgical context itself. Look for a moment at the representation of the Nativity of Christ in iconography. There the rocks appear as mountains and become as sharp as if they had been cut out by a knife. They turn towards the very center of the picture, to the main event, the Nativity. In addition, the trees and bushes bow before the infant Jesus. Thus, suddenly we are brought into another reality, not only to a pre-Adamic situation of all cosmic nature, but even to an eloquent manifestation whereby the whole of creation acknowledges the lordship of the infant Christ.

Thus, the manger becomes the offering of all the *oikumene* — both spiritual and material — to the Logos. Indeed, human beings and all visible creation have a certain association and a deep interdependence. Symeon the New Theologian says that because of Christ's appearance in the flesh, "each of us becomes a second ornament — *kosmos* — of God. Man is made great within this small visible world." (*Sermon* 4, in *Apatheia*; SC 129,64). "While through his soul one communicates with the heavenly powers, with his body, as part of the creation, he is connected to the things of the earth," John Chrysostom stated (*De prophetarum obscuritate hom.* 2, 5; PG 56.182)

Although eternal and imperishable, man carries with him all the parts of the whole. Within such possibilities, man is marching towards his final goal, his deification — *theosis* — having as his fellow-traveler his bodily structure and consequently the whole of creation.

Man is created according to God's image in order to contain within himself the archetype, through the incarnation of Christ. Thus, he becomes the link between the invisible and the visible world. Material creation does not remain on the side, indifferent, neutral, or passive before the great event of Christ's incarnation in history. The nativity manger constitutes the proof and the witness of creation's restoration and its return to its original state. Nature, thus, is offered as an oblation to its Lord. God accepted willingly to become man in the midst of fallen creation in order to show that from now on all are redeemed and equally share the blessings of his love. Any nativity iconography excluding the presence of the material cosmos reduces the meaning of redemption by only introducing the concept of its narrow effect, as if the divine economy were seeking the reconciliation and atonement of the individual only while excluding the salutary effect upon the whole of nature. At the same time, such a depiction would betray an ignorance of the previously existing harmony in the relationship between God and creation before the fall. That is why the material world is never absent in icons when the different historical stages of Christ's humanity are being portrayed.

From the moment of Christ's incarnation, man is no longer a simple inhabitant upon the earth, nor a simple consumer of produced goods whose task ends with his death. He becomes the steward, as well as the administrator of the whole world, and of all the hidden powers, provided that he uses them to serve his ultimate and supreme calling. In addition, he is promoted to becoming a partner and a collaborator with God in his plan for the world. Man is not placed on earth to be a mere spectator, occupying space and time with no purpose, while wasting his energies in futility and impotence. Space, as such, is neither a certain measured place where he lives and works as a closed-in, isolated being, nor the place wherein he seeks his own exclusive pleasure, comfort, and interest. This is exactly what animals seek to do when they fight to secure their own territory, always defensive against other, rival animals. Space for Christians takes on the meaning of meeting others, of *koinonia* and fellowship, of personal sharing and participation during this lifetime. Incarnation, therefore, is nothing other than the beginning of the realization of the task set forth from the very beginning of time by God, namely, to assemble into the one body of his Son. Thus, Maximos the Confessor wrote, confirming the fact that we all became quite different men: "The creation is one . . . but this oneness will be carried out by stages, with complementary features and marching together to perfection, thus sailing to the fullness of existence" (*Ambiguorum liber*; PG 91.1312B).

When we take into account the above anthropological considerations, we can easily understand the role of the Church on earth and its historical contribution to humanity. The Church is the extension of the incarnation in time and space, the continuous communication and imparting of the temporal to the timeless, of the created to the uncreated. Consequently, the Church consists of baptized believers who are struggling for the defense of their identity in the midst of a polluted, selfish, and hostile world; it cannot be considered as a "remote, peaceful oasis," cut off from the world. Quite the opposite, their place is to stay in this world and to witness to the fact that light exists behind the darkness, generosity, and self-giving in spite of egoism, and purity where iniquity prevails. Each Christian, and the Church as a whole, thus becomes a permanent leaven, an agent of and for the re-conversion of all creation to its true itinerary, and an instrument of sanctification in all aspects of life. While not despising this world or creation, God's people persist in their struggle to be separated from evil and to heal and restore that which is distorted.

Indeed, the birth of Christ is the most decisive of all historical events. For this reason, short of the triumph of an alien world-religion, man will continue to divide history at the point where Christ entered it. The centrality of Christ in universal history, and consequently that of his followers, is based in the first instance upon an appreciation of what his epiphany accomplished. Christ brought eternity into time and set in order all human affairs in the light of God. More than that — in whatever terms it may be defined — his advent was a divine visitation to the race of man. It is all the more striking, therefore, that what took place in Christ should be combined with an error as to when exactly it took place.

An essential part of the Christian faith is that the unassuming

may very well also be the most eventful and that when God's wisdom
and love entered the world it did not necessarily conform to or comply with man's expectations. A human, dubious attitude towards God's
gift shows that God neither esteems nor despises the things to which
men attach honor, wealth, power, knowledge. There is room at the
cradle of the Child for the wise men from the East as well as for the
shepherds, and room even for Herod, if he but lay aside his cruelty
and come to worship. God looks not to some outward distinctions,
but to the heart. His gift is for the despised and the humble. Just
because it is God's love that comes, it chooses the simplest means
and offers itself first to those who, whether wise or simple, know that
God gives himself and does not impose himself. The institutions of
Caesar Augustus gave the ancient world stability for several generations. The epiphany of Christ restored its lost youth. This *philanthropia* of God is at work continuously in our very midst today as
of old, but again it goes unnoticed. Only to the humble and the loving is the secret available, for they alone are ready to welcome the
divine visitation in its simplicity and so to recognize it in its hidden
poverty. God reveals his saving plan through his *kenosis,* this unusual
method for us humans. In the midst of Christ's way to the cross, the
Orthodox hymnography sings that he remains for us believers the
"joy of all": "Christ, the joy of all, the truth, the light, the life, the
resurrection of the world, did through his goodness manifest himself
to those on earth, and he became a pledge of the resurrection and
grants to all divine forgiveness" (*Saturday of St. Lazarus, Collect.*).

41. Conclusion

In view of a general crisis of spiritual values and moral decay, both in East and West, interaction and mutual assistance is necessary. True ecumenism consists not only in long-term theological dialogues; beyond that lie an urgent cooperation and mutual help, by offering one other what one preserves as the most precious legacy and resource.

The increasing concern for patristic studies, for research and better knowledge of the ascetic writings of the fathers of the desert, the impressive acceptance of icons as part of worship and deep meditation, the frequent reference to the liturgical sources and the theological thinking of the Orthodox world, are signs of a hopeful longing and of a vacuum to be filled. So many treasures have been ignored or misunderstood since the great schism and the subsequent reformation of the sixteenth century. Without any feeling of superiority or arrogance, it is the imperative duty of the Orthodox to bring to light these hidden sources and to offer a dynamic picture of the new image of the true Christian, living in such a liturgical, patristic setting.

All that the east possesses, in reality, constitute a common heritage, to be shared by all Christ's faithful, apart from whether they live in the West or in the East. With the expansion of communications, of increasing circulation, of tourism, of diffusion of ideas and conceptions, Christianity should find what is common, belonging to all, and enter into a process of sharing and of together feeding the deep hunger of our innermost being. This challenging necessity would help the Christian family to improve considerably the quality of desacralized life and make witness more effective and more solid.

In this respect, Christian worship may become a catalyst. Worship has its theology. Christ's incarnation with all its manifestations, which are so closely related to the life of the baptized person, suddenly become contemporary events seen before us with the eyes of faith, so that the faithful participate empirically in them. The earthly life from Bethlehem, to Gethsemane, to Thabor, the mountain of his transfiguration, these and other events, can be seen and experienced within the Church, where the redeeming life of Jesus is experienced. In the *Prothesis*, we are before Bethlehem. On the altar we face Golgotha. In the Baptistry we see Jordan, and all these events join together and lead to the climax of God's economy, that is *anastasis*.

Together all the ineffable events together which brought redemption and sonship to sinful humanity are precisely articulated in the liturgical feasts, celebrated on given days throughout the liturgical year. In this way, the faithful meet Christ personally as well as communally. All are enabled to become his disciples, walking with him, listening to his words. They are invited to make the miracles performed by Christ their own, and, above all, the miracle of miracles: his resurrection. All these particular episodes of his life are composed in one unity during each eucharistic assembly. There Christ comes down again, through *anamnesis* and the subsequent *epiklesis,* making us partakers of his life. Maximos the Confessor summarized this divine action after having commented on the different stages of the liturgy:

> The holy reception of the life-giving sacraments brings about a resemblance to him, which effects a communion and identity with him by participation, after which the human person is deemed fit to be changed out of a man into God. For we believe ourselves to have had a share in the gifts of the Holy Spirit here in this present life through the grace embraced in faith; and we believe that, having kept his commandments as well as we are able, we shall, in the next world, really in fact gain possession of those gifts in the reality of a divine person; this is what we believe, in accordance with the unfailing hope proper to our faith, and the firm, unimpeachable guarantee of him who made the promise; we pass over from the grace of faith to the grace of vision, Jesus Christ our God and Savior clearly transforming us into himself. He rids us of the symptoms of corruption and grants us the original, archetypal mysteries represented here to the senses under symbols (*De Mystagogia* 24).

The above patristic reflection confirms that God intervenes, transcending time and space, so that the worshiper lives beyond time limitations. He experiences what is ever present, eternal, endless. He finds himself in a time without boundaries, the eternal time of God. The theological value and dynamism of the eucharist is based on the resurrection. Although God's love is manifested now, however, we live the past too, and even more, we experience in part, the other dimension of time: the future, what will be in the after-death life.

God's kingdom begins now in his Church, and is extended beyond the time of this age, a foretaste offered during the eucharist. In such a setting with moving feelings, the prevailing doxological character of our liturgy is understandable, full of optimism and joy. These two elements abundant in Orthodox worship, rather weak in the Western worship, have attracted deep concern in the West. Many people proposed even to restore them in their own liturgy by substantial modifications. Orthodoxy, in humility, may display the richness and beauty of this liturgical treasure, working for its implementation in Western thought and piety.

Concerning the great question of the testing and verification of faith, Christ has a word whose significance is far-reaching: "He that does the will of God shall know the doctrine whether I came from God, or whether I speak from myself" (Jn 7.17). Knowledge, therefore, of the Gospel depends on knowledge and intimate communion with God. Is the life and work of Jesus to be assessed in the same way as that of any other personality in history? Is Christ only a dead fact, stranded on the shore of the oblivious years or are his teachings and works — his life and death — the eternal message of God to the souls of men in every century? In other words, is he limited by history, or is he the climax of history?

Christ himself said that this supreme question could be answered only in a life of action, not merely in life of contemplation. The men and women who would follow the will of God, as he revealed it, would have an answer to the question. The testing is in the laboratory of life, in the field of challenging opportunities. Christian experience does not always say the same thing. There are varieties in it, as people differ from each other in so many ways. But beyond all those variations, which in themselves are a sign of life, a vast consensus of judgment maintains that "no man spake like this man," and that he is "the way, the truth, and the life" for all humanity.

This testimony of experience is the unity underlying all the varieties of interpretation, a unity which gathers into one fellowship the people of different races, cultures, and ages. A clash between the creeds sometimes seems confusing to the mind, but to this fundamental question there is a harmony of assent which is the bond of unity surpassing all differences.

What challenges each of us today is precisely that love of Christ and his deep concern for the salvation of all. His love and message must be known and proclaimed in the strongest terms to each soul. We are all responsible. In such a gathering we feel Christ's presence and his urgent appeal, saying to each one of us, as St. Jerome puts it:

Do, please, preach the Gospel as much in the rural countryside as in the busy urban cities. And in the castles, too, that is amidst the well-off as to the poor, too. Do not be overly impressed by the mighty of the upper classes but more by the salvation of the faithful. Jesus was passing through cities with one aim entrusted to him by the Father, and an utmost desire to save the people by his teaching." (*In Evang. Matth. comment.* 1,9,35; PL 26.60B)

The dynamics of suffering

From the point of view of time's length, Christ's sufferings may be longer, if one adds the attacks of his enemies and the unfriendly attitude of the world. But his glory never left him, so that he always saw the adversities as part of the process toward glory. You might object that there could not be much in common between hanging on the cross and sitting at the right hand of God. But they have at least this in common, that both are glorious, though, of course, in different ways, just as the first budding of the elm tree is very different from its later state when it is laden with its burden of leaves, of the first blades of corn are different, as Christ himself said, from the full ear of wheat. One is the glory of vigorous effort and promise, the other is the glory of a purpose fully achieved. So, also, Christ's suffering is glorious because of the effort he had to make to accept it and to bear it.

Suffering is never to be thought of as good in itself. It is only good because it can achieve something which can be achieved in any other way. But there are two very different kinds of suffering. Both can do good, but only one is glorious. We may suffer because we have brought it on ourselves by sin or silliness, and then God lets us suffer in order to make it easier for us to avoid being sinful or silly in the future, just as pains in the body show us that something is the matter with us and that we need curing.

There is an ancient Greek saying that to suffer is to learn — *pathos mathos,* and this is very true, if we allow it to teach us. But there is quite a different kind of suffering. It is suffering for others. We all know how different this feels. If you have a lot of luggage in a heavy bag and must carry it for yourself, it seems a terrible nuissance. But if you are carrying somebody else's bag, even though it is heavy, it is often a real pleasure. To help an old woman with her basket, or a young woman who has three children to look after and a lot of parcels as well, is often no trouble at all, and even when it is a trouble, it is a great satisfaction to have done it.

We believe this pleasure is part of our original goodness, just as it is part of our original sin to say, as we are rather inclined to say, that we do not see why we should suffer for this or that instead of somebody else or when it is somebody else's fault. But there is often every reason why we should suffer, partly because it will be really satisfying, and partly because it may be the only way some job can be done or some remedy be found.

This suffering is, in fact, part of God's plan for the world we spend our lives in. The whole plan is nothing less than glorious, and the height of the glory surrounds Christ in heaven. He has suffered the most of all for us, and he has won the greatest glory. The New Testament is full of this thought: "Christ also has once suffered for sins, the just for the unjust, that he might bring us to God" (1 Pet 3.18; cf. Heb 1.3 Rom 8.16-18.

Although we are alienated sinnes, nevertheless God intends us for glory. We are to be the objects of a transformation. We must fix our thoughts and feelings upon Christ, and then "we all, with unveiled face reflecting as a mirror the glory of the Lord, are transformed into the same image from glory to glory, even as from the Lord the Spirit" (2 Cor 3.18). That is it. "When I awake up after your likeness, I shall be satisfied with it" (Ps 17.16).

"Beloved, now are we the sons of God." We have already seen what comes of being sons of God in the above passage of St. Paul from Romans. Saint John puts it in another way: "Beloved, now are we the sons of God, and it does not yet appear what we shall be; but we know that, when he shall appear, we shall be like him; for we shall see him as he is" (I Jn 3.2). How glorious that will be.

First comes Good Friday, and after forty days the Ascension. It is the time of year when we watch with a thrill from day to day the bursting forth of nature in field and bush and nest. It makes us think this earth of ours is hopeful, full of promise. If at the same season we fix our thoughts where our faith would have them, on the glorified and glorious Savior of humanity, we ought to feel sure that in this hopeful world the men and women for whom Christ died are the most promising part of all.